CASEBOOK SERIES

GENERAL EDITOR: A. E. Dyson

PUBLI

Jane
Jane
Jane
B. C.
Willia
Charl
Emily
Brow
Bunya
Byron
Chau
Coleri
TY
Conra
Dicke
Donn
Georg
Georg
T. S.
T. S.
so
T. S.
Farqu
AN
Henr
E. M
Hard
Gera
Jonso
James
John
D. H.
D. H.
Marl
The N
Milto
Milto
John

Peacock: *The Satirical Novels* LORNA SAGE
Pope: *The Rape of the Lock* JOHN DIXON HUNT
Shakespeare: *Antony and Cleopatra* JOHN RUSSELL BROWN
Shakespeare: *Coriolanus* B. A. BROCKMAN
Shakespeare: *Hamlet* JOHN JUMP
Shakespeare: *Henry IV Parts I and II* G. K. HUNTER
Shakespeare: *Henry V* MICHAEL QUINN
Shakespeare: *Julius Caesar* PETER URE
Shakespeare: *King Lear* FRANK KERMODE
Shakespeare: *Macbeth* JOHN WAIN
Shakespeare: *Measure for Measure* C. K. STEAD
Shakespeare: *The Merchant of Venice* JOHN WILDERS
Shakespeare: *Othello* JOHN WAIN
Shakespeare: *Richard II* NICHOLAS BROOKE
Shakespeare: *The Sonnets* PETER JONES
Shakespeare: *The Tempest* D. J. PALMER
Shakespeare: *Troilus and Cressida* PRISCILLA MARTIN
Shakespeare: *Twelfth Night* D. J. PALMER
Shakespeare: *The Winter's Tale* KENNETH MUIR
Shelley: *Shorter Poems and Lyrics* PATRICK SWINDEN
Spenser: *The Faerie Queene* PETER BAYLEY
Swift: *Gulliver's Travels* RICHARD GRAVIL
Tennyson: *In Memoriam* JOHN DIXON HUNT
Thackeray: *Vanity Fair* ARTHUR POLLARD
Webster: *'The White Devil' and 'The Duchess of Malfi'* R. V. HOLDSWORTH
Virginia Woolf: *To the Lighthouse* MORRIS BEJA
Wordsworth: *Lyrical Ballads* ALUN R. JONES AND WILLIAM TYDEMAN
Wordsworth: *The Prelude* W. J. HARVEY AND RICHARD GRAVIL
Yeats: *Last Poems* JON STALLWORTHY

The English Novel: Developments in Criticism since Henry James STEPHEN HAZELL
The Romantic Imagination JOHN SPENCER HILL

TITLES IN PREPARATION INCLUDE

Dickens: *'Hard Times', 'Great Expectations' and 'Our Mutual Friend'* NORMAN
  PAGE
Hardy: *Poems* JAMES GIBSON AND TREVOR JOHNSON
Jonson: *'Every Man in His Humour' and 'The Alchemist'* R. V. HOLDSWORTH
Shakespeare: *'Much Ado about Nothing' and 'As You Like It'*
  JOHN RUSSELL BROWN
Sheridan: *'The Rivals', 'The School for Scandal' and 'The Critic'*
  WILLIAM RUDDICK

Poetry Criticism: Developments since the Symbolists A. E. DYSON
Drama Criticism: Developments since Ibsen ARNOLD P. HINCHLIFFE

Thackeray

Vanity Fair

A CASEBOOK

EDITED BY

ARTHUR POLLARD

M

First published 1978 by
THE MACMILLAN PRESS LTD
London and Basingstoke
Associated companies in Delhi Dublin
Hong Kong Johannesburg Lagos Melbourne
New York Singapore and Tokyo

Printed in Great Britain by
REDWOOD BURN LIMITED
Trowbridge & Esher

British Library Cataloguing in Publication Data

Thackeray, 'Vanity Fair'. – (Casebook series).
  1. Thackeray, William Makepeace. Vanity Fair –
Addresses, essays, lectures
  I. Pollard, Arthur, b. 1922 II. Series
823'.8   PR5618

ISBN 0-333-21513-3
ISBN 0-333-21514-1 Pbk

CONTENTS

Acknowledgements   7

General Editor's Preface   9

Introduction   11

Part One: *Earlier Comments*

1. Opinions and Reviews

CHARLOTTE BRONTË (1848), p. 25 – JOHN FORSTER
(1848), p. 26 – ROBERT BELL (1848), p. 28 – ELIZABETH
RIGBY, LADY EASTLAKE (1848), p. 30 – THEODORE
MARTIN (1853), p. 32

2. Letters of Thackeray (1847, 1848)   33

Part Two: *Later Comments*

ANTHONY TROLLOPE (1879), p. 41 – W. C.
BROWNELL (1901), p. 45 – CHARLES WHIBLEY
(1903), p. 47 – PERCY LUBBOCK (1921), p. 51 – G. K.
CHESTERTON (1930), p. 57

Part Three: *Illustrations and Source Material*

U. C. KNOEPFLMACHER: 'Thackeray's Masks'
(1971)   65

JULIET McMASTER: 'Sir Pitt's Proposal' (1971)   69

GORDON N. RAY: 'Two Thackeray Originals?' (1952)   71

G. AND K. TILLOTSON: 'Thackeray: Historical
Novelist' (1963)   83

Part Four: *Modern Studies*

GORDON N. RAY: *Vanity Fair*: One Version of the
Novelist's Responsibility (1950)   95

DOROTHY VAN GHENT: 'The "Omniscient Author"
Convention and the "Compositional Centre" Function' (1953)   114

KATHLEEN TILLOTSON: 'The Debatable Land between
the Middle Classes and the Aristocracy' (1954)   127

G. ARMOUR CRAIG: On the Style of *Vanity Fair* (1958)   143

A. E. DYSON: An Irony Against Heroes (1966)   163

IOAN M. WILLIAMS: 'The Role of the Narrator'
(1968)   183

EDGAR F. HARDEN: The Discipline and Significance of
Form (1967)   188

BARBARA HARDY: Rank and Reversal (1972)   214

Select Bibliography   229

Notes on Contributors   231

Index   233

ACKNOWLEDGEMENTS

The editor and publishers wish to thank the following who have kindly given permission for the use of copyright material: G. K. Chesterton, extracts from 'Introduction to *Vanity Fair*' in *A Handful of Authors*, reprinted by permission of Miss Dorothy Collins and A. P. Watt & Son; G. Armour Craig, essay 'On the Style of *Vanity Fair*', reprinted from H. C. Martin (ed.): *Style in Prose Fiction: English Institute Essays 1958* (New York: Columbia University Press, 1959), by permission of the author and publisher; Edgar F. Harden, article on 'The Discipline and Significance of Form in *Vanity Fair*', *P.M.L.A.*, LXXXII (1967) 530−41, reprinted by permission of the Modern Language Association of America; Barbara Hardy, extracts from *The Exposure of Luxury* (1972) pp. 23−6, 27−37, reprinted by permission of the publisher, Peter Owen, London; U. C. Knoepflmacher, extract from *Laughter and Despair*, p. 63, © by The Regents of the University of California 1971, reprinted by permission of the University of California Press; Percy Lubbock, extract from *The Craft of Fiction*, pp. 97−106, reprinted by permission of Jonathan Cape Ltd on behalf of the Executors of the Estate of Percy Lubbock; Juliet McMaster, extract from *Thackeray: The Major Novels*, pp. 32−3, © University of Toronto Press 1971, reprinted by permission; Gordon N. Ray, extracts from *The Buried Life* (1952, for the Royal Society of Literature) pp. 37−47, and from *Essays by Divers Hands* (1950, for the Royal Society of Literature) pp. 342−56, reprinted by permission of the Oxford University Press; Geoffrey and Kathleen Tillotson (eds), extract from Introduction to *Vanity Fair* (Riverside Editions B66), reprinted by permission of Houghton Mifflin Company,

Boston, U.S.A.,© 1963 by Geoffrey and Kathleen Tillotson; Kathleen Tillotson, extract from *Novels of the Eighteen-Forties* (1954) pp. 234–56, reprinted by permission of the Oxford University Press; Dorothy Van Ghent, extract from *The English Novel: Form and Function* (New York: Holt, Rinehart and Winston, 1953), reprinted by permission of C.B.S. International Publishing; Charles Whibley, extract from *William Makepeace Thackeray* (1903) pp. 93–7, reprinted by permission of William Blackwood & Sons Ltd; Ioan M. Williams, extracts from *Thackeray* (1968) pp. 67–71, 75–6, reprinted by permission of Evans Bros Ltd.

The publishers have made every effort to trace all the copyright-holders, but if they have inadvertently overlooked any they will be pleased to make the necessary arrangement at the first opportunity.

GENERAL EDITOR'S PREFACE

The Casebook series, launched in 1968, has become a well-regarded library of critical studies. The central concern of the series remains the 'single-author' volume, but suggestions from the academic community have led to an extension of the original plan, to include occasional volumes on such general themes as literary 'schools' and genres.

Each volume in the central category deals either with the one well-known and influential work by an individual author, or with closely related works by one writer. The main section consists of critical readings, mostly modern, collected from books and journals. A selection of reviews and comments by the author's contemporaries is also included, and sometimes comment from the author himself. The Editor's Introduction charts the reputation of the work or works from the first appearance to the present time.

Volumes in the 'general themes' category are variable in structure but follow the basic purpose of the series in presenting an integrated selection of readings, with an Introduction which explores the theme and discusses the literary and critical issues involved.

A single volume can represent no more than a small selection of critical opinions. Some critics are excluded for reasons of space, and it is hoped that readers will pursue the suggestions for further reading in the Select Bibliography. Other contributions are severed from their original context, to which some readers may wish to turn. Indeed, if they take a hint from the critics represented here, they certainly will.

A. E. DYSON

For Ruth Green

INTRODUCTION

Vanity Fair has never ceased to be a problem to readers and critics. Why it is so can best be summed up in two quotations. Geoffrey and Kathleen Tillotson began their Introduction to the Norton edition (which must now be regarded as the standard text) with the words, 'Thackeray was a born narrator – his stories can put us in possession of two or more personages, engage them in interaction and, when that is over, leave us with the aesthetic satisfaction of having witnessed the inevitable.' But Thackeray can also digress and delay. The second passage is from A. E. Dyson's essay in *The Crazy Fabric*: '*Vanity Fair* is surely one of the world's most devious novels, devious in its characterisation, its irony, its explicit moralising, its exuberance, its tone. Few novels demand more continuing alertness from the reader' (see below, Part Four). These two quotations suggest a tension between the tale and the teller. They also serve to remind us that nobody is more adept than Thackeray in attracting – and tantalising – the reader.

Much of the story that he had to tell came from barely disguised people and incidents of his own acquaintance. What he found and made of persons, time and history is illustrated in the sections which are included from the Tillotsons' introduction and from Gordon N. Ray's *The Buried Life*, a minute and impressive investigation of Thackeray's personal background and the uses he made of it. William Makepeace Thackeray was born in Calcutta in 1811, the son of Richard Thackeray, a senior civilian of the East India Company, and his wife Anne (*née* Becher). His father died in 1815 and Thackeray returned home a year later, arriving in England in May 1817 and going to school in Southampton. After sad experience there he moved to another school in Chiswick and in 1822 to Charterhouse. His mother and step-father, Major-General Carmichael-Smyth, whom she had married in March 1817, had also returned to England and Thackeray spent some time with them before going up to Trinity College, Cambridge, in 1829. There he was on the fringe of the Apostles, the famous group which included Tennyson, Hallam and FitzGerald, the last of whom became a lifelong friend. He left Cambridge after a year, travelled in Germany and settled for a short while in Weimar. He was back in England in May 1831 to study law; a year later he was in Paris, then by the beginning of 1833 in England once more. Gambling lost him most of his own fortune and, a little later, in 1837, an unsuccessful newspaper venture part of his step-father's as well. He went to Paris to study art, and there he met Isabel Shawe, whom he married in August 1836. He thereby acquired a wife, who gave him three daughters (one of whom died in infancy), and a neurotic and hostile mother-in-law, who provided the basis for several of Thackeray's characters in that role. To add to his failures and other troubles Isabel became insane in 1841, leaving him to rear his two young daughters.

Thackeray's literary career began and ended with that characteristically Victorian phenomenon the literary periodical. *Fraser's Magazine*, and less frequently *Punch*, gave him an outlet for his comic journalism and for the short novels such as *Catherine* and *Barry Lyndon* which filled the ten or so years before the appearance of *Vanity Fair* in 1847–8. This, like most of his major novels (*Esmond* is the exception), was published in monthly parts, and he only returned to the periodical with his last three works (*Lovel the Widower*, *Philip* and *Denis Duval*) which, together with the essays forming *Roundabout Papers*, appeared in the *Cornhill Magazine*, the editorship of which he assumed at its inception in 1860.

Thackeray apparently started *Vanity Fair* around the turn of the year 1844–5, and by 8 May, probably on a sight of the opening chapters, Colburn had refused it. Not until January 1846 did the project re-emerge. He then wrote that Bradbury and Evans had 'engaged [him] to write a monthly story at 60£ a number' (*Letters*, ed. Gordon N. Ray, vol. II, p. 225). Due to appear in May, the new novel did not, in fact, commence publication until January 1847. The manuscript of the first thirteen chapters shows that Thackeray made a number of important additions and revisions, chief of which was the insertion of chapter 5. The serial publication ran to twenty monthly parts, divided into groups of chapters and indicated in this volume in the appendix to E. F. Harden's article 'The Discipline and Significance of Form in *Vanity Fair*'. Though its present sub-title, 'A Novel Without a Hero', was the name by which Thackeray referred to the work before 'Vanity Fair' occurred to him, the work was published in its monthly parts with a different sub-title – 'Pen and Pencil Sketches of Society', the pen for writing, the pencil for drawing. Thackeray's sketches provide their own commentary, and not least important of these are the differing title-pages of the parts and the completed novel, for they tell us something about the narrator (for remarks on these see the extracts from Knoepflmacher and McMaster). The jester is both comic and sad – just another tantalising example of Thackeray's ambiguity, or 'deviousness'.

Part-publication has been blamed for the alleged shapelessness of *Vanity Fair*. A contemporary reviewer, Robert Bell, called it 'a novel without a plan' (see below, Part One, section 1), and Charles Whibley turned this comment into denigration: 'The story grew as it chose, from month to month, and dragged its author after it. And this explains its failure to stop when it should' (see below, Part Two). Two things serve to suggest an apparent lack of structural discipline. One is the narrator's intrusive, occasionally fairly lengthy and sometimes seemingly digressive comment; the other is what I may call Thackeray's elastic attitude to time, by which he causes the pressure of events sometimes to intensify and at others allows it to slacken. Thus, whereas the Waterloo period and, to a lesser extent, the Steyne affair produce a heightened impression, the last sections of the book seem to run on a looser rein. Action and reaction are succeeded by a kind of stasis. But surely Thackeray is being true to life here. He is a novelist who sees in the past the seeds of the present, a writer who by contrast with the biblical phrase appears to believe that those who sow in joy shall reap in tears – fleeting pleasures followed by a long and bitter harvest; not the gladness of the Psalms but the *Vanitas Vanitatum* of Ecclesiastes.

Thackeray gave hostages to his critics. He wrote, 'Our history is destined in this chapter [25] to go backwards and forwards in a very irresolute manner seemingly.' The disarming but subtle catch is in that final adverb. It is dangerous to take Thackeray at his word. Though Bell thought the novel lacked a plan, he did recognise the 'two distinct narratives which not only never interfere with each other, but frequently help each other on'. Later critics have seen relationships such as the principle of contrast which Myron Taube detects ('Contrast as a Principle of Structure in *Vanity Fair*', *Nineteenth Century Fiction*, XVIII (1963) 119–35) and the 'highly articulated' connections seen by Edgar F. Harden (see below, Part Four). The narrative pattern of these relationships is succinctly described in Kathleen Tillotson's phrase 'the converging and diverging, parallel and contrasting fortunes of the two girls' (see below, Part Three). She is arguing for progress in the story. It is the converse of the point I was making in the last paragraph. We survey the panorama of the past in a kind of stasis, but in the present the dynamic of life goes forward with ever new experience. The only difference is that age constantly redisposes the balance of past and present, of static and dynamic.

The 'two distinct narratives' provide a plan of sorts. It is possible to see the contrast of good and bad between Amelia and Becky, Dobbin and Osborne, but we can go no further. Rawdon is better than Becky or Steyne, but good and bad are not the right categories here – and the end for Amelia and Dobbin is anything but happy, as Thackeray's savage response to Mrs Liddell's desire for their ultimate marriage (quoted by various critics in this volume) makes clear. The novelist even went so far as to say, 'Dont you see how odious all the people are in the book (with exception of Dobbin)' (Letter to his mother, 2 July 1847). Yet many Victorians must have shared Mrs Liddell's simplified view. In so doing they may have been misled by the novel's title, recalling as it did the simple categories of good and evil in Bunyan's allegory, but the title, we need to remember, recalls only one incident of that pilgrim's progress, his visit to a place where, to use Thackeray's quotation of Scripture in the letter to

his mother, men were 'living without God in the world'. Ioan
Williams argues that the title may have been suggested by
Carlyle's essay on Boswell's *Life of Johnson*: in this, Carlyle, in
distinguishing great men from ordinary, described the latter as
being, 'in the grand Vanity-Fair of the world, blinded by the
mere Shows of things' and in that sense not men but puppets (see
below, Part Four).

Those Victorian critics who, unlike Mrs Liddell, saw that they
could not divide the characters of *Vanity Fair* into good and bad
were frustrated by this inability. Elizabeth Rigby, Lady Eastlake, complained that they were 'too like our every-day selves
and neighbours to draw any distinct moral from'. She saw but
failed to appreciate the 'puzzling cross-light of good in evil, and
evil in good'. To compound the problem, the obvious rogues
were clearly more attractive than the seemingly virtuous.
Thackeray himself anticipated those who would not 'care a fig'
for Amelia, adding that the postulated 'unknown correspondent'
would say, 'She is *fade* and insipid' (ch. 12); whilst Trollope
would in due course write, 'Becky Sharp and Rawdon Crawley
are the real heroine and the hero of the story. . . . It is by them
that [the reader] will judge the book when he has read it' (see
below, Part Two).

Becky's struggle in a hard world takes her over some twenty-
odd years from an artist's den in Soho to the Court of George IV
and then from there to seedy lodgings at second-rate Continental
spas and the hell of dull provincial respectability in Cheltenham.
In giving us what Gordon Ray has called the 'immense
panorama of English life', Thackeray has provided a social range
without parallel in the English novel. Sometimes the character
does not even appear – Jenkins, for example, Commissioner of
the Tape and Sealing-Wax Office: how does he manage, the
narrator wonders, his three men and a carriage, his boys at Eton,
the girls with their governesses, the annual holiday – and all that
on £1200 a year and his wife with no portion of her own?
Exactness of nuance is matched by accuracy of awareness of a
way of life. That accuracy of awareness is evident again in the
brief and incidental descriptions of the Miss Pinkertons and their
boarding school at the beginning of the novel and of Mr Moss

and his bailiff's 'mansion' in Cursitor Street where Rawdon
spends a short, uncomfortable imprisonment for debt (ch. 53).
The main area of interest lies, however, in what W. C. Roscoe
called 'the debatable land between the middle classes and the
aristocracy' (*National Review*, Jan 1856), an area within which
Gordon Ray has described Thackeray's attitude thus: 'He was
fascinated by the aristocratic outlook – no attitude is more often
explored in his books – but he could not identify himself with it in
the manner of Disraeli, for he recognised that it had become an
anachronism in a prevailingly middle-class world' (see below,
Part Four). This is true as far as it goes, but it does not recognise
middle-class aspiration after aristocratic status. The Marquis of
Steyne may be degenerate, but it does not prevent the lesser
aristocracy from accepting his invitations; and others would have
done – 'In a word, everybody went to wait upon this great
man – everybody who was asked'. Then Thackeray with his
penetrating and cynical (if you like) view of human nature adds,
'As you the reader (do not say nay) or I the writer hereof would
go if we had an invitation' (ch. 47). He returns to the theme in the
next chapter: 'Mrs Frederick Bullock, for instance, would have
gone on her knees from Mayfair to Lombard Street, if Lady
Steyne and Lady Gaunt had been waiting in the City to raise her
up and say, "Come to us next Friday".'

But Becky Sharp had made it – against all the odds and by her
own unaided efforts. This is one reason why we admire her,
whatever be the means she has used. Like Volpone, she is the
knave who triumphs in a world of would-be knaves who are
really only gulls. As she herself says, her success has come
'because I have brains . . . and almost all the rest of the world are
fools' (ch. 41). Becky is *déclassée* and as such can both by her
action and by her words be used by Thackeray to comment on
the behaviour and pretensions of others. Thus at Brussels after
Lady Bareacres (Thackeray's names are usually indicative) has
snubbed Amelia, her hostess, and declared to her daughter, 'We
needn't know them in England, you know' (ch. 28), it is Becky
with the foresight to possess horses during the Waterloo panic
who exquisitely reduces the suppliant Lady Bareacres to tears of
anger after she has 'even offered to invite Becky to Bareacres

House'. Becky sneers at this helpless woman who at the ball on the eve of the battle had moved arrayed in diamonds (now sewn in her and her husband's clothes) (ch. 32). Ten years later they meet again at Lord Steyne's and Becky reminds her of the occasion, concluding, 'I hope your Ladyship's diamonds are safe' – to which Thackeray adds, 'Everybody's eyes looked into their neighbour's. The famous diamonds had undergone a famous seizure, it appears, about which Becky, of course, knew nothing' (ch. 49). Did she not? Those parenthetic insertions are very suspicious.

If Becky does this to the aristocracy, she is quite as ruthless with middle-class pretensions, and most of all with George Osborne. It looks as though the infatuated Jos Sedley might propose to the penniless orphan, Becky. Mrs Sedley objects, only for her housekeeper to remind her of her own and her husband's origins. None, however, is more vehement in opposition than George, who is engaged to Jos's sister, Amelia. Thackeray has taken care to pinpoint the pretension before he describes the detail: 'we are only discoursing at present about a stockbroker's family in Russell Square. . . . Suppose we had laid the scene in Grosvenor Square, with the very same adventures . . . how Lord Joseph Sedley fell in love, and the Marquis of Osborne became attached to the Lady Amelia' (ch. 6). He is also satirising the 'silver-fork' novel here, but the main thrust is against middle-class social-climbing. Osborne, as Becky thinks, succeeds in frightening Jos away. She has her revenge severally and at length. When, later, George condescendingly enquires how she likes her 'new place' as a governess to Sir Pitt Crawley, Becky replies, 'We are not so wealthy in Hampshire as you lucky folks of the City. But then I am in a gentleman's family – good old English stock' (ch. 14). At Brussels as the centre of attraction she uses him to arouse General Tufto's jealousy and then, receiving his note proposing elope-ment, hidden in a bouquet of flowers, allows George to know that she is aware that it is there, but no more. She produces the note, years after his death, to bring Amelia to her senses about Dobbin. She calls Osborne 'that low-bred cockney dandy'. She ends a devastating tirade by saying he 'gave it me under your nose, the day before he was shot – and served him right!'

Here Becky has moved from social to moral commentary.
Whatever we may think about her and whatever she herself may
do, she always knows and recognises the truth not only about
others and the world she lives in but also about herself. She has
many qualities; she is intelligent, resilient, energetic, good-
humoured and totally lacking in snobbery. Above all, and in
contrast with all the other characters, her unfailing perception of
the truth means that she alone has self-understanding. This also
means, of course, that she is the most self-consciously wicked
character in the book. 'I think I could be a good woman if I had
five thousand a year', she says (ch. 41); unfortunately for her she
must contrive (and she does) 'how to live well on nothing a year'
(ch. 36, chapter-title). Thus placed, she is both a reflection and a
victim of the material values of the society in which she lives. It is
when she has reached the zenith of her career that our sympathy
begins to wane. Thackeray uses children to point the condem-
nation. Amelia in widowhood is a doting mother; Becky, by
contrast, in her social success neglects her husband and maltreats
her child, preferring Lord Steyne to them both.

The beginning and the end of the Steyne affair each carry the
question 'Was Rebecca guilty or not?' (chs 44, 53). With the first
we read, 'The servants' hall had pronounced against her'; with
the second, as the French maid is picking up the trinkets from
Lord Steyne, now scattered in disarray around Becky, Thackeray
writes, 'What *had* happened? Was she guilty or not? She said not;
but who could tell what was truth which came from those lips?'
Steyne has sneered at her protestations of innocence to her
husband; all the circumstantial evidence is against her, but
Thackeray never answers the question. He has been accused of
'casuistry' (see G. Armour Craig's essay, Part Four below; and
Russell Fraser, 'Pernicious Casuistry: A Study of Character in
Vanity Fair', *Nineteenth Century Fiction*, XII (1958)), but here may
well be the supreme irony of all, that Becky with her self-
knowledge and her ruthless exposure of others is unable to face
the truth of her own crisis. But in any case we do not really need to
know. The history of her character is more revealing than the
morality of an isolated experience. Nor should we ignore the
piquancy that lies in the agency of Becky's downfall, engineered

all unknowingly by the rescue of Rawdon from the hands of the bailiffs by the intervention of Becky's pious and, in her opinion, all too stupid sister-in-law, Lady Jane Southdown.

Amelia's weak, 'virtuous' world stands in contrast to the raw opportunism of Becky's. It is a world, however, of conventional values, rarely examined and rarely tested. When trial comes, Amelia's parents fail, whilst she herself shows a stoic courage that must have done much to sustain her in the regard of Victorian readers. In his treatment of her Thackeray provides a set of variations on the sentimental, and we need to remember that the Victorians were more susceptible to pathos than is our own, less pervious century. Even so, the famous ambiguity is at work and is not always easy to unravel. On George's return to Amelia's lonely bed after the revels of the Waterloo Ball, 'Two fair arms closed tenderly round his neck as he stooped down. "I am awake, George", the poor child said with a sob fit to break the little heart that nestled so closely by his own' (ch. 29); and when Amelia, having in her poverty surrendered her son to the care of his grandfather, sees him being taken to church one Sunday, she follows him there: 'she sat in a place where she could see the head of the boy under his father's tombstone' but 'could not see him for awhile, through the mist that dimmed her eyes' (ch. 50). Thackeray is pulling out the stops. Both these passages end a part, the eighth and the fourteenth respectively; but we should be careful about suspecting him of deliberately exaggerating. Amelia's devotion to both her husband and her child is (and is meant to be) admirable.

What is reprehensible is the excess which results in her prolonged mourning (even this the Victorians might admire) and her blindness to the comparable devotion of Dobbin to herself. He notably lacks the dash of Osborne and Crawley, and his self-effacing fidelity to Amelia, both before and after George's death, takes a lot of believing. It looks, however, as though he has stunned her into the world of reality when he threatens to go away – 'She didn't wish to marry him but she wished to keep him'; but whether she would have settled this problem with herself we never know, for at this point Becky enters, and dispels the illusion another way by revealing the truth about Osborne.

Amelia is Dobbin's idol, the object of his whole life, and, as Thackeray remarked to his mother, she is not worth it and he would have to find that out. She is his particular illusion in Vanity Fair, and the disillusion for them both is a slow and painful process, typical of much well-mannered but thoroughly bored and passionless domesticity.

Which brings us to Thackeray's alleged cynicism – 'Ah! *Vanitas Vanitatum!* which of us is happy in this world?' This is the text to confirm the record that Dobbin and Amelia did not live happy ever after. Thackeray is famous for his sardonic views on marriage, blighted, as he thought it, by the influence of money, the intervention of parents, the illusions of romance. In *The Newcomes* he even compared it to Hindu *suttee*. Worldly success likewise is not the joy it seems when viewed from afar. When Becky has reached the pinnacle of her climb, her 'former acquaintances hated and envied her; the poor woman herself was yawning in spirit. "I wish I were out of it," she said to herself. "I would rather be a parson's wife and teach a Sunday School than this; or a sergeant's lady, and ride in the regimental waggon; or, O how much gayer it would have been to wear spangles and trousers, and dance before a booth at a fair" ' (ch. 51). We return to the last lines of the book: 'Which of us has his desire? or, having it, is satisfied?' Yes, there is a degree of cynicism. We cannot do without illusions, and we suffer when the bubbles burst – but surely not all is lost, for, matching all this as life goes on, there is the courage to live as it is shown in a Dobbin or a Rawdon Crawley. Not high adventure or noble achievement, granted; but steady persistence, stoic determination, clear-sighted recognition. Thackeray, like Swift, had no illusions; nor could he afford them to or for others. Similarly, he saw that, as life was far too complicated to provide pure happiness, so also it was too complex to permit simple justice. The best are flawed and the worst not always vile. Mixed motives, sometimes misunderstood, bid us beware of mistaking *Vanity Fair* for the simple allegory that it is not; and Thackeray is quick to remind us that we ourselves are no different from his characters.

Dorothy Van Ghent objects to 'two orders of reality . . . clumsily getting in each other's way: the order of imaginative reality, where Becky lives, and the order of historical reality, where William Makepeace Thackeray lives' (see below, Part Four). We cannot pronounce on Thackeray's morality until we have discussed the role and significance of the narrator in *Vanity Fair*. The authorial voice, the 'I' which personifies the 'Mrs Grundy of each respected reader's private circle' (ch. 36) is an intrusive commentator but a treacherous guide, for Thackeray breaches the usual complicity between satirist and reader by refusing to stick to a particular point of view. For one thing we need to identify the narrator. Is it really Thackeray himself? Or is the narrator an *altera persona*? Is Thackeray the puppet-master? And what control does the master exercise? Complaint has been made about what is at one time included and at another omitted. We can be told Becky's secrets one moment and denied Amelia's the next. But many an author does this. The only difference is that Thackeray, like Fielding before him, tells us he is doing it. As James complained of Trollope, it reminds us that it is only a story, but in Thackeray's case it seems worse because of his insistence that the characters are puppets. What this does, however, is to remind us of the element of accident and the arbitrary in human life. This helps to heighten the significance, but not necessarily the reliability, of the narrator's comment. Sometimes this is mellow, as when the narrator contemplates the fallen Sedleys (ch. 38); sometimes it is obviously pedantic, as in the advice, 'Be cautious, then, young ladies; be wary how you engage' (ch. 18); sometimes, as of Amelia's sacrifices for young George, it seems outrageously exaggerated: 'O you poor women! O you poor secret martyrs and victims, whose life is a torture . . . every man who watches your pains, or peers into those dark places where the torture is administered to you, must pity you – and – and thank God that he has a beard.' We need a careful ear, as we listen to the comment. Thus the last of these remarks emerges into the mature reflection that 'the hidden and awful Wisdom which apportions the destinies of mankind is pleased so to humiliate and cast down the tender, good, and wise; and to set up the selfish, or foolish, or the wicked. Oh, be humble, my brother, in your prosperity!' (ch. 57).

'. . . the destinies of mankind'! *Vanity Fair* is a vast novel in time and range and *dramatis personae*, above all in the scope of its theme. It required a puppet-master to organise the plethora of apparently inconsequential incident and recollection; it demanded a commentator to bring all this detail into something approaching *sub specie aeternitatis*. But, though he may reflect, as in life itself, out of mature wisdom and deep sympathy, his voice is not that of God; it is neither omniscient nor infallible. We cannot always take the tone and the moralising at its face-value. We cannot be sure that he knows or feels fully enough; and we must be ever on the alert for irony and exaggeration. We must constantly judge the narrator. He may be Mrs Grundy; or Thackeray may be being devious. He was always loath to over-simplify. Life isn't like that. *Vanity Fair* offers an ever renewed challenge and an ever heightened reward to the sensitive reader. Amid the ordinarinesses of its people and events we are left in the company of our informed but not inerrant guide to contemplate the infinite variety of experience, to savour nuances and appreciate attitudes, to ponder enigmas and wrestle with unanswered questions. Life *is* like that.

PART ONE

Earlier Comments

1. OPINIONS AND REVIEWS

Charlotte Brontë (1848)

. . . You mention Thackeray and the last number of *Vanity Fair*. The more I read Thackeray's works the more certain I am that he stands alone – alone in his sagacity, alone in his truth, alone in his feeling (his feeling, though he makes no noise about it, is about the most genuine that ever lived on a printed page), alone in his power, alone in his simplicity, alone in his self-control. Thackeray is a Titan, so strong that he can afford to perform with calm the most herculean feats; there is the charm and majesty of repose in his greatest efforts; *he* borrows nothing from fever, his is never the energy of delirium – his energy is sane energy, deliberate energy, thoughtful energy. The last number of *Vanity Fair* proves this peculiarly.[1] Forcible, exciting in its force, still more impressive than exciting, carrying on the interest of the narrative in a flow, deep, full, resistless, it is still quiet – as quiet as reflection, as quiet as memory; and to me there are parts of it that sound as solemn as an oracle. Thackeray is never borne away by his own ardour – he has it under control. His genius obeys him – it is his servant, it works no fantastic changes at its own wild will, it must still achieve the task which reason and sense assign it, and none other. Thackeray is unique. I *can* say no more, I *will* say no less. . . .

SOURCE: extract from letter to W. S. Williams, 29 March 1848; in *Life and Letters of Charlotte Brontë*, Shakespeare Head edition (1932), vol. II, p. 200.

NOTE

1. The 'last number' was the fifteenth (chs 51–3), published at the beginning of March 1848.

John Forster (1848)

. . . We love [Dobbin] from the first page to the last; from his gawky beginnings at school, through his inadequate rewards during life, to his doubtful happiness at the close. He is always kind, loving, truthful, heroical-hearted; a gentleman. The ineffable Peggy O'Dowd, too, is always welcome; whether brushing her husband's accoutrements and preparing his cup of coffee while he takes his natural rest before the battle of Waterloo, or plotting and planning to marry the major with Glorvina, or watching tenderly over the sick bed of the desolate Amelia, or breaking off the intrigue between the lieutenant and the surgeon's wife, or quarrelling with all the other ladies of the regiment, or dancing down an interminable succession of military men and civilians in an Irish jig. Nor less is her quiet, submissive, gallant, and good-natured husband worthy of her. The poor curate at Brompton, Miss Clapp, Miss Swartz, Jemima, Miss Briggs, Lady Jane, and others, are also people we can take to our heart, and in whose society we edify. Perhaps the noblest conception of all, however, is the manner in which the good qualities of the manly but battered old *roué*, Rawdon, ignorant and uneducated except by vice, are developed under the combined influence of paternal affection, adversity, and occasional association with the good.

Still it cannot be denied that it is in those characters where great natural talents and energy are combined with unredeemed depravity that the author puts forth his full powers, and that in the management and contemplation of them he seems absolutely to revel. The Marquis of Steyne is a magnificent picture; his fiendish sagacity, energy, absorbing self-indulgences, and contemptuous tramplings upon everything human and divine, fascinate while they revolt. It is in like manner impossible to escape being charmed with the indomitable buoyancy, self-possession, and *aplomb* of the little adventuress, Becky, even while we are conscious of her utter depravity. She commits every conceivable wickedness; dishonours her husband, betrays her friend, degrades and embrutes herself, and finally commits a murder; without in the least losing those smart, good-tempered, sensible manners and ways, which ingratiate her with the reader in spite of all their atrocities. In this we may think the art questionably employed, but it is not to be denied that it is very extraordinary art; and it is due to Mr Thackeray to add that he has been careful to explain the blended good and evil in this woman by very curious and impressive early details of the circumstances of her birth and bringing up. Nor is it so much with respect to these exceptional characters that we feel inclined to complain of the taunting, cynical, sarcastic tone that too much pervades the work, as with respect to a preponderance of unredeemed selfishness in the more common-place as well as the leading characters, such as the Bullocks, Mrs Clapp, the Miss Dobbinses even, and Amelia's mother. We can relish the shrewd egoism of Miss Crawley; can admire, while we tremble at, the terrible intentness of Mrs Bute Crawley, who writes her husband's sermons, drills her daughters, and persecutes with selfish sycophancy till everybody flies from her; we can bow with awe and veneration before Lady Southdown, that miraculous compound of Lady Bountiful and Lady Macbeth; we can triumph completely over such fribblers as Sir Pitt Crawley the second, and Tapeworm; we see what power there is in making young Osborne so heartless, old Osborne so hateful, old Sedley so contemptible; but we feel that the atmosphere of the work is overloaded with these exhalations of human folly and wicked-ness. We gasp for a more liberal alternation of refreshing breezes of unsophisticated honesty. Fielding, after he has administered a sufficient dose of Blifil's choke-damp, purifies the air by a hearty laugh from Tom Jones. But the stifling ingredients are adminis-tered by Mr Thackeray to excess, without the necessary relief.

It is exclusively in an artistical point of view that we offer this criticism. It would be unjust in the extreme to impute an immoral tendency to *Vanity Fair*. Vice and folly are never made alluring in it, though all justice is done to their superficial meretricious charms. Mr Thackeray's moral is true and just. It is the victims of such adventurers as Becky who are made so mainly by their own faults and follies. Unsuspicious virtue and innocence – as in the case of Dobbin and Amelia – have a charm in their own simple integrity that unconsciously baffles her spells. It is the vices of her victims that subject them to her power – whether their vices be inherent, gross, and revolting, as in the case of Sir Pitt Crawley; or superinduced on a naturally better, but ignorant and uneducated nature, as in the case of poor Rawdon; or feeble and degrading, as in that compound of silly vanity and selfishness, Joseph Sedley; or merely insipidly heartless and unthinking, as with young Osborne. But this moral is insisted upon with a pertinacity, and illustrations of it are heaped upon us with a redundant profusion, unalleviated by a sufficient amount of more gratifying images, that seems to us to go beyond the limits of the pleasurable, and consequently of true art.

SOURCE: extract from review in *The Examiner*, 22 July 1848.

Robert Bell (1848)

... *Vanity Fair* is a movable wardrobe, without hearts or understandings beneath. But there still remains the question – important to all Art that addresses itself to the laudable business of scourging the foibles and criminalities of mankind – Is there any den of vice so utterly depraved, any round of intercourse so utterly hollow and deceitful, that there is not some redeeming feature lurking somewhere, under rags or tinsel?

This revolting reflex of society is literally true enough. But it does not shew us the whole truth. Are there not women, even in *Vanity Fair*, capable of nobler things than are here set down for them? Are they all schemers or *intrigantes*, worldwise, shuffling, perfidious, empty-headed? With the exception of poor Amelia, whose pale lustre shines out so gently in the midst of these harpies, there is scarcely a woman in *Vanity Fair* from whom we should not shrink in private life as from a contagion. And poor Amelia goes but a short way to purify the foul atmosphere. The author has given her a heart, but no understanding. If he has made her patient and good, loving, trusting, enduring, he has also made her a fool. Her meekness under suffering, her innocent faith in the evils which she lacks sagacity to penetrate, constantly excite our pity; but the helpless weakness of her character forces the sentiment to the verge of that feeling to which pity is said to be akin. . . .

Looking back upon this story, we are struck more than ever by the simplicity of its conduct. It is not constructed upon a legitimate principle, or upon any principle at all. It is a novel without a plan, as without a hero. There are two distinct narratives running through it, which not only never interfere with each other, but frequently help each other on. Shoals of characters are drafted through its pages, but they never crowd or jostle each other, or produce the slightest confusion of action or obscurity of incident. The whole business of the fiction moves on before us, with as little reference to a beginning, middle, or end, as the progress of one's own life. The established usages of novels are entirely set aside. Instead of winding up with the merry marriage bells, as if all human interest in the personages of a story terminated in Doctors' Commons, the real interest does not fairly begin until the marriage bells have done their office. Nor is this interest kept up by factitious means. There are no extraneous sources opened as we go along – no episodes to relieve the route – no superfluous characters to strew it with variety. The interest is progressive and complete to the end. . . . The originality of the treatment, the freshness and fluency of the style, and the absence of peculiarities in the diction or terms of expression, inspire it with the charm of perpetual variety. No writer was ever less of a mannerist, and few writers have displayed within the compass of a single story more fertility of invention, or a more accurate knowledge of life. . . .

SOURCE: extracts from review in *Fraser's Magazine*, September 1848.

Elizabeth Rigby, Lady Eastlake (1848)

... With few exceptions the personages are too like our every-
day selves and neighbours to draw any distinct moral from. We
cannot see our way clearly. Palliations of the bad and disappointments in the good are perpetually obstructing our judgment, by
bringing what should decide it too close to that common standard
of experience in which our only rule of opinion is charity. For it is
only in fictitious characters which are highly coloured for one
definite object, or in notorious personages viewed from a
distance, that the course of the true moral can be seen to run
straight – once bring the individual with his life and circumstances closely before you, and it is lost to the mental eye in the
thousand pleas and witnesses, unseen and unheard before, which
rise up to overshadow it. And what are all these personages in
Vanity Fair but feigned names for our own beloved friends and
acquaintances, seen under such a puzzling cross-light of good in
evil, and evil in good, of sins and sinnings against, of little to be
praised virtues, and much to be excused vices, that we cannot
presume to moralise upon them – not even to judge
them – content to exclaim sorrowfully with the old prophet,
'Alas! my brother!' Every actor on the crowded stage of *Vanity
Fair* represents some type of that perverse mixture of humanity in
which there is ever something not wholly to approve or to
condemn. There is the desperate devotion of a fond heart to a
false object, which we cannot respect; there is the vain, weak
man, half good and half bad, who is more despicable in our eyes
than the decided villain. There are the irretrievably wretched
education, and the unquenchably manly instincts, both contend-
ing in the confirmed *roué*, which melt us to the tenderest pity.
There is the selfishness and self-will which the possessor of great
wealth and fawning relations can hardly avoid. There is the
vanity and fear of the world, which assist mysteriously with pious
principles in keeping a man respectable; there are combinations
of this kind of every imaginable human form and colour,

redeemed but feebly by the steady excellence of an awkward man, and the genuine heart of a vulgar woman, till we feel inclined to tax Mr. Thackeray with an under estimate of our nature, forgetting that Madame de Staël is right after all, and that without a little conventional rouge no human complexion can stand the stage-lights of fiction.

. . . Becky was a thrifty dame, and liked to despatch two birds with one stone. And she was honest, too, after a fashion. The part of wife she acts at first as well, and better than most; but as for that of mother, there she fails from the beginning. She knew that maternal love was no business of hers – that a fine frontal development could give her no help there – and puts so little spirit into her imitation that no one could be taken in for a moment. She felt that that bill, of all others, would be sure to be dishonoured, and it went against her conscience – we mean her sense – to send it in.

In short, the only respect in which Becky's course gives us pain is when it locks itself into that of another, and more genuine child of this earth. No one can regret those being entangled in her nets whose vanity and meanness of spirit alone led them into its meshes – such are rightly served; but we do grudge her that real sacred thing called *love*, even of a Rawdon Crawley, who has more of that self-forgetting, all-purifying feeling for his little evil spirit than many a better man has for a good woman. We do grudge Becky *a heart*, though it belong only to a swindler. Poor, sinned against, vile, degraded, but still true-hearted Rawdon! – you stand next in our affections and sympathies to honest Dobbin himself. It was the instinct of a good nature which made the Major feel that the stamp of the Evil One was upon Becky; and it was the stupidity of a good nature which made the Colonel never suspect it. He was a cheat, a black-leg, an unprincipled dog; but still 'Rawdon *is* a man, and he hanged to him,' as the Rector says . . .

SOURCE: extracts from review in the *Quarterly Review*, December 1848.

Theodore Martin (1853)

. . . That Mr. Thackeray may have pushed his views to excess, we do not deny. He might, we think, have accomplished his object quite as effectually by letting in a little more sunshine on his picture, and by lightening the shadows in some of his characters. Without any compromise of truth, he might have given us somebody to admire and esteem, without qualifications or humiliating reserves. That no human being is exempt from frailties, we need not be reminded. The 'divine Imogen' herself, we daresay, had her faults, if the whole truth were told; and we will not undertake to say, that Juliet may not have cost old Capulet a good deal of excusable anxiety. But why dash our admiration by needlessly reminding us of such facts? There is a wantonness in fixing the eye upon some merely casual flaw, after you have filled the heart and imagination with a beautiful image. It is a sorry morality which evermore places the death's-head among the flowers and garlands of the banquet. In *Vanity Fair*, Mr. Thackeray has frequently fallen into this error; and he has further marred it by wilfully injuring our interest in the only characters which he puts forward for our regard. Anxious to avoid the propensity of novelists to make Apollos of their heroes, and paragons of their heroines, he has run into the opposite extreme and made Dobbin – the only thoroughly excellent and loveable character in the book, – so ungainly as to be all but objectionable, and his pet heroine, Amelia, so foolishly weak as to wear out our patience.

This is all the more vexatious, seeing that the love of Dobbin for Amelia is the finest delineation of pure and unselfish devotion within the whole range of fiction. Such love in woman has often been depicted, but Mr. Thackeray is the first who has had the courage to essay, and the delicacy of touch to perfect, a portraiture of this lifelong devotion in the opposite sex. It is a favourite theory of his, that men who love best are prone to be most mistaken in their choice. We doubt the truth of the position;

and we question the accuracy of the illustration in Dobbin. He would have got off his knees, we think, and gone away long before he did; at all events, having once gone, the very strength of character which attached him to Amelia so long would have kept him away. Why come back to mate with one whom he had proved unable to reach to the height of the attachment which he bore her? Admirable as are the concluding scenes between Amelia and the Major, we wish Mr. Thackeray could have wound up his story in some other way, for nothing is, to our minds, sadder among the grave impressions left by this saddening book, than the thought that even Dobbin has found his ennobling dream of devotion to be a weariness and a vanity. It is as though one had ruthlessly trodden down some single solitary flower in a desert place.

SOURCE: extract from article in the *Westminster Review*, April 1853.

2. LETTERS OF THACKERAY

1. TO HIS MOTHER, MRS CARMICHAEL-SMYTH, 2 July 1847

. . . Of course you are quite right about Vanity Fair and Amelia being selfish – it is mentioned in this very number. My object is not to make a perfect character or anything like it. Dont you see how odious all the people are in the book (with exception of Dobbin) – behind whom all there lies a dark moral I hope. What I want is to make a set of people living without God in the world (only that is a cant phrase) greedy pompous mean perfectly self

satisfied for the most part and at ease about their superior virtue.
Dobbin & poor Briggs are the only 2 people with real humility as
yet. Amelia's to come, when her scoundrel of a husband is well
dead with a ball in his odious bowels; when she has had sufferings,
a child, and a religion – But she has at present a quality above
most people whizz: LOVE – by w^{h.} she shall be saved. Save me,
save me too O my God and Father, cleanse my heart and teach
me my duty.

I wasn't going to write in this way when I began. But these
thoughts pursue me plentifully. Will they ever come to a good
end? I should doubt God who gave them if I doubted that. . . .

II. TO THE DUKE OF DEVONSHIRE, 1 May 1848

My Lord Duke, – Mrs. Rawdon Crawley, whom I saw last week,
and whom I informed of your Grace's desire to have her portrait,
was good enough to permit me to copy a little drawing made of
her 'in happier days', she said with a sigh, by Smee, the Royal
Academician.

Mrs. Crawley now lives in a small but very pretty little house in
Belgravia, and is conspicuous for her numerous charities, which
always get into the newspapers, and her unaffected piety. Many
of the most exalted and spotless of her own sex visit her, and are of
opinion that she is a *most injured woman*. There is no *sort of truth* in
the stories regarding Mrs. Crawley and the late Lord Steyne. The
licentious character of that nobleman alone gave rise to reports
from which, alas! the most spotless life and reputation cannot
always defend themselves. The present Sir Rawdon Crawley
(who succeeded his late uncle, Sir Pitt, 1832; Sir Pitt died on the
passing of the Reform Bill) does not see his mother, and his
undutifulness is a cause of the deepest grief to that admirable
lady. 'If it were not for *higher things*', she says, how could she have
borne up against the world's calumny, a wicked husband's
cruelty and falseness, and the thanklessness (sharper than a
serpent's tooth) of an adored child? But she has been preserved,
mercifully preserved, to bear all these griefs, and awaits her
reward *elsewhere*. The *italics* are Mrs. Crawley's own.

She took the style and title of Lady Crawley for some time after Sir Pitt s death in 1832; but it turned out that Colonel Crawley, Governor of Coventry Island, had died of fever three months before his brother, whereupon Mrs. Rawdon was obliged to lay down the title which she had prematurely assumed.

The late Jos. Sedley, Esq., of the Bengal Civil Service, left her two lakhs of rupees, on the interest of which the widow lives in the practices of piety and benevolence before mentioned. She has lost what little good looks she once possessed, and wears false hair and teeth (the latter give her rather a ghastly look when she smiles), and – for a pious woman – is the best-crinolined lady in Knightsbridge district.

Colonel and Mrs. W. Dobbin live in Hampshire, near Sir R. Crawley; Lady Jane was godmother to their little girl, and the ladies are exceedingly attached to each other. The Colonel's *History of the Punjaub* is looked for with much anxiety in some circles.

Captain and Lt.-Colonel G. Sedley-Osborne (he wishes, he says, to be distinguished from some other branches of the Osborne family, and is descended by the mother's side from Sir Charles Sedley) is, I need not say, well, for I saw him in a most richly embroidered cambric pink shirt with diamond studs, bowing to your Grace at the last party at Devonshire House. He is in Parliament; but the property left him by his Grandfather has, I hear, been a good deal overrated.

He was very sweet upon Miss Crawley, Sir Pitt's daughter, who married her cousin, the present Baronet, and a good deal cut up when he was refused. He is not, however, a man to be permanently cast down by sentimental disappointments. His chief cause of annoyance at the present moment is that he is growing bald, but his whiskers are still without a gray hair and the finest in London.

I think these are the latest particulars relating to a number of persons about whom your Grace was good enough to express some interest. I am very glad to be enabled to give this information, and am –

Your Grace's very much obliged servant,

W. M. Thackeray.

P.S. – Lady O'Dowd is at O'Dowdstown arming. She has just sent in a letter of adhesion to the Lord-Lieutenant, which has been acknowledged by his Excellency's private secretary, Mr. Corry Connellan. Miss Glorvina O'Dowd is thinking of coming up to the Castle to marry the last-named gentleman.

P.S. 2.– The India mail just arrived announces the utter ruin of the Union Bank of Calcutta, in which all Mrs. Crawley's money was. Will Fate never cease to persecute that suffering saint?

III. TO ROBERT BELL, 3 September 1848

My dear Bell

Although I have made a rule to myself never to thank critics yet I like to break it continually, and especially in the present instance for what I hope is the excellent article in Fraser [quoted above, section 1 – Ed.]. It seems to me very just in most points as regards the author: some he questions as usual – If I had put in more fresh air as you call it my object would have been defeated – It is to indicate, in cheerful terms, that we are for the most part an abominably foolish and selfish people 'desperately wicked' and all eager after vanities. Everybody is you see in that book, – for instance if I had made Amelia a higher order of woman there would have been no vanity in Dobbins falling in love with her, whereas the impression at present is that he is a fool for his pains that he has married a silly little thing and in fact has found out his error rather a sweet and tender one however, *quia multum amavit* I want to leave everybody dissatisfied and unhappy at the end of the story – we ought all to be with our own and all other stories. Good God dont I see (in that may-be cracked and warped looking glass in which I am always looking) my own weaknesses wickednesses lusts follies shortcomings? in company let us hope with better qualities about which we will pretermit discourse. We must lift up our voices about these and howl to a congregation of fools: so much at least has been my endeavour.

You have all of you taken my misanthropy to task – I wish I could myself: but take the world by a certain standard (you know what I mean) and who dares talk of having any virtue at all? For instance Forster [the relevant passage is quoted above, section 1 – Ed.] says After a scene with Blifil, the air is cleared by a laugh of Tom Jones – Why Tom Jones in my holding is as big a rogue as Blifil. Before God he is – I mean the man is selfish according to his nature as Blifil according to his. In fact I've a strong impression that we are most of us not fit for – never mind.

Pathos I hold should be very occasional indeed in humourous works and indicated rather than expressed or expressed very rarely. In the passage where Amelia is represented as trying to separate herself from the boy – She goes upstairs and leaves him with his aunt 'as that poor Lady Jane Grey tried the axe that was to separate her slender life' [ch. 50] I say that is a fine image whoever wrote it (& I came on it quite by surprize in a review the other day) that is greatly pathetic I think: it leaves you to make your own sad pictures – We shouldn't do much more than that I think in comic books – In a story written in the pathetic key it would be different & then the comedy perhaps should be occasional. Some day – but a truce to egotistical twaddle. It seems to me such a time ago that V F was written that one may talk of it as of some body elses performance. My dear Bell I am very thankful for your friendliness & pleased to have your good opinion.

SOURCE: extracts from Gordon N. Ray (ed.), *The Letters and Private Papers of William Makepeace Thackeray* (1945–6).

PART TWO

Later Comments

Anthony Trollope (1879)

. . . This special fault was certainly found with *Vanity Fair* at the time. Heroines should not only be beautiful, but should be endowed also with a quasi celestial grace, – grace of dignity, propriety, and reticence. A heroine should hardly want to be married, the arrangement being almost too mundane, – and, should she be brought to consent to undergo such bond, because of its acknowledged utility, it should be at some period so distant as hardly to present itself to the mind as a reality. Eating and drinking should be altogether indifferent to her, and her clothes should be picturesque rather than smart, and that from accident rather than design. Thackeray's Amelia does not at all come up to the description here given. She is proud of having a lover, constantly declaring to herself and to others that he is 'the greatest and the best of men', – whereas the young gentleman is, in truth, a very little man. She is not at all indifferent as to her finery, nor, as we see incidentally, to enjoying her suppers at Vauxhall. She is anxious to be married, – and as soon as possible. A hero too should be dignified and of a noble presence; a man who, though he may be as poor as Nicholas Nickleby, should nevertheless be beautiful on all occasions, and never deficient in readiness, address, or self-assertion. *Vanity Fair* is especially declared by the author to be 'a novel without a hero', and therefore we have hardly a right to complain a deficiency of heroic conduct in any of the male characters. But Captain Dobbin does become the hero, and is deficient. Why was he called Dobbin, except to make him ridiculous? Why is he so shamefully ugly, so shy, so awkward? Why was he the son of a grocer? Thackeray in so depicting him was determined to run counter to the recognised taste of novel readers. And then again there was the feeling of another great fault. Let there be the virtuous in a novel and let there be the vicious, the dignified and the undignified, the sublime and the ridiculous, – only let the virtuous, the dignified, and the sublime be in the ascendant.

Edith Bellenden, and Lord Evandale, and Morton himself would
be too stilted, were they not enlivened by Mause, and Cuddie,
and Poundtext. But here, in this novel, the vicious and the absurd
have been made to be of more importance than the good and the
noble. Becky Sharp and Rawdon Crawley are the real heroine
and hero of the story. It is with them that the reader is called
upon to interest himself. It is of them that he will think when he is
reading the book. It is by them that he will judge the book when
he has read it. There was no doubt a feeling with the public that
though satire may be very well in its place, it should not be made
the backbone of a work so long and so important as this. A short
story such as *Catherine* or *Barry Lyndon* might be pronounced to
have been called for by the iniquities of an outside world; but this
seemed to the readers to have been addressed almost to
themselves. Now men and women like to be painted as Titian
would paint them, or Raffaelle, – not as Rembrandt, or even
Rubens.

Whether the ideal or the real is the best form of a novel may be
questioned, but there can be no doubt that as there are novelists
who cannot descend from the bright heaven of the imagination to
walk with their feet upon the earth, so there are others to whom it
is not given to soar among clouds. The reader must please
himself, and make his selection if he cannot enjoy both. There are
many who are carried into a heaven of pathos by the woes of a
Master of Ravenswood, who fail altogether to be touched by the
enduring constancy of a Dobbin. There are others, – and I will
not say but they may enjoy the keenest delight which literature
can give, – who cannot employ their minds on fiction unless it be
conveyed in poetry. With Thackeray it was essential that the
representations made by him should be, to his own thinking,
lifelike. A Dobbin seemed to him to be such a one as might
probably be met with in the world, whereas to his thinking a
Ravenswood was simply a creature of the imagination. He would
have said of such, as we would say of female faces by Raffaelle,
that women would like to be like them, but are not like them.
Men might like to be like Ravenswood, and women may dream
of men so formed and constituted, but such men do not exist.
Dobbins do, and therefore Thackeray chose to write of a Dobbin.

So also of the preference given to Becky Sharp and to Rawdon Crawley. Thackeray thought that more can be done by exposing the vices than extolling the virtues of mankind. No doubt he had a more thorough belief in the one than in the other. The Dobbins he did encounter – seldom; the Rawdon Crawleys very often. He saw around him so much that was mean! He was hurt so often by the little vanities of people! It was thus that he was driven to . . . overthoughtfulness about snobs . . . . It thus became natural to him to insist on the thing which he hated with unceasing assiduity, and only to break out now and again into a rapture of love for the true nobility which was dear to him, – as he did with the character of Captain Dobbin.

It must be added to all this that, before he has done with his snob or his knave, he will generally weave in some little trait of humanity by which the sinner shall be relieved from the absolute darkness of utter iniquity. He deals with no Varneys or Deputy-Shepherds, all villany and all lies, because the snobs and knaves he had seen had never been all snob or all knave. Even Shindy probably had some feeling for the poor woman he left at home. Rawdon Crawley loved his wicked wife dearly, and there were moments even with her in which some redeeming trait half reconciles her to the reader.

Such were the faults which were found in *Vanity Fair*; but though the faults were found freely, the book was read by all. Those who are old enough can well remember the effect which it had, and the welcome which was given to the different numbers as they appeared. Though the story is vague and wandering, clearly commenced without any idea of an ending, yet there is something in the telling which makes every portion of it perfect in itself.

. . . To the end [Becky] is the same, – utterly false, selfish, covetous, and successful. To have made such a woman really in love would have been a mistake. Her husband she likes best, – because he is, or was, her own. But there is no man so foul, so wicked, so unattractive, but that she can fawn over him for money and jewels. There are women to whom nothing is nasty, either in person, language, scenes, actions, or principle, – and Becky is one of them; and yet she is herself attractive. A most wonderful sketch, for the perpetration of which all Thackeray's power of combined indignation and humour was necessary!

The story of Amelia and her two lovers, George Osborne and Captain, or as he came afterwords to be, Major, and Colonel Dobbin, is less interesting, simply because goodness and eulogy are less exciting than wickedness and censure. Amelia is a true, honest-hearted, thoroughly English young woman, who loves her love because he is grand, – to her eyes, – and loving him, loves him with all her heart. Readers have said that she is silly, only because she is not heroic. I do not know that she is more silly than many young ladies whom we who are old have loved in our youth, or than those whom our sons are loving at the present time. Readers complain of Amelia because she is absolutely true to nature. There are no Raffaellistic touches, no added graces, no divine romance. She is feminine all over, and British, – loving, true, thoroughly unselfish, yet with a taste for having things comfortable, forgiving, quite capable of jealousy, but prone to be appeased at once, at the first kiss; quite convinced that her lover, her husband, her children are the people in all the world to whom the greatest consideration is due. Such a one is sure to be the dupe of a Becky Sharp, should a Becky Sharp come in her way, – as is the case with so many sweet Amelias whom we have known. But in a matter of love she is sound enough and sensible enough, – and she is as true as steel. I know no trait in Amelia which a man would be ashamed to find in his own daughter.

She marries her George Osborne, who, to tell the truth of him, is but a poor kind of fellow, though he is a brave soldier. He thinks much of his own person, and is selfish. Thackeray puts in a touch or two here and there by which he is made to be odious. He would rather give a present to himself than to the girl who loved him. Nevertheless, when her father is ruined he marries her, and he fights bravely at Waterloo, and is killed. 'No more firing was heard at Brussels. The pursuit rolled miles away. Darkness came down on the field and the city, – and Amelia was praying for George, who was lying on his face, dead, with a bullet through his heart.'

Then follows the long courtship of Dobbin, the true hero, – he who has been the friend of George since their old school-days;

who has lived with him and served him, and has also loved Amelia. But he has loved her, – as one man may love another, – solely with a view to the profit of his friend. He has known all along that George and Amelia have been engaged to each other as boy and girl. George would have neglected her, but Dobbin would not allow it. George would have jilted the girl who loved him, but Dobbin would not let him. He had nothing to get for himself, but loving her as he did, it was the work of his life to get for her all that she wanted.

George is shot at Waterloo, and then come fifteen years of widowhood, – fifteen years during which Becky is carrying on her manoeuvres, – fifteen years during which Amelia cannot bring herself to accept the devotion of the old captain, who becomes at last a colonel. But at the end she is won. 'The vessel is in port. He has got the prize he has been trying for all his life. The bird has come in at last. There it is, with its head on its shoulder, billing and cooing clean up to his heart, with soft outstretched fluttering wings. This is what he has asked for everyday and hour for eighteen years. This is what he has pined after. Here it is, – the summit, the end, the last page of the third volume.'

The reader as he closes the book has on his mind a strong conviction, the strongest possible conviction, that among men George is as weak and Dobbin as noble as any that he has met in literature; and that among women Amelia is as true and Becky as vile as any he has encountered. . . .

SOURCE: extracts from *Thackeray* (London, 1879) pp. 92–5, 104–6.

W. C. Brownell (1901)

. . . the one reason for insisting on 'objectivity' in art is that it is often the condition of illusion – the illusion of reality in virtue of which art is art and not itself reality, the mere material of art. If Thackeray's 'subjectivity' destroyed illusion it would indeed be

inartistic. The notable thing about it is that it deepens illusion.
The reality of his 'happy, harmless fable-land' is wonderfully
enhanced by the atmosphere with which his moralizing enfolds
it, and at the same time the magic quality of this medium itself
enforces our sense that it *is* fable-land, and enables us to savor *as*
illusion the illusion of its art. Nothing could establish the edifice of
his imaginative fiction on so sound a basis as those confidences
with the reader – subtly inspired by his governing passion for
truth – in which he is constantly protesting that it is fiction after
all.

. . . It is the moral and social qualities, of course, that unite
men in society, and make it something other than the sum of the
individuals composing it. Thackeray's personages are never
portrayed in isolation. They are a part of the *milieu* in which they
exist, and which has itself therefore much more distinction and
relief than an environment which is merely a framework. How
they regard each other, how they feel toward and what they think
of each other, the mutuality of their very numerous and vital
relations, furnishes an important strand in the texture of the story
in which they figure. Their activities are modified by the air they
breathe in common. Their conduct is controlled, their ideas
affected, even their desires and ambitions dictated, by the
general ideals of the society that includes them. So far as it goes,
therefore, – and it would be easy to exaggerate its limitations,
which are trivial in comparison, – Thackeray's picture of society
is the most vivid, as it is incontestably the most real, in prose
fiction. The temperament of the artist and satirist combined, the
preoccupation with the moral element in character, – and in
logical sequence, with its human and social side, – lead naturally
to the next step of viewing man in his relations, and the
construction of a miniature world. And in addition to the high
place in literature won for him by his insight into character,
Thackeray's social picture has given him a distinction that is
perhaps unique. . . .

[There is a strong sense of life in Thackeray.] It appears in its
intensity in *Vanity Fair*, in its variety in *The Newcomes*, in its
immitigability in *Pendennis*, with a definiteness and reality to be
found elsewhere only in the few great classics of literature. The

tension of *Vanity Fair* is almost oppressive. The first-fruits of Thackeray's maturity, after the Titmarsh period, and coming as it did into the world of fiction occupied by the writers burlesqued in the 'Novels by Eminent Hands', its substitution of truth for convention had something almost fierce in it. The title alone, the few words 'Before the Curtain', the last paragraph of the book, pointed its felicity of extreme pertinence, and any one could see that a new power in fiction had arisen. But it is not its satiric force that has preserved it. It has the perennial interest of fundamental spontaneity, and its tinge of Juvenalian color merely accentuates its positive and constructive quality. Life in it is tremendously real, whatever its goal. It is not a fairy-tale, and things are far from what they seem. Any episode or incident or subordinate character of the story shares its intensity. The unedifying career of Jos Sedley, for example, is grimly vital. I remember no book which is, like *Vanity Fair*, a portrayal of life rather than purely a satire that is so free from triviality.

Source: extracts from *Victorian Prose Masters* (London, 1901) pp. 8–9, 29, 33.

Charles Whibley (1903)

... The story grew as it chose, from month to month, and dragged its author after it. And this explains its failure to stop when it should. The logical end of the book is Rawdon Crawley's appointment to the Governorship of Coventry Island, and the regathering of the threads – over 150 pages – is a wanton and tedious operation.

So far as its construction goes, *Vanity Fair* is a novel of adventure, of adventure in society, where hearts and banks are broken more easily than heads or dynasties; and despite his own declaration that he wanted to make 'a set of people living without God in the world', the book has not a plan or motive in the sense that Balzac and the moderns have understood it. For Thackeray, although he might, an he chose, have studied the *Comédie Humaine*, remained old-fashioned to the end, and let his personages wander up and down as they listed, content if only he could now and again slip in a sentiment, or castigate a favourite vice on his own account. But the charge commonly brought against *Vanity Fair* that it is heartless and cynical cannot be sustained for a moment. A novel of manners does not exhaust the whole of human life, and Thackeray had a perfect right to choose such puppets for his shows as aroused his keenest interest. Nor is the book merely a novel of manners; it is a satire as well. The author does not ask his readers to profess sympathy with his ruffians. He demands no more than an appreciation of a witty presentment and of deft draughtsmanship. If he had suppressed the sentiment, which ever rose up in his heart, *Vanity Fair* might have been as un-moral as *The Way of the World*, and what a masterpiece it would have been! Even Amelia, a very Niobe of tears, is drawn with a cold contempt, and I am not certain that she is not as savage a piece of satire as Becky herself.

But Thackeray, though he loved to masquerade as a man of the world, could not help looking even at his own creations with an eye of pity or dislike. He plays the same part in his books as is played in Greek tragedy by a chorus of tiresome elders, and it is this constant intrusion which gives certain passages in *Vanity Fair* a rakish, almost a battered, air. The reader would never dream of taking such persons as Rawdon and his Aunt seriously, were he not told to do so by the author of their being. The reader, had he been allowed, would have been content with an artistic appreciation. But, says Thackeray, 'as we bring our characters forward, I will ask leave, as a man and a brother, not only to introduce them, but occasionally to step down from the platform and talk about them; if they are good and kindly, to love them, and shake them by the hand'. And that is what he is too often – a man and a brother; he forgets the impartiality of the artist, and goes about babbling with his own puppets.

These excesses of sentiment are plain for all to see. They interrupt the progress of the story with irritating frequency. They put a needless accent upon what is called the 'cynicism' of Thackeray, and confuse the very simple method of the book.

'Picture to yourself, oh fair young reader', exclaims the author of Miss Crawley, 'a worldly, selfish, graceless, thankless, religionless old woman, writing in pain and fear, and without her wig. Picture her to yourself, and ere you be old, learn to love and pray.' The reference to the wig betrays an animus which should never disturb a novelist's serenity, and Miss Crawley is otherwise so well drawn that she might safely be left to point her own moral. So on another page he reminds us, with his eye upon the obvious, that 'the bustle, and triumph, and laughter, and gaiety which Vanity Fair exhibits in public do not always pursue the performer into private life.' And from this point of view he defines the purpose of his romance. 'This, dear friends and companions', so he writes in his most intimate style, 'is my amiable object – to walk with you through the Fair, to examine the shops and the shows there; and that we should all come home after the flare, and the noise, and the gaiety, and be perfectly miserable in private.' But why should we be miserable – in private or public – about that in which our interest is, or should be, purely artistic?

However, he is so closely set upon disquisition that he cannot refrain the hand of sentiment even from the character of Rawdon Crawley, whose rough, amiable brutality might have been pictured without a flaw. When the guardsman, who shot Captain Marker, visits Queen's Crawley with his Rebecca, even he, under the auspices of Thackeray, is somewhat abashed. 'What recollections of boyhood and innocence might have been flitting across his brain?' asks the novelist. 'What pangs of dim remorse and doubt and shame?' If elsewhere the excellent Rawdon is drawn with justice, no pangs of remorse or shame would have flitted across his brain, and the character is weakened by each attempt made by the author's sentimentality to weaken that 'spirit of oneness' which should animate it. We resent the interpolation of moral comment, even when Amelia is the moralist's excuse. 'By heavens! it is pitiful,' exclaims Thackeray, 'the bootless love of women for children in Vanity Fair.' What is all this but a confession of weakness. A story which needs annotation fails of its main purpose, and the reader may justly feel irritated who is not left to form his own conclusions.

It is especially in satire that sermonising has no place, for satire is of itself a method of reproof. Though Aristophanes at times laid aside the lash for the lyre, he knew the limits of his *genre* too well to lapse into moral discourses. But Thackeray acts the sheep-dog to his own characters. He plays propriety before them, very much as Miss Briggs ensured the public respectability of Becky Sharp. And when he is angry with them, he scolds them with almost a shrewish tongue. But, despite this concession to his own and the popular taste, Thackeray – with *Vanity Fair* – well deserved the place which he won in the literature of his age. Its style, peculiarly simple and straightforward, was free both from rhetoric and ornament. It suppressed all the tricks of the novelist, and threw what discredit it could upon fine writing. At the same time, it was various enough to express the diverse persons and changing emotions which are the material of the book. The characters are as distinguished as the style. Seldom in the history of English romance had a more genteel company been gathered together, and even when it is disreputable, it is still the best of bad company. Moreover, it is characteristic of the author that for all his moralisings he is most sincerely interested in his blackguards. He cares so little himself for Amelia that he cannot expect to awake an appreciation in his readers; while Dobbin, for all his nobility, is purposely awkward where he is not ridiculous.

But Becky Sharp, always the central figure of the book, is drawn with a firmer hand and brighter colours. You must travel far indeed before you find so good a portrait of the incarnate minx. When she is off the stage the action languishes; the squalor of Queen's Crawley, the grimness of Gaunt House, hold our attention merely as they affect the true heroine of the book. . . .

SOURCE: extract from *William Makepeace Thackeray* (London, 1903) pp. 92 – 7.

Percy Lubbock (1921)

. . . Though the fullness of memory is directed into a consecutive tale, it is not the narrative, not its order and movement, that chiefly holds either Thackeray's attention or ours who read; the narrative is steeped in the suffusion of the general tone, the sensation of the place and the life that he is recalling, and it is out of this effect, insensibly changing and developing, that the novel is created.

For a nearer sight of it I go back to Vanity Fair. The chapters that are concerned with Becky's determined siege of London – 'How to live well on nothing a year' – are exactly to the point; the wonderful things that Thackeray could do, the odd lapse of his power when he had to go beyond his particular province, both are here written large. Every one remembers the chapters and their place in the book. Becky, resolutely shaking off old difficulties for the moment, installs herself with her husband in the heart of the world she means to conquer; she all but succeeds, she just fails. Her campaign and its untimely end are to be pictured; it is an interlude to be filled with stir and glitter, with the sense of the passage of a certain time, above all with intimations of insecurity and precarious fortune; and it is to lead (this it must do) to a scene of final and decisive climax. Such is the effect to be drawn from the matter that Thackeray has stored up – the whole hierarchy of the Crawleys, Steyne, Gaunt House, always with Becky in the midst and to the fore. Up to a point it is precisely the kind of juncture in which Thackeray's art delights. There is abundance of vivid stuff, and the picture to be made of it is highly functional in the book. It is not merely a preparation for a story to follow; it is itself the story, a most important part of it. The chapters representing Becky's manner of life in Curzon Street make the hinge of her career; she approaches her turning-point at the beginning of them, she is past it at the end. Functional, therefore, they are to the last degree; but up to the very climax, or the verge of it, there is no need for a set scene of

dramatic particularity. An impression is to be created, growing
and growing; and it can well be created in the loose panoramic
style which is Thackeray's paramount arm. A general view, once
more, a summary of Becky's course of action, a long look at her
conditions, a participation in her gathering difficulties – that is
the nature and the task of these chapters, that is what Thackeray
proceeds to give us.

He sets about it with a beautiful ease of assurance. From his
height he looks forth, takes in the effect with his sweeping vision,
possesses himself of the gradation of its tone; then, stooping
nearer, he seizes the detail that renders it. But the sense of the
broad survey is first in his thought. When he reflects upon Becky's
life in London and all that came of her attempt to establish herself
there, he is soon assailed by a score of definite recollections, tell-
tale incidents, scraps of talk that show how things were going
with her; but these, it would seem, arise by the way, they spring
up in his mind as he reviews the past. They illustrate what he has
to say, and he takes advantage of them. He brushes past them,
however, without much delaying or particularizing; a hint, a
moment, a glance suffices for the contribution that some event or
colloquy is to make to the picture. Note, for example, how
unceremoniously, again and again, and with how little thought
of disposing a deliberate scene, he drifts into his account of
something that Becky said or did; she begins to talk, you find
there is some one else in the room, you find they are in a certain
room at a certain hour; definition emerges unawares in a
brooding memory. Briefly, to all appearance quite casually, the
little incident shows itself and vanishes; there is a pause to watch
and listen, and then the stream sets forward again, by so much
enriched and reinforced. Or in a heightened mood, as in the
picture of the midnight flurry and alarm of the great desolate
house, when old Pitt Crawley is suddenly struck down, still it is as
though Thackeray circled about the thought of the time and
place, offering swift and piercing glimpses of it, giving no
continuous and dramatic display of a constituted scene.

That foreshortening and generalizing, that fusion of detail,
that subordination of the instance and the occasion to the broad
effect, are the elements of the pictorial art in which Thackeray is

so great a master. So long as it is a matter of sketching a train of life in broad free strokes, the poise and swing of his style are beyond praise. And its perfection is all the more notable that it stands in such contrast with the curious drop and uncertainty of his skill, so soon as there is something more, something different to be done. For Becky's dubious adventure has its climax, it tends towards a conclusion, and the final scene cannot be recalled and summarized in his indirect, reminiscential manner. It must be placed immediately before us, the collapse of Becky's plotting and scheming must be enacted in full view, if it is to have its proper emphasis and rightly round off her career. Hitherto we have been listening to Thackeray, on the whole, while he talked about Becky – talked with such extraordinary brilliance that he evoked her in all her ways and made us see her with his eyes; but now it is time to see her with our own, his lively interpretation of her will serve no longer. Does Becky fail in the end? After all that we have heard of her struggle it has become the great question, and the force of the answer will be impaired if it is not given with the best possible warrant. The best possible, better even than Thackeray's wonderful account of her, will be the plain and immediate *performance* of the answer, its embodiment in a scene that shall pass directly in front of us. The method that was not demanded by the preceding phases of the tale is here absolutely prescribed. Becky, Rawdon, Steyne, must now take the matter into their own hands and show themselves without any other intervention. Hitherto, practically throughout, they have been the creatures of Thackeray's thought, they have been openly and confessedly the figures of *his* vision. Now they must come forward, declare themselves, and be seen for what they are.

And accordingly they do come forward and are seen in a famous passage. Rawdon makes his unexpected return home from prison, and Becky's unfortunate disaster overtakes her, so to say, in our very presence. Perhaps I may seem to exaggerate the change of method which I note at this point; but does it not appear to any one, glancing back at his recollection of the book, that this particular scene is defined and relieved and lighted differently, somehow, from the stream of impressions in which it is set? A space is cleared for it, the stage is swept. This is now no retrospective vision, shared with Thackeray; it is a piece of present action with which we are confronted. It is strictly dramatic, and I suppose it is good drama of its kind. But there is more to be said of it than this – more to be said, even when it has been admitted to be drama of rather a high-pitched, theatrical strain. The foot-lights, it is probably agreed, seem suddenly to flare before Becky and Rawdon, after the clear daylight that reigned in Thackeray's description of them; they appear upon the scene, as they should, but it must be owned that the scene has an artificial look, by comparison with the flowing spontaneity of all that has gone before. And this it is exactly that shows how and where Thackeray's skill betrays him. He is not (like Dickens) naturally inclined to the theatre, the melodramatic has no fatal attraction for him; so that if he is theatrical here, it is not because he inevitably would be, given his chance. It is rather because he must, at all costs, make this climax of his story conclusively *tell*; and in order to do so he is forced to use devices of some crudity – for him they are crude – because his climax, his *scène à faire*, has been insufficiently prepared for. Becky, Rawdon, Steyne, in all this matter that has been leading up to the scene, have scarcely before been rendered in these immediate terms; and now that they appear on their own account they can only make a sure and pronounced effect by perceptibly forcing their note. A little too much is expected of them, and they must make an unnatural effort to meet it.

My instance is a small one, no doubt, to be pressed so far; in lingering over these shades of treatment a critic, it may be thought, loses sight of the book itself. But I am not trying, of course, to criticize Vanity Fair; I am looking for certain details of method, and the small instance is surely illuminating. It shows how little Thackeray's fashion of handling a novel allowed for the big dramatic scene, when at length it had to be faced – how he neglected it in advance, how he refused it till the last possible moment. It is as though he never quite trusted his men and women when he had to place things entirely in their care, standing aside to let them act; he wanted to intervene continually, he hesitated to leave them alone save for a brief and belated half-hour. It was perverse of him, because the men and women would have acquitted themselves so strikingly with a better chance; he gave them life and vigour enough for much more independence than they ever enjoyed. The culmination of Becky's adventure offered a clear opening for full dramatic effect, if he had chosen to take advantage of it. He had steadily piled up his impression, carefully brought all the sense of the situation to converge upon a single point; everything was ready for the great scene of Becky's triumph in the face of the world, one memorable night of a party at Gaunt House. It is incredible that he should let the opportunity slip. There was a chance of a straight, un-hampered view of the whole meaning of his matter; nothing was needed but to allow the scene to show itself, fairly and squarely. All its force would have been lent to the disaster that follows; the dismay, the disillusion, the snarl of anger and defiance, all would have been made beforehand. By so much would the effect of the impending scene, the scene of catastrophe, have been strength-ened. There would have been no necessity for the sudden heightening of the pitch, the thickening of the colour, the incongruous and theatrical tone.

Yet the chance is missed, the triumphal evening passes in a confused haze that leaves the situation exactly where it was before. The episode is only a repetition of the kind of thing that has happened already. There are echoes of festive sound and a rumour of Becky's brilliance; but the significant look that the actual facts might have worn and must have betrayed, the look that by this time Thackeray has so fully instructed his reader to catch – this is not disclosed after all. There is still nothing here but Thackeray's amusing, irrepressible conversation *about* the scene; he cannot make up his mind to clear a space before it and give the situation the free field it cries out for. And if it is asked what kind of clarity I mean, I need only recall another page, close by, which shows it perfectly. Becky had made an earlier appearance at Gaunt House; she had dined there, near the beginning of her social career, and had found herself in a difficulty; there came a moment when she had to face the frigid hostility of the noble ladies of the party, alone with them in the drawing-room, and her assurance failed. In the little scene that ensues the charming veil of Thackeray's talk is suddenly raised;

there is Becky seated at the piano, Lady Steyne listening in a
dream of old memories, the other women chattering at a
distance, when the jarring doors are thrown open and the men
return. It is all over in half a page, but in that glimpse the story is
lifted forward dramatically; ocular proof, as it were, is added to
Thackeray's account of Becky's doubtful and delicate position.
As a matter of curiosity I mention the one moment in the later
episode, the evening of those strangely ineffective charades at
Gaunt House, which appears to me to open the same kind of rift
in the haze; it is a single glimpse of Steyne, applauding Becky's
triumph. He is immediately there, an actor in the show, alive and
expressive, but he is alone; none of the others so emerges, even
Becky is only a luminous spot in the dimness. As for the relation of
the three, Steyne, Becky, and her husband, which is on the point
of becoming so important, there is nothing to be seen of it.

  Right and left in the novels of Thackeray one may gather
instances of the same kind – the piercing and momentary shaft of
direct vision, the big scene approached and then refused. It is
easy to find another in Vanity Fair. Who but Thackeray could
have borne to use the famous matter of the Waterloo ball, a
wonderful gift for a novelist to find in his path, only to waste it, to
dissipate its effect, to get no real contribution from it after all? In
the queer, haphazard, polyglot interlude that precedes it
Thackeray is, of course, entirely at home; there it is a question of
the picture-making he delights in, the large impression of things
in general, the evocation of daily life; Brussels in its talkative
suspense, waiting for the sound of the guns, feeding on rumour,
comes crowding into the chapter. And then the great occasion
that should have crowned it, into which the story naturally and
logically passes – for again the scene is not a decorative patch,
the story needs it – the Waterloo ball is nothing, leaves no image,
constitutes no effect whatever; the reader, looking back on the
book, might be quite uncertain whether he had been there or not.
Nobody could forget the sight of Lady Bareacres, sitting under
the *porte cochère* in her horseless carriage – of good Mrs. O'Dowd,
rising in the dawn to equip her warrior for battle – of George
Osborne, dead on the field; but these are Thackeray's flashes of
revelation, straight and sure, and they are all the drama, strictly

speaking, that he extorts from his material. The rest is picture, stirringly, vivaciously reflected in his unfailing memory – with the dramatic occasion to which it tends, the historic affair of the 'revelry by night', neglected and lost. . . .

SOURCE: extract from *The Craft of Fiction* (London, 1921), reprinted in Traveller's Library edition (1926) pp. 97–106.

G. K. Chesterton (1930)

The rising generations, when confronted with *Vanity Fair*, as with the *Iliad*, the *Book of Job* or other works, are fully entitled to be struck, or even repelled, by the appearance of something old-fashioned; so long as they remember that they will not go on rising very long, before they become old-fashioned themselves. But in the matter of the form of fiction, fashions follow each other today with rather bewildering rapidity. *Vanity Fair* might have appeared somewhat formless to some of the old supporters of the classical unities; it might again have appeared somewhat formless to the exact artistry of the school and generation of Stevenson; but even if it were much more formless than it is, it could hardly reach the superb ecstasy of formlessness, which is admired in many of the long realistic novels of today. As a matter of fact, it is far less formless than it looks. The narrative style of the novelist is garrulous and therefore discursive. Indeed the way in which the tale is told is in a rather special sense the manner of gossip. It is gossip not only in being casual and allusive; but also in actually being indirect. Much of the story comes to us by rùmour; tales are told by one club man to another club man; we might say by one Thackeray to another Thackeray. He often manages to suggest more than he is prepared to say, by putting up some jolly old snob to say it. The method of gossip has a certain realism; it suggests the same figure seen from many sides; like a single man seen in all the mirrors of the London club. It will at least be well if the

younger critic realises that Thackeray's style, which seems to be
one of drawling and dawdling irrelevancy, is not an accident but
an artistic method, suitable to his special purposes; and that
sometimes his very irrelevance is as relevant as a conjurer's
patter. In more direct and economical stylists, such as Stevenson,
we know what the author thinks of the character; and possibly
what the character thinks of the other character whom he marries
or murders with a cutlass. In books like *Vanity Fair*, it is very
necessary that we should also know what the World thinks of the
character; for indeed in *Vanity Fair* the chief character is the
World. It would be an exaggeration to say that the World is the
villain of the piece; but it may well be said that in this sense it is a
novel without a hero. The theme of it is what the old comic
dramatist called *The Way of the World*; and a sort of satiric but not
too severe judgment on it, for the way in which it treats all its
characters, including the comparatively rare heroes and villains.
For this purpose it is necessary that the club of Thackeray, like
the island of Prospero, should be 'full of voices'; and that we
should get a general sense of much that is mere talk, or even mere
echoes. For instance; I doubt if it would have been possible to
convey the historic but rather unique position of the few very
great, because very rich, English Dukes or Marquises (who were
something quite different from mere nobility or gentry, in the
sense in which any squire or soldier might happen to have a title);
it would have been impossible to suggest the strange public
position of a man like Lord Steyne, without all those scattered
allusions to him and momentary glimpses of him, in the distance,
on the high places of English social life. That sort of man is
Somebody through all the nobodies who never knew him. We
should not feel it enough by being suddenly introduced into his
presence; we have to feel that his very absence is as impressive as
his presence. All this gossip about the great House of Gaunt is
deliberate and even delicate, and without it we should not get the
distance or the perspective that points to the ultimate scene; or
feel the full force of that splendid blow which the obscure and
stupid husband struck, leaving the scar which Lord Steyne
carried till his death.

Allowing for this wandering style (which as I say is often artful as well as artless), I repeat that there is a real form in *Vanity Fair*, the lines of which are kept more carefully than in much modern fiction. The pattern or outline of the story consists of the parallel or divergent careers of two girls, who start together from the same school in the first chapter. Vanity Fair, or the fashion of this world that passes away, is tested by its treatment of these two types and tests the types in its turn. One is the celebrated Becky Sharp, the adventuress with many of the attractions of adventure; courageous, humorous, quick-witted, but under these natural defences somewhat hard and entirely cynical; one of those children of the poor who are born with a curious moral conviction of a right to possess riches and to rob the rich. The other is a more normal young woman of the sort that most would call ordinary; not demanding much from life, but expecting at the best a happiness of the sort called sentimental; and in all her views of existence at the best traditional, and at the worst conventional. I may remark here that I think it was one of Thackeray's real mistakes that he made her hold on such things rather conventional than traditional. Indeed in this case he was too conventional himself. He was so occupied with his contrasted pattern, with the good golden-haired heroine on one side and the wicked red-haired heroine on the other, that he made the golden-haired heroine a great deal less heroic than she might reasonably have been. It is not stating the alternative of vice and virtue fairly to make the vicious person a wit and imply that the virtuous person must be a fool. If he had been less anxious to make her a pathetic figure, she would have been more of a tragic figure.

Indeed, I think one disadvantage about *Vanity Fair*, especially today, is that one or two of these weak exaggerations occur very early in the book: and some greater passages only towards the end. Amelia is made at the very beginning a mere pink and white doll to be a foil to Becky; and if she represents a rather stale and vapid sort of sentimental comedy, her brother, Jos Sedley, represents a rather stale and vulgar sort of sentimental farce. I never could understand, even in youth, why that fat and featureless buck was allowed to sprawl across so much of the opening of the story; and I think it is rather a false note to make Becky deliberately set her cap at him. I imagine Miss Sharp as already knowing the world well enough not to waste herself on so socially fourth-rate a figure. It almost seems as if the Sedley family were more unfairly treated by Thackeray than by fortune; since the brother is vulgarised merely that he may be a slightly more vulgar copy of the dandy Osborne; while the sister suffers throughout from that first water-colour sketch of the two school girls, in which Amelia is given all the water and Rebecca all the colour.

But, allowing for this, which I confess to thinking a mistake, we can still trace the clear outline and the largely convincing logic in the contrast of the two heroines. The contrast is of importance, for it involves the chief debates about Thackeray: the sense in which he was wrongly called cynical; the sense in which he may rightly be called sceptical. First of all, any number of idiots doubtless did call him cynical, because the story of these two girls was not what they called a moral tale; by which they meant the grossly immoral tale which tells, in the teeth of Job and Jesus Christ, the lie that the virtuous are rewarded with wealth. It is not, certainly, in that sense, a story of the Idle and Industrious Apprentice. It is certainly not modelled on the disgusting morals of 'Pamela or Virtue Rewarded'. But (and this is the important point) neither is it made to enforce the opposite modern moral of 'Amelia or Virtue Punished'. There are many twisted and poisoned writers today, who would have played out the whole play with the opposite anti-moral purpose; leaving the wicked Becky in the blaze of the candelabra of Gaunt House and the kind Amelia picking up bits of coal, with a smut on her nose. This tragic trick (which was only too attractive to Thomas Hardy) is quite as much of a refusal to see life steadily and see it whole as the opposite artifice of the most artificial happy ending. It is not probable, but improbable, that Becky, with her desperate double or triple life, would have remained the Queen of Society for ever. It is not probable, but improbable, that anyone with the virtues and old connections of Amelia would have found absolutely none of her old friends ready to patch up her life for her. The point is that it is a sort of patching up in both cases. And with that we come near to the real meaning of Thackeray and the real moral of *Vanity Fair*.

The general inference from *Vanity Fair* is that life largely deceives and disappoints *all* people, bad and good; but that there is a difference, and that is (though the stupid optimist could not see it) rather on the side of the good. If we judge even Becky's life by the ambitious flights and flirtations of the beginning she is a ragged and disreputable failure at the end. If we judge Amelia's life by the romantic hopes of her first engagement, she is a stunned and helpless victim at the end. But if we compare the failure of Becky with the failure of Amelia, we see something that is profoundly true and is the chief truth of *Vanity Fair*, though most of the critics have missed it. The simpler, more innocent and more bewildered person is still capable of settling down into some sort of consolation and contentment; whereas she who has hardened herself against scandal or remorse has also hardened herself against hope.

A good novelist always has a philosophy; but a good novel is never a book of philosophy. The moral philosophy of Thackeray unites him rather with the old moralists than with the modern pessimists. He says, as his favourite authors, Solomon and Horace, would say, that life is in a sense vanity. He would never admit, in the sense of more modern authors like Zola and Dreiser, that life is also vileness. His view may be called stoic or sceptic or anything else rather than pessimist. But because he was a novelist and a narrative artist, and not merely a man with a theory, it is true that there did appear in his works something of a personal note, not to be explained by any impersonal system. There is, when all is said and done, something which haunts the air and discolours the very scenery of *Vanity Fair* though it has never been satisfactorily stated or explained. It is a vivacious book, passing chiefly through scenes of gaiety and fashion; it is often witty and satirical; it contains a great deal of humorous interlude and comic characterisation; some of it, as I have noted, being even too broadly comic. But it is not a *jolly* book; even when it is for the moment a funny book. There really is something about it faintly acid and antagonistic; and that something did belong partly to Thackeray the man, as well as to Thackeray the philosopher.

. . . we may say of Thackeray what he said of Swift; that there did remain at the back of his mind, in spite of all apparent scepticism, a noble but rather dark reality that is of the substance of religion. The Victorian Age had made it vague; the tradition of classical scholarship had made it seem almost heathen; but it was there, by the unanswerable test that applies to all the prophets and the saints. Thackeray thought the world *false*; which alone proves the presence of something contrasted with it which is true. Despite the superficial irritability which I have described, and which accounts for some of his lighter and less convincing sneers, it is true that he was too great a man to be godless and that he did not in his heart doubt that the injustices of the earth stand in contrast with a real justice. That is why I say that he stands rather with the ancient moralists than with the modern pessimists. It is true that this phrase also has been used incessantly and invariably wrongly. He himself confessed to a tendency to moralise; and many modern readers will doubtless repeat with far fiercer contempt this charge of moralising. But as a fact, it is not moralising at all. It is not strictly even philosophising. It is repeating old proverbs like the burden of an old song. It is not surprising that people once called it cynical and now call it sentimental. 'Oh, it's the old story' is a sentence that can easily be said, both in a cynical and a sentimental tone. Thackeray was penetrated through and through with the conviction that this story is only the old story; and no criticisms can anticipate him on that. But its importance is that, like many old stories, it is in its way a great tragedy; and tragedy is that point when things are left to God and men can do no more.

SOURCE: extracts from Introduction to *Vanity Fair* (Limited Edition Club, U.S.A., 1930); reprinted in *A Handful of Authors* (London, 1953).

PART THREE

Illustrations and Source Material

U. C. Knoepflmacher

'THACKERAY'S MASKS' (1971)

Vanity Fair is a novel that forces the reader into a constant process of questioning. The Showman delights in puncturing the complacency of his audience. He refuses to instruct us in what to think or how to react to the bustling fair before us; he tells us that he can at best point out its 'shops' and 'shows' – to make us laugh and yet to force us also to 'be perfectly miserable in private' (ch. 18). In the original title page of his novel, Thackeray drew a jester expounding on the follies of an audience which lives in a topsy-turvy world (in the background of the drawing is the Duke of York standing upside down on his column in Waterloo Place) and which possesses the same donkey ears that adorn the jester's cap. The title page for the completed novel in 1848 shows a rather different design. The jester now leans on a box of puppets and looks at his own image in a cracked mirror. In chapter 9, at the end of a passage in which the narrator has mocked the value that all men, including himself, place on money, Thackeray introduces a third picture of his Showman. The jester's stick is still in evidence, but the clown's comic mask is removed. Exposed is a sketch of the face of William Makepeace Thackeray himself. The mask is smiling, the face is doleful and melancholic – beneath laughter lies a quiet despair.

SOURCE: extract from *Laughter and Despair* (Berkeley, Calif., 1971) p. 63.

[For the illustrations discussed here, see pp. 66–8– Ed.]

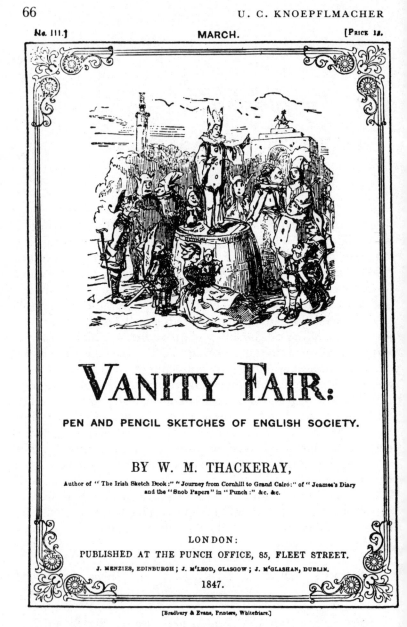

No. III.]   MARCH.   [Price 1s.

VANITY FAIR:

PEN AND PENCIL SKETCHES OF ENGLISH SOCIETY.

BY W. M. THACKERAY,

Author of "The Irish Sketch Book:" "Journey from Cornhill to Grand Cairo:" of "Jeames's Diary and the "Snob Papers" in "Punch:" &c. &c.

LONDON:
PUBLISHED AT THE PUNCH OFFICE, 85, FLEET STREET.

J. MENZIES, EDINBURGH; J. M'LEOD, GLASGOW; J. M'GLASHAN, DUBLIN.

1847.

[Bradbury & Evans, Printers, Whitefriars.]

Cover of the serialised edition, published in monthly parts: issue no. III of March 1847.

A Novel without a Hero.

BY

WILLIAM MAKEPEACE THACKERAY.

Title page of the first edition of the completed novel, 1848.

'Showman' motif at the conclusion of chapter 9, 1848 edition.

Juliet McMaster

'SIR PITT'S PROPOSAL' (1971)

. . . emphasis on the incongruity between romance and reality,
or between the pose and the truth is both subject and technique
in *Vanity Fair*. Frequently the reader is ironically invited to see the
sordid facts of the lustful and rapacious world through the rose-
coloured spectacles of the novel of sentiment. In the number

' . . . the old man fell down on his knees and leered at her like a satyr'. Sir Pitt Crawley
proposes to Becky.

following the scene of old Sir Pitt's proposal to Becky the writer
congratulates himself that 'every reader of a sentimental turn
(and we desire no other) must have been pleased with the tableau
with which the last act of our little drama concluded; for what
can be prettier than an image of Love on his knees before
Beauty?' (ch. 15). We are meant to enjoy the contrast between
this image and the one we had been left with: the leering old satyr
before the scheming adventuress. But at the same time we must
appreciate the extent of its justice: now if ever is the moment of
sentiment in the lives of these two worldly sinners. The scene is
indeed an emotional crisis in Becky's life – she 'wept some of the
most genuine tears that ever fell from her eyes' (ch. 14). And Sir
Pitt's avowal, 'You shall do what you like; spend what you like;
and 'av it all your own way. I'll make you a zettlement. I'll do
everything reglar' is no doubt as sincere a profession of love as he
has made in his life. . . .

SOURCE: extract from *Thackeray: The Major Novels* (Manchester and Toronto, 1971) p. 32.

Gordon N. Ray

'TWO THACKERAY ORIGINALS?'
(1952)

The truth that an artist's strength and weakness are inseparable, that the merits of a method imply concomitant defects, receives further demonstration when we turn to certain of *Vanity Fair*'s secondary characters. In a recent essay on this novel Mr. V. S. Pritchett, whose views I cite as representative of informed contemporary taste, selects two figures for particular praise. He describes old Miss Crawley as 'the greatest character in the book'; and of Jos Sedley he inquires, 'What is more perfect than the career of this buffoon?' How did Thackeray come to conceive these figures? What relation do they bear to his personal history?

Miss Crawley in her essentials is Thackeray's maternal grand mother, an account of whose lively, not to say scandalous, career I have pieced together from family papers and Commonwealth Relations Office records. Nothing certain is known of the lineage of Harriet Cowper, but there is a tradition in the Thackeray family that she had some Asiatic blood. Born about 1770, she married John Harman Becher in Calcutta in 1786 and bore him four children during the next nine years. Throughout this period Becher was in the civil service of the East India Company. That he was highly regarded by his superiors is attested by his appointment in 1794 to the collectorship of the Twenty-Four Pergunnahs, the large and wealthy district near Calcutta later supervised by Thackeray's father. Yet in 1797 he is described as 'out of employ'. And when he drew up his will two years later, he was a broken bankrupt, stripped of his possessions and in near expectation of death. Indeed, this pathetic document includes a plea to his creditors that he may be allowed to leave a few

mementos to his relations: a family Bible, odd volumes of
Shakespeare, and certain plain gold rings in each of which is to be
engraved the inscription: 'This from poor Jack'. Becher was
buried in Calcutta in 1800.

Nowhere in his will does Becher mention his wife. Again family
tradition explains the omission. It tells us that Mrs. Becher tired
of her husband and left him some time before his death. Whether
her departure was the cause or result of his ruin has not
transpired. Nothing is known of Mrs. Becher, in any event, until
1802, when she figures as the wife of Captain Charles Christie in
the will of that officer. We may note, however, that though
Christie's duties kept him continuously in Bengal after his arrival
in India in 1781, his marriage to Mrs. Becher is not entered in the
Bengal *Ecclesiastical Records*. If she lived under Christie's 'pro-
tection' while her husband survived, she may not have found it
convenient to legalize the connection after Becher's death. At this
time Anglo-Indian society took a very lenient view of marital
irregularities.

Christie died in 1804, leaving his lady a small property. But life
was by no means over for her. Still hardly thirty-five, she
possessed considerable personal advantages. In 1806 we find
record of her marriage to Captain Edward William Butler of the
Bengal Artillery. By this step she must have retrieved altogether
her position in the easy-going Calcutta world. Captain Butler
was an officer of means, who had behind him twenty-three years
of service in India. Nor was he in a position very forcibly to
reproach Mrs. Butler for past peccadillos. Four natural children
had been born to him by native mistresses, and three of these
children survived.

In 1807 Captain and Mrs. Butler sailed for England on
furlough. Whatever may have been the attitude of the Becher
family towards her in the years that followed her desertion of her
husband, she received a warm welcome upon her reappearance
as a respectable matron of assured fortune. When she returned to
India with Captain Butler two years later, she took two of her
daughters by John Becher with her; and the third followed within
a few months.

For the next ten years Lt.-Colonel Butler, as he shortly

became, held various important positions in Bengal. The Becher girls made excellent marriages in the army and the civil service; but continued to be closely associated with the Butlers, for the Colonel was usually attached to a command where at least one of Mrs. Butler's children lived near at hand. Butler died in 1819. Though insolvent, he was luckily a participator in two insurance schemes for the families of officers; and Mrs. Butler, with an income of nearly £500 a year, found herself possessed of a comfortable independence. For a time she lived with her daughters. Then tiring of the narrow round of back-country society, the indefatigable lady, now fifty years old, set off alone on 'four or five months dreary travelling' to Calcutta. Two years later she followed her oldest daughter to England, her younger children having died in the interval.

The problem of caring for Mrs. Butler, home to stay after nearly thirty-five years in India, rather puzzled her family. The breathless response of her sister-in-law, Miss Anne Becher, to her initial proposal to return home, hints at their forebodings.

Tell your mother [she wrote to Mrs. Carmichael-Smyth] if she comes to England to be as near as she can we will do all we can towards contributing to her comfort, if that could be done by her living with us we would do so, but our house won't allow of it & says dear Granny I never could expect her to put up with all my whims.

And, indeed, when Mrs. Butler arrived, her relatives found her a most imperious, crotchety, and perverse lady. But they need not have feared that she would be a burden to the family. Restless as ever, she did not remain long with any of them. Apart from a year or so at Larkbeare, while Thackeray was a boy, she kept on the move constantly, living in a variety of boarding houses and hotels in England and France, accompanied on her travels by a companion and a maid.

Thackeray first came to know her intimately after he lost his fortune in 1833. She came generously to his aid with a series of loans; and while he was trying to make himself a painter in 1834 and 1835, he lived for nearly a year with her. Though they were fond of each other, he was made to feel the full force of her uncertain temper. He told his mother on one occasion 'I am at this moment writhing under the stripes of her satire, and the public expression of her wrath.' Again we find him speaking of the 'bad words' which 'with a wonderful eloquence and ingenuity are wrung into my ears by G.M.' Yet their quarrels were soon made up; and even after Thackeray moved into his own quarters, he continued to 'walk stoutly up three times a week to be scolded' by her.

Mrs. Butler remained at Paris near Mrs. Carmichael-Smyth after Thackeray married and settled in London. She was visiting him in London at the time that Isabella's affliction declared itself, most unfortunately as it turned out. Expecting to be treated with distinguished consideration and unaware of the tragedy that she was witnessing, she grew angry because Isabella did not answer when spoken to. Explaining to his mother that 'the poor thing did not do this from sulkiness but from sheer absence and depression', Thackeray added that his grandmother was after all 'a sad pestering old body'.

Thackeray lived with Mrs. Butler again for a time in 1841, while Isabella was undergoing treatment in Paris. He was her favourite relative, and she was most generous to him during this second period of trouble. Indeed, her generosity was later one cause of disagreement between Thackeray and his cousin Mary Graham, also Mrs. Butler's grandchild, to whom she had not been by any means so liberal. There is real cordiality in Thackeray's description of her in 1841 as 'a hale, handsome old lady of seventy, the very best dressed and neatest old lady in Paris'.

Her health failed in the years that followed; and when she made her last visit to Thackeray in 1847, she was very worn and tired. His daughter remembered her as 'an old lady wrapped in Indian shawls . . . [who] rarely spoke, and was almost always in her room'. But she still occasionally rallied to bully her great-grandchildren, and she still took pleasure in her three o'clock dinner. When oppressed by ill health, she devoted herself to books of devotion. Otherwise she remained quite as worldly as she had been when a young lady in Calcutta. The fragments of her correspondence that have survived bear witness to her determined sprightliness of manner even in her late seventies. I cite a note to Eugénie Crowe, a young lady of Thackeray's acquaintance whose beauty and ingenuousness had pleased Mrs. Butler.

My grandson [she writes] has invited his two *young friends* The Reverend Lionel Delamere and Captain Frederic Delancy (*of the Blues*) to dine with us on *Friday* – They perfectly well remember you *at Rome* – Both are *bachelors*: both are *very rich* and one I think very handsome – . Bess however prefers the Captain. [Bess Hamerton was Mrs. Butler's Companion.]

Could you not *settle this dispute* – and come to us for a few days before *the great ball?*. . . .
Believe me your sincere
Louisa Matilda Butler
P.S. You *must come*. I will take no denial.

Now, this note is significant, not only because it underlines Mrs. Butler's lively interest in society in extreme old age, but also for its reference to the Reverend Lionel Delamere and for its signature. Delamere figures in *Vanity Fair* as a friend of Miss Crawley's companion Briggs; and though Mrs. Butler's name was Harriet, she has here signed herself Matilda, the name that Thackeray gave to Miss Crawley in his novel. It is evident that Mrs. Butler knew very well that her grandson was sketching her in *Vanity Fair* and was by no means displeased by the knowledge. Indeed, the success of *Vanity Fair* enchanted her, not least because it took Thackeray into the best society. 'I tell G.M. of the Lords I meet,' he wrote to his mother; 'it delights the old lady hugely.' In the autumn of 1847 Mrs. Butler returned to Paris, where she died on the first of November. Thackeray was her executor, and found upon examining her estate that nearly the whole of her fortune had been dissipated.

In *Vanity Fair* Thackeray gives Miss Crawley a lurid past in France and England rather than in India; and he makes her a much richer and grander person than Mrs. Butler. Miss Crawley has a fortune of £70,000, 'a balance at her banker's which would have made her beloved anywhere', in contrast to Mrs. Butler's mere

£500 a year. Miss Crawley maintains a house in Park Lane and moves in the best society, while Mrs. Butler frequented chiefly the third-rate company of Parisian or provincial English boarding houses. But, *toutes proportions gardées*, Miss Crawley is just such another old worldling as Mrs. Butler.

Despite her advanced years, she is luxurious, vain, and imperious, living for gossip and amusement. Though long past the inflammatory age herself, she delights to hear of other people's love affairs and finds an added spice in them if they are illicit. 'That was the most beautiful part of dear Lord Nelson's character,' she tells Becky. 'He went to the deuce for a woman.' It is Rawdon's reputation as a rake that makes him her favorite nephew. The capitalist of her family, she expects her eccentricities and selfishness to be forgiven for the sake of her money, and regards the careful attendance provided by her relatives and companions when she is ill as merely her just due. When very sick, she is frightened into spurts of piety. But for the most part she is a shrewd and self-possessed old woman of the world, gauging people and their motives with precision, and knowing how to make herself respected and obeyed.

Thackeray knew few women better than Mrs. Butler; her character had few secrets from him. He had a certain fondness for her, he regarded her foibles and eccentricities with forbearance, but he felt none of the emotional attachment to her that he did to Isabella. In drawing her as Miss Crawley he accordingly makes no attempt to excuse her weaknesses, as he does those of Amelia, but portrays her with a cool detachment. Consequently, there is no disparity, as in Amelia's case, between what Miss Crawley does and what Thackeray says about her actions. His valedictory to her in the October number of *Vanity Fair* may stand as an example of the impartiality with which he habitually judges her: 'Peace to thee, kind and selfish, vain and generous old heathen! – We shall see thee no more.' Thackeray's portrait of Miss Crawley is thus quite perfect, as far as it goes, always consistent, always controlled; yet contrasted with his picture of Amelia, it is limited and superficial.

Finally, let us consider Jos Sedley, the other character in *Vanity*

Fair praised especially by Mr. Pritchett. His 'original' can be identified with quite as much certainty as can Amelia's and Miss Crawley's.

Our cue comes this time from Henry Beveridge, the father of the present Lord Beveridge. Beveridge came out to India in 1858. Among the friends that he made was Merrick Shawe, Thackeray's brother-in-law, who had himself been in India since 1834. 'He was informed by Mr. Shawe,' Beveridge later recalled, ' . . . that the character [of Jos Sedley] was an over-coloured picture of George Trant Shakespear.'

Shakespear was Thackeray's cousin. Born in India two years before Thackeray, he had preceded him home by several months. He was among Thackeray's companions in misery at the Arthurs' school in Southampton; indeed, Thackeray later told a common relative, Mrs. Irvine, 'I can remember George coming in and flinging himself down on my bed the first night.' There a friendship between the two began, which continued at Charterhouse School and was not entirely broken off until George went out to India as a writer in the East India Company's service in 1829.

George remained in India for fourteen years, rising steadily in the service, but seeing employment almost exclusively in remote provincial outposts. Nuddea, Moorshedabad, Pubna, Dinagepore, the Soonderbunds, Midnapore and Hidgellee were some of the localities in which he successively served as magistrate, collector and commissioner. It was not until early in 1843 that he was granted permission to return to England on furlough.

George was then thirty-three years old and a very odd fish. Of 'rotund form and rolling gait', he was known in his family as the '*Polar Bear*'. That this nickname pleased him is attested by a set of verses, written to celebrate an occasion auspicious in Shakespear annals, in which he pleasantly describes himself as a part of 'the brute creation', whose joy leads him to 'shuffle' with 'gambols rude'. For the rest, he was a great consumer of food, liquor, and tobacco; and a confirmed bachelor, skittish as a colt with unmarried women. His family and close friends accepted him as an acknowledged eccentric and felt real fondness for him. His sister Selina, meeting him for the first time in 1838 at the age of eighteen (such late encounters among near kin were a not uncommon chance of Anglo-Indian life), admitted that he 'had been so much in the jungles that he was shy', but found him 'witty and amusing when alone with us'. Similarly William Ritchie four years later described him as 'a fat, shy, eccentric, but most witty, entertaining old fellow'.

In January, 1843, George joined his sister Augusta and her husband John Low aboard the East Indiaman *India* bound for Suez. Augusta kept a journal of their experiences, in which her brother figures characteristically. On the first leg of their journey, he was constantly seasick; and Augusta had to note regretfully that there was 'no good saying of his to relate'. In Madras reviving spirits led him into a typical blunder. With Low he presented himself at the Club House; but only his brother-in-law gained admittance, since George did not belong either to the Bengal or Bombay club and could not claim exchange privileges. Augusta writes :

Low says poor George drove off with his servant, looking piteously at him & saying – 'I am rejected.' However, it appears he made himself very comfortable at a Punch House, where he played billiards at a very old table, full of holes, with a little black boy, who he says gave him ten & beat him.

Re-embarked on the *India*, George was still harried by misfortune.

George has lost four caps made by Messrs. Gibson & Co. overboard [Augusta notes], also the straw hat which was too small for Low, and he is now obliged to wear a strange thing on his head like a little horn.

Unceasing seasickness and a painful fall reduced him to profound depression.

I saw George to-day [Augusta notes with unfailing sprightliness after a spell of particularly heavy weather]; he . . . declares . . . whenever he is put on shore, there he will remain, and never go on board another vessel. He says also he will leave off cheroots and beer.

These good resolutions did not survive the temptations of port. George amused himself ashore at Aden by spending 'about £30 in beer and supplies' to see him through the few days that remained of the voyage. He also mounted 'a very short, stout little poney' to visit the fortifications that the Turks were building in expectation of Arab raids, where he was nearly shot for his pains by suspicious Turkish guards.

Arrived at length at Suez, the passengers of the *India* betook themselves to vans 'like butchers' carts', except for 'the addition of a chintz covering over the top'. In these conveyances they headed across the desert to Cairo. One of the stations at which they spent the night was in the charge of a pretty Englishwoman from Kent, who had married an Arab.

She was most civil and tripped about in a light and airy way [writes Augusta]. George however was quite put out by her politeness, and said, as we drove off: 'Sooner than have that pretty damsel flitting about him, he would have fled across the desert on foot.'

When the party reached Cairo, George and the Lows visited a slave market, where a number of fat and cheerful Abyssinian woman were exposed for sale.

On one of the women saying something [Augusta relates], they all laughed, and they told us it was because she had said she would like to be bought by that 'young man'.

This was George! George said her selection was 'a great trial'.

He was further harassed during the boat trip from Cairo to Alexandria. The cook that he hired for the journey came aboard tipsy; and later in the trip, while George was ashore endeavoring unsuccessfully to shoot quail, this miscreant 'got at his wine and drank three bottles of sherry, after which I saw him [says Augusta] sitting knocking his head against a leg of mutton, George's sad and sole remains of Messrs. Hill's provisions'.

George parted company from the Lows at Alexandria. He proceeded to London in a leisurely fashion, arriving there in time to become a member of the Oriental Club late in 1843. By the following June he and Thackeray had renewed their boyhood friendship, though hardly on the old basis of intimacy. In that month Thackeray mentions to an aunt that he has seen George twice, adding, 'we have besides exchanged cards genteelly'. And in July Thackeray reports having had tea with George, 'whose selfishness is delightfully characteristic'.

Three months later George died in Geneva, it is said by his own hand. What caused this abrupt transition from farce to melodrama in his history remains obscure. In any event, though his savings from his lucrative Indian employments had been substantial enough to allow him to return to England and live in London in considerable style, less than £600 was turned over to his heirs in 1845.

When the reader first encounters Jos Sedley in *Vanity Fair* he has just returned to England after eight years in the employment of the East India Company. The whole of this period was passed in solitude as collector of Boggley Wollah, Thackeray tells us, a remote outpost 'situated in a fine, lonely, marshy, jungly district'.

He was lazy, peevish, and a *bon-vivant* [Thackeray continues]; the appearance of a lady frightened him beyond measure; hence it was but seldom that he joined the paternal circle in Russell Square, where there was plenty of gaiety, and where the jokes of his good-natured old father frightened his *amour-propre*. His bulk caused Joseph much anxious thought and alarm; now and then he would make a desperate attempt to get rid of his superabundant fat; but his indolence and love of good living speedily got the better of these endeavours at reform, and he found himself again at his three meals a day. He never was well dressed; but he took the hugest pains to adorn his big person, and passed many hours daily in that occupation. His valet made a fortune out of his wardrobe: his toilet-table was covered with as many pomatums and essences as ever were employed by an old beauty: he had tried, in order to give himself a waist, every girth, stay, and waistband then invented. Like most fat men, he *would* have his clothes made too tight, and took care they should be of the most brilliant colours and youthful cut. When dressed at length, in the afternoon he would issue forth to take a drive with nobody in the Park; and then would come back in order to dress again and go and dine with nobody at the Piazza Coffee-house. He was as vain as a girl; and perhaps his extreme shyness was one of the results of his extreme vanity.

This sharp, merciless vignette no doubt represents George Shakespear as Thackeray saw him in their several encounters in 1844. One might think, from the evidence of Augusta Low's diary, that Thackeray had suppressed some of George's more amiable traits, his cleverness, his affection for his family, and his appreciation of the comic aspects of his own character. But perhaps Augusta's testimony was colored by a sister's partiality. Thackeray's picture of Jos may be substantially what any unbiased observer would have seen in George Shakespear. In any event, the chapters that follow develop these traits in action, and a richly comic figure emerges, in portraying whom Thackeray only once deviates from the strictest and most objective realism. It is in the final episode of Jos's career that Thackeray thus taxes his reader's faith. Jos dies at Aix-la-Chapelle, where he has for some time been living with Becky. It is discovered that his fortune has been dissipated, and that he has left behind him only an insurance policy made out equally to Becky and to Amelia. There can be no doubt Thackeray means it is to be understood that Becky has encompassed Jos's death. Witness the illustration entitled 'Becky's second appearance in the character of Clytemnestra', in which she lurks behind a curtain, knife in hand, while the sick and terrified Jos pleads with Dobbin to come and live near him. Witness the names that Thackeray gives to the firm of solicitors who press Becky's claim to Jos's insurance: Messrs. Burke, Thurtell, and Hayes – each christened after a famous murderer. We have seen how George Shakespear's career ended on a minor key with his suicide at Geneva. Forgetting momentarily the requirements of verisimilitude, Thackeray seems to have acted on this hint in bringing Jos Sedley violently to his long home.

Apart from this single lapse, Thackeray's portrait of Jos is faultless. He knows the type perfectly and presents it without praise or blame. He does not excuse Jos's weaknesses, as he does Amelia's; nor does he pursue them with scorn and anger, as he does Becky's. But he can be neutral and dispassionate in

contemplating Jos only because he does not take him seriously.
Understanding thoroughly what goes on in Jos's head, he does
not think it worth his while to enter into Jos's state of mind. The
reason is that as a rule he cares to describe the feelings of his
characters in detail, to penetrate to the deeper levels of their
experience, only when he draws them from persons with whom
he had lived on terms not merely of intimacy, but of close
personal attachment. If Thackeray's portraits of Miss Crawley
and of Jos Sedley are both very nearly flawless, they are yet mere
sketches when compared with his portrait of Amelia, which is not
flawless at all. To note these two orders of characterization is to
wonder if impartiality may not be too dearly bought when it
entails the sacrifice of sympathy and penetration, as it usually
does in Thackeray's fiction.

SOURCE: extract from *The Buried Life* (Oxford, 1952)
pp. 37–47.

G. and K. Tillotson

'THACKERAY: HISTORICAL NOVELIST' (1963)

Thackeray is most nearly a historical novelist in the Waterloo chapters. . . . he was treating an event vivid in the memory of many of his readers – 'How many thousand times . . . the battle of Waterloo has been discussed after dinner' – and doubtless drawing much from conversation with his elders from childhood onwards: 'you and I, who were children when the great battle was won and lost, are never tired of hearing and recounting the history of that famous action'.

The figure of Napoleon was early impressed on his imagination; as a child, voyaging from India, he had had 'the Corsican ogre' pointed out to him on St Helena. In 1843, he himself took 'that well-known journey which almost every Englishman of middle rank has travelled since', and 'went to survey with eagle glance the field of Waterloo'; anecdotes of this visit appear both in the sketch published in January 1845 (when he had already begun his novel) and in chapter 28. But his main source for the Brussels and Waterloo chapters was a very recently published work, G. R. Gleig's *Story of the Battle of Waterloo* (1847), which he read as soon as it came out. To this comprehensive and picturesque work, which incorporates many earlier sources, including much of Siborne's *History*, he owed not merely military facts, but much of the vivid detail of the background of Brussels before and after the battle. Compare, for example, his description in chapter 28 of its 'liveliness and splendour', gambling, dancing, feasting, 'a theatre where a miraculous Catalani was delighting all hearers', 'a perpetual military festival', with Gleig's picture of a city which 'swarmed . . . with visitors not of the military order', engaged in 'dinners, soirées, balls, theatrical amusements, concerts' (including Catalani) and 'rounds of morning calls and evening parties'. His source gave ample warrant for his 'brilliant train of camp-followers . . . dancing and feasting . . . up to the very brink of battle'. Repeatedly, and most naturally (since Amelia, Rebecca, and Peggy O'Dowd are all in their different ways born 'camp-followers'), he has given to Gleig's generalised description a personal and particular application, so that the truth of imagination and the truth of history reinforce one another. The Duchess's famous ball on the eve of the battle, its implicit irony providing obvious opportunities for the novelist, is the background for the 'bouquet-scene' in which the intrigue between George and Rebecca comes to a head; the atmosphere changes dramatically when George, 'wild with elation', drinking and 'rattling away to the people around' is approached by Dobbin, 'pale and grave', with the news: ' "The enemy has passed the Sambre and our left is already engaged. Come away. We are to march in three hours.' " This is the novel's individual version of Gleig's 'It had been hinted to the Generals of division and brigade, that, one by one, as the night drew on, they should take their leave . . . by and bye General after General withdrew from the Duchess's party.'

At home, after making his preparations, George looks at Amelia who is feigning sleep, and the chapter and the number end with the words

At that moment a bugle from the Place of Arms began sounding clearly, and was taken up through the town; and amidst the drums of the infantry, and the shrill pipes of the Scotch, the whole city awoke.

This recalls Gleig's

Light after light had been extinguished in chamber and in hall, and sleep seemed to have established his dominion over the city, when a bugle-call, heard first in the Place d'Armes, on the summit of the Montagne du Parc, and taken up and echoed back through various quarters of the town, roused all classes of people in a moment . . . the bugle-call was soon followed by the rolling of drums and the screaming of bagpipes.

At the end of chapter 31, on the following day when only the 'non-combatants' remain in Brussels, 'at half-past two . . . the dinner hour arrived'; Jos's spirits rise with the meal and he drinks the regiment's health:

> But all of a sudden, Isidor started, and the Major's wife laid down her knife and fork. The windows of the room were open, and looked southward, and a dull distant sound came over the sun-lighted roofs from that direction. 'What is it?' said Jos.
> 'Why don't you pour, you rascal?'
> '*C'est le feu!*' said Isidor, running to the balcony.
> 'God defend us; it's cannon!' Mrs. O'Dowd cried, starting up, and followed too to the window. A thousand pale and anxious faces might have been seen looking from other casements. And presently it seemed as if the whole population of the city rushed into the streets.

Again, Thackeray is simply dramatising Gleig's account:

> About half-past two or three in the afternoon the noise of firing came back upon the breeze. Then were the streets filled again with anxious listeners. Men and women ran to the Park . . . and . . . there greeted them there a tumult of battle so incessant that it resembled more the sound of distant thunder than the noise of a cannonade.

Jos's panic search for horses and his expensive half-hour with Rebecca is but a single, comically elaborated instance of the general situation as presented by Gleig:

> Then might be seen in the passages of hotels, in the gate-ways of private houses, and about stable-yards, delicate women as well as timid men rushing half-dressed as from instant destruction. 'Let the carriage be got ready immediately – the French are upon us.' 'Who will get me four horses – two horses – one horse?' 'I will give any price for a vehicle so that it be brought immediately.'

> All ranks were confounded, all distinctions levelled, all common forms neglected. Gentlemen and servants, lords and common soldiers, British and foreigners were all upon an equality, elbowing each other without ceremony, and addressing each other without apology. . . . English reserve seemed no longer to exist.

The actual events needed no adapting; as we have said above, Thackeray's personages seem to fulfil their natures in taking part in them, and the novel coalesces with history as by felicitous coincidence. 'Waterloo' is a landmark in all their lives; Jos is 'Waterloo Sedley' to the end. Its influence overhangs the whole novel; through its repercussions, Thackeray pursues and deepens the contrast between Amelia and Rebecca, and in the concluding scene between them reverts to the incident of the bouquet at the ball. But after 1815, the story no longer hangs 'on to the skirts of history', and the change of mode is evident in the treatment of the one 'notorious personage' who does figure in the action – Lord Steyne.

Only in a limited sense does he represent the third Marquis of Hertford; the *roman à clef* is one more category into which *Vanity Fair* refuses to fit. As Henry Kingsley said, Lord Steyne is 'too perfect a character ever to have existed; he is so perfect, that we have to argue ourselves out of the belief that he is drawn from life. . . . People have tried to represent the wicked nobleman often enough. Let them try no more. Lord Steyne is in the field'.

Thackeray's fiction required a 'wicked nobleman', but with a footing in life as well as melodrama, and also in a particular phase of life – that of the wealthy, dissolute and influential Regency aristocrat, representative of an age that had vanished but was fresh in memory. The obituary notices of the Marquis of Hertford in 1842 and the scandalous revelations in the litigation following his will supplied both picturesque details and what seemed a representative truth, embodying the common image of grossness, grandeur, cynically manipulated power. The facts showed up the shallowness of ordinary fashionable novelists, whom Thackeray humorously rebuked for not being immoral enough: 'they have not the unconscious wickedness, the delightful want of principle, which the great fashionable man possesses, none of the grace and ease of vice . . . what mere literary head could have invented Monsieur Suisse and his noble master?'[1]

By borrowing some of the authentic monstrosity of life and combining it with his own invention, Thackeray created a character who belongs as it were to the borderland between historic fact and his own fiction. Lord Steyne contributes more than any other single character to the novel as a picture of its time; from him flows much of the authentic sense of period that colours it. At the same time he is completely assimilated to the action, as ally and antagonist of Becky; and to the moral, as a massive illustration of 'Vanity Fair', not only in himself but by the way others regard him. Thackeray preserves his 'legendary' impression by keeping him a little remote and mysterious: not introducing him formally, but planting him in the Curzon Street circle as if he had been there for a long time, and surrounding him in a web of hearsay and gossip. (It is Tom Eaves, not the author, who reports on the doings at Gaunt House.) He has selected from the character and career of Lord Hertford such details as suit his purposes – his early association with the Prince Regent, his lavish entertainments, his lackeys and hangers-on, his French mistress, his sojourns abroad, his honours and public offices, the disputes over his will, – and has invented or modified others. The factual basis is composite; some particulars of his father's and his mother's careers are transferred to him, and details of several family mansions are combined in Gaunt Square. Both physically and morally the picture is darkened; his political activities – not all disreputable – are virtually suppressed; his intellectual interests survive only in the charades; and for the notorious Maria Fagniani, 'Old Q's daughter' (an upstart not unlike Becky) whom he married but soon separated from, Thackeray substitutes a helpless and pathetic wife, with an imaginary Welsh ancestry, for contrast and relief. In order to contain his career within the novel, his death is advanced from 1842 to 1830; but Thackeray comes nearest to fact, since fact was itself almost a sufficient satire, in the summary of his career. His art in the handling of a source is nowhere better illustrated in a small space than by a comparsion of the well-known passage in chapter 64 with this account in the *Annual Register:*

At his town residence, Dorchester House, Park-lane, in his 65th year, the Most Hon. Francis Charles Seymour Conway, third Marquess of Hertford and Earl of Yarmouth (1793), Earl of Hertford and Viscount Beauchamp of Hache (1750), and fourth Lord Conway, Baron of Ragley, co. Warwick, all titles in the peerage of England; also Baron

Conway, of Killultah, co. Antrim (1703), in the peerage of Ireland;
K.G., G.C.H.; Knt. of St. Anne of Russia; a Privy Councillor; Custos
Rotulorum of the co. of Antrim; Warden of the Stanneries, Steward and
Vice-Admiral of the Duchy of Cornwall and Chief Commissioner for
managing the affairs of that Duchy; Lieutenant-Colonel Commandant
of the Militia corps of Cornwall and Devonshire Miners; Vice-Admiral
of the Coast of Suffolk; M.A. &c. &c.

Many old memories would be revived by such a notice as this,
encountered by Thackeray's readers only a few years before; and
it is characteristic of his general method in depicting the past to
make use especially of what has recently been revived or
extended into the present, appealing to his readers' sense of
change and continuity. Much of the detailed 'local colour' of the
novel is of this kind; when George drives down Piccadilly on the
way to his wedding there is no Achilles statue or triumphal arch
or 'equestrian monster'; all these tributes to the Duke of
Wellington, familiar or execrated in the London of the eighteen-
forties, lay in the future in 1815 – a future in which George would
have no part. His honeymoon is spent at Brighton – 'Brighton,
that always looks brisk, gay, and gaudy, like a harlequin's
jacket – . . . Brighton, which used to be seven hours distant
from London at the time of our story; which is now only a
hundred minutes off; and which may approach who knows how
much nearer, unless Joinville comes and untimely bombards it.'

It is a further justification of the author's commentary that it is
so often used to relate past and present; sometimes in a long
passage of wistful reflection, like the recollection of coach travel
that concludes chapter 7, sometimes in an almost unnoted
reminder, that soda-water or orange-blossoms or varnished boots
were still unknown, and the waltz 'then newly imported'. The
effect is to make the half-remembered past seem both near and
remote; and by dwelling particularly, as is natural in 'Vanity
Fair', on changes in externals – architecture, costume, and
popular entertainment – Thackeray suggests the transience and
pathos of fashion. Nothing dates so quickly or recalls a past age so
sharply as its sentimental popular songs; and Thackeray not only
mentions songs and kinds of song reminiscent of his period, such

as Dibdin's, Moore's, and Thomas Haynes Bayly's, and the vapid ditties which form Miss Swartz's limited repertoire, but supplies two of his own for Becky to sing. 'Ah! bleak and barren was the moor' and 'The Rose upon my Balcony' are not burlesques but, as Ray says, 'distillations of the sentimental ballads of the day'.

Vauxhall Gardens is the outstanding example of a past fashion of entertainment recaptured in its one-time brightness and novelty; the modern reader is unaware of all this meant to readers of *Vanity Fair* in the forties, when the Gardens indeed survived, but in dingy decline. One of Dickens's *Sketches by Boz* had described a desperate attempt to revive them by daytime opening; *Punch* in 1841 had reported 'a last look at the long-expiring gardens'. Bankruptcy, sales of effects, and changes of management all emphasised the contrast with past glories; many must have felt with Laman Blanchard: 'The days of my youth, where are they? . . . buried for ever in dark Vauxhall.' Invited to re-live his youth in Thackeray's sixth chapter, the reader would find all the most familiar particulars: the gilt cockleshell and the hermitage, the fireworks and the tight-rope act, and what had already been the subjects of inumerable jokes, 'the hundred thousand *extra* lamps', the obsequious Simpson, Master of Ceremonies, the almost invisible ham, the rack punch. The Battle of Borodino and the panorama of Moscow tie the scene to a particular year; it is the setting for a crucial episode in the fortunes of the personages; but at the same time it is a vivid glimpse of social history and an appeal to the sentiment of reminiscence.

Thackeray has many other references to recreations and entertainments popular at this period; to gambling, prize-fights, Exeter 'Change with its elephant, and to clubs, coffee-houses, theatres, opera-houses, shops, and restaurants. Theatrical entertainment ranges from *The Forty Thieves*, with Miss Decamp's dance, to *Jean de Paris* and *La Sonnambula*. The reading of the time is represented by *Cecilia*, *Udolpho*, and *The Orphan of the Forest*, by Miss Crawley's wicked French novels and the tracts urged upon her by Mrs. Bute; the maidservant reads *Fatherless Fanny* (still popular in the 1840s), and Amelia buys Georgy a copy of Maria Edgeworth's *Parent's Assistant* and of Thomas Day's *Sandford and*

Merton. A well-known painter of the time is correctly referred to before 1815 as 'Mr. Lawrence'; and at about the right date, Becky buys a print of his famous portrait of the King. In the text, though not in the illustrations, Thackeray pictures the buckskins and hessians, the shoulder-knots, the gigot sleeves and huge tortoiseshell combs of the time. Even the coinage of the Napoleonic war is recalled by Osborne's reference to a 'dollar'.

Such references are scattered here and there, never laboured but arising from the action and in the dialogue; they came naturally to one whose sense of the period arose from observation and memory, reinforced by 'looking back to a file of the newspapers of the time', and turning the pages of old *Annual Registers, European Magazines*, and *Journal des Modes*. But most comes from memory, the active affectionate memory seen in the *Roundabout Papers*; the 'lazy idle boy' recalled there was in fact 'one of the people on whom nothing is lost'. He had also his elders' memories to draw on; in childhood he was constantly with much older people, coming from India to a 'dear little old Hampshire town inhabited by the wives, widows, daughters of navy captains, admirals, lieutenants . . . like a novel of Jane Austen's'. From a school in Chiswick he went to Charterhouse in the heart of the city, the London of 'Tom and Jerry', where he feasted his eyes on Cruikshank's caricatures in the shop windows, and joined a crowd scene on the stage at Drury Lane in a performance before the King. Whether in London, Paris, or 'Pumpernickel' (Weimar), or hearing regimental gossip in County Down, or talking to his grandmother a worldly, selfish old lady with a past, or his fat, shy, eccentric cousin George Shakespear, back from India on furlough in 1844 and staying at the Oriental Club, he was absorbing details which reappear in the novel.

In many earlier sketches and stories he had already begun to people the world of *Vanity Fair*, and for his supernumeraries and background he often borrows from himself; Tufto, Deuceace, Cinqbars, Loder, Sir Huddlestone Fuddlestone, Bareacres, Miss Wirt, and even the inspired name of Crawley, had all appeared before, the mock tracts were familiar to *Punch* readers, and Pumpernickel, as 'Kalbsbraten', had been the scene of some of the FitzBoodle stories in *Fraser's*. The repeated allusions ratify each other and contribute, like the genealogies and family histories, to our sense of a ramifying, proliferating world with its roots in the past. 'This fair is no new-erected business, but a thing of ancient standing.'

SOURCE: extract from Introduction to Norton edition of *Vanity Fair* (London, 1963). pp. xxix – xxxviii.

NOTE

1. Article in *Foreign Quarterly Review*, Jan 1844. Suisse was Hertford's valet, represented by Thackeray's 'Fiche'. 'The Marquess of Borgia' and 'Centsuisse' also appear in chapter 17 of the *Book of Snobs*.

PART FOUR

Modern Studies

Gordon N. Ray

VANITY FAIR: ONE VERSION OF THE NOVELIST'S RESPONSIBILITY (1950)

My title, I am afraid, has an old-fashioned ring. The novelists of today who best know their job believe with André Gide that 'the moral issue for the artist is not that he should present an idea that is useful but that he should present an idea well'.[1] They have relinquished their ethical role by eliminating themselves, and therefore the question of responsibility to their readers, from their books. Their credo is summed up by Evelyn Waugh in an article on Graham Greene's *The Heart of the Matter*. Greene's style is functional, not at all 'specifically literary', he writes. 'The words are simply mathematical symbols for his thought. Moreover, no relation is established between writer and reader. The reader has not had a conversation with a third party such as he enjoys with Sterne or Thackeray.' There is not even an observer through whose eyes events are seen. The technique employed is that of the cinema, with Greene as director and producer. 'It is the modern way of telling a story.'[2]

Victorian novelists, on the other hand, cherished the relation of writer to reader and pondered very seriously their moral obligation to their audience. Of them all Thackeray has been most severely reproached by later critics for intruding upon his stories in the character of guide, philosopher and friend. But perhaps it has been too hastily assumed that the advantage in this particular must lie with the modern novelist. At any rate, instead of taking it for granted that Thackeray's penchant for moral commentary is an excrescence, unhappily all too common among the naïve and primitive novelists who lived before Henry

James, I propose to inquire how he came to entertain his conception of the novelist's responsibility, how his work was altered by it, how it affected his standing with his readers, and how it is related to his intellectual position in his age.

I

When the first monthly number of *Vanity Fair* appeared in January, 1847, Thackeray had for ten years earned his living by his pen; yet what reputation he had achieved hardly extended beyond his fellow-writers and a small audience of discriminating readers. Because they were either anonymous or written over one or another of his various *noms de plume*, his long series of brilliant contributions to *Fraser's Magazine, Punch* and the *Morning Chronicle* had little cumulative effect. The 'great stupid public',[3] as he called it, passed him by indifferent. 'Mrs. Perkins's [Ball] is a great success – the greatest I have had – very nearly as great as Dickens,' he remarked of the first of his Christmas books in December of 1846, 'that is Perkins 500, Dickens 25,000 – only that difference!'[4]

The reception accorded the yellow-wrappered parts of *Vanity Fair* was at first hardly more encouraging. But gradually they began to be talked about. Friendly paragraphs underlined their excellence in *Fraser's Magazine*, the *Scotsman* and the *North British Review*. In July, after the seventh monthly number had appeared, the *Sun* hailed Thackeray as 'the Fielding of the nineteenth century'.[5] By September Mrs. Carlyle was convinced that *Vanity Fair* 'beats Dickens out of the world'.[6] A long panegyric by Abraham Hayward in the *Edinburgh Review* of January, 1848, sealed the success of the novel. 'There is no use denying the matter or blinking it now', Thackeray wrote a few days later. 'I am become a sort of great man in my way – all but at the top of the tree: indeed there if the truth were known and having a great fight up there with Dickens.'[7]

How is one to account for this sudden and splendid elevation to eminence of a writer who had been regarded a year earlier, so Henry Kingsley relates, as 'a man known certainly to some extent, but who was thought to have had sufficient trial, and to have found his métier as a clever magazine writer'?[8] What was the element hitherto lacking in Thackeray's books which explains the immense prestige of *Vanity Fair* with Victorian readers? A glance at his career before 1847 may answer these questions.

Connop Thirlwall said of the England of Thackeray's youth: 'Society possesses two or three strong, stiff frames, in which all persons of liberal education who need or desire a fixed place and specific designation must consent to be set.'[9] Thackeray obstinately sought success outside these frames. Abandoning the university after five terms and the Inns of Court after a few months, he tried his fortune as an artist and as a journalist, both employments then well beyond the social pale. He discovered before long that he could not draw well enough to succeed as a painter; and he later confessed that *'what I wrote was bad and poor stuff for many years'*.[10] Meanwhile, not wholly by his own fault, he had lost the modest fortune on which he had relied for a competence while he pursued his unconventional path. He was consequently exposed for many years to the distresses and humiliations of shabby gentility. When a happy marriage and recognition as a periodical writer began to promise compensation for earlier misfortunes, his wife became insane. It is not surprising that Thackeray accumulated from these experiences what Taine calls 'a treasure of mediated hatred'.

His history as a writer was hardly more propitious. Coming to literary maturity in the eighteen-thirties, an age of uncertain taste and uninspiring example, he turned decisively away from prevailing formulas for the novel, which seemed to him either childish or unwholesome. It was his endeavour, he said in a rare statement of purpose, 'to work as an artist telling the truth and morbidly perhaps eschewing humbug'.[11]

Telling the truth to Thackeray meant describing life as he had seen it during the bitter years since he came of age. 'He was created,' he told Dr. John Brown, 'with a sense of the ugly, the odd, of the meanly false, of the desperately wicked; he laid them bare: them under all disguises he hunted to death.'[12] The first readers of *The Yellowplush Papers, Catherine, Denis Haggarty's Wife,* and *Barry Lyndon* not unnaturally found the themes that Thackeray's experience suggested to him low and sordid.

The second part of his programme, even morbidly to eschew humbug, led him to tell his stories substantially without commentary; for as a young man he was inclined to identify humbug with moralizing. Whenever he could, he adopted a dramatic disguise. The opinions of Yellowplush, George Fitz-Boodle and Barry Lyndon are intended for the most part to characterize these worthies; not to convey Thackeray's judgments. In more than one of his critical essays of the middle eighteen-forties, Thackeray explicitly stated that it is not the novelist's business to teach.

> If we want instruction [he wrote of Lever's 'St. Patrick's Eve'], we prefer to take it from fact rather than from fiction. We like to hear sermons from his reverence at church, to get our notions of trade, crime, politics and other national statistics from the proper papers and figures; but when suddenly, out of the gilt pages of a pretty picture book, a comic moralist rushes forward, and takes occasion to tell us that society is diseased . . . persons who wish to lead an easy life are inclined to remonstrate against this literary ambuscadoe.[13]

To a public eager for guidance from its literary mentors, this attitude recommended Thackeray hardly more than did his subject matter.

Moreover, the disappointments of Thackeray's life sometimes goaded him to savage and devil-may-care protest. We find him resolving to contribute to *Punch* in 1842, at a time when that magazine was still identified in the public mind with the notorious *Age* and *Satirist* newspapers, because it offered him 'a great opportunity for unrestrained laughing, sneering, kicking and gambadoing'.[14] He made little effort, indeed, to ensure success by conciliating his audience. *The Book of Snobs* was designed from beginning to end to prick its readers out of their complacency. And none of Thackeray's earlier books lacks many passages in the same vein, of which the following imaginary after-dinner conversation from *The Irish Sketch-Book* may stand as an example:

One word more regarding the Widow Fagan's house. When Peggy brought in coals for the drawing-room fire, she carried them – in what do you think? 'In a coal-scuttle, to be sure,' says the English reader, down on you as sharp as a needle.

No, you clever Englishman, it wasn't a coal-scuttle.

'Well, then, it was in a fire-shovel,' says that brightest of wits, guessing again.

No, it *wasn't* a fire-shovel, you heaven-born genius; and you might guess from this until Mrs. Snooks called you up to coffee, and you would never find out. It was in something which I have already described in Mrs. Fagan's pantry.

'Oh, I have you now, it was the bucket where the potatoes were: the thlatternly wetch!' says Snooks.

Wrong again – Peggy brought up the coals – in a CHINA PLATE!

Snooks turns quite white with surprise, and almost chokes himself with his port. 'Well,' says he, 'of all the *wum* countwith that I ever wead of, hang me if Ireland ithn't the *wummetht*. Coalth in a plate! Mawyann, do you hear that? In Ireland they alwayth thend up their coalth in a plate!'[15]

Stung by such taunts as this, it mattered little to the average Englishman that none of Thackeray's works after 1840 was without many touches of profound insight and tenderness. Such mitigations were forgotten, and the reader was left with the prevailing impression of a brilliant but forbidding talent which made him uneasy while it amused him. He regarded Thackeray as a writer for whom he could feel no affection and with whom he could achieve little solidarity.

II

If Thackeray had continued in this vein, he would hardly have written *Vanity Fair*. But late in 1846 he experienced a change of heart, the culmination of a progressive reconciliation to life, which can be compared with John Stuart Mill's awakening from Benthamite Utilitarianism twenty years earlier. Attention is directed to it by a letter which Thackeray wrote to Mark Lemon, the editor of *Punch*, in February of 1847. His subject was the last paragraph of 'The Snobs of England': 'To laugh at such is

Mr. Punch's business. May he laugh honestly, hit no foul blow, and tell the truth when at his very broadest grin – never forgetting that if Fun is good, Truth is still better, and Love is best of all.'[16]

What I mean [he explained to Lemon], applies to my own case and that of all of us – who set up as Satirical-Moralists – and having such a vast multitude of readers whom we not only amuse but teach. . . . A few years ago I should have sneered at the idea of setting up as a teacher at all, and perhaps at this pompous and pious way of talking about a few papers of jokes in *Punch* – but I have got to believe in the business, and in many other things since then. And our profession seems to me to be as serious as the Parson's own.[17]

What happened to Thackeray in the eighteen-forties affords at least a partial explanation of his altered attitude towards the writer's task. After the break-up of his marriage he fell into a life of Bohemian bachelorhood, living in lodgings and finding his amusement in taverns, clubs, or the homes of his friends. It was a hectic, rootless existence, which he was by no means self-sufficient enough to enjoy. In June of 1845 family circumstances at last made it possible for his mother to bring his two daughters to visit him in London. They stayed only a few days, and after their departure, Thackeray wrote to his mother: 'I wish you had never come that's the truth – for I fancied myself perfectly happy until then – now I see the difference: and what a deal of the best sort of happiness it is God's will that I should lose. Whitebait dinners are all very well but – hang the buts – it is those we are always sighing after'.[18]

He set his heart on re-establishing his home; and fourteen months later he realized his desire. The society of his daughters, aged nine and six, brought him to an attitude of mind quite different from that which he had displayed among his rough and sometimes raffish 'companions . . . over the bottle'.[19] He wrote to his mother in December, 1846:

Now they [his daughters] are with me I am getting so fond of them that I can understand the pangs of the dear old mother who loses them. . . . Continual thoughts of them chase I don't know how many wickednesses out of my mind: Their society makes many of my old amusements seem trivial and shameful. What bounties are there of Providence in the very instincts which God gives us. . . . Remember the children are in their natural place: with their nearest friend working their natural influence: getting and giving the good let us hope, which the Divine Benevolence appointed to result from the union between parents and children.[20]

The revolution that Thackeray's reunion with his family worked in his scale of values radically altered his conception of what fiction ought to be. By good fortune the fragmentary manuscript of the early chapters of *Vanity Fair* survives in the Pierpont Morgan Library to show exactly what happened. It would appear that Thackeray began his novel early in 1845 and soon completed enough for two monthly parts. These eight chapters he wrote in his slanting hand. When Colburn and two or three other publishers refused 'Pen and Pencil Sketches of English Society', as the story was first called, Thackeray laid his manuscript temporarily aside. By March of 1846 Bradbury and Evans had accepted it; but other work intervened, and Thackeray did not return to his novel until the last months of that year. The changes that he made at this time are readily identifiable, for they were entered, perhaps at the printer's request, in his more legible upright hand.

Thackeray's revisions everywhere bear the mark of his new view of fiction. For the noncommittal 'Pen and Pencil Sketches of English Society' he substituted the pregnant phrase 'Vanity Fair', in itself a judgment on the life that he was describing. Here and there in his earlier narrative, which was almost as devoid of authorial intrusion as *Barry Lyndon*, he introduced passages of moral commentary. The next to the last chapter of 'Pen and Pencil Sketches of English Society', for example, had originally been devoted entirely to Becky's first letter to Amelia from Queen's Crawley. In his revision Thackeray added six concluding paragraphs which sum up the serious and responsible view that he had come to take of novel-writing.

And, as we bring our characters forward [he wrote], I will ask leave, as a man and a brother, not only to introduce them, but occasionally to step down from the platform, and talk about them: if they are good and kindly, to love them and shake them by the hand: if they are silly, to laugh at them confidentially in the reader's sleeve: if they are wicked and heartless, to abuse them in the strongest terms which politeness admits of.

Otherwise you might fancy it was I who was sneering at the practice of devotion, which Miss Sharp finds so ridiculous; that it was I who laughed good-humouredly at the reeling old Silenus of a baronet – whereas the laughter comes from one who has no reverence except for prosperity, and no eye for anything beyond success. Such people there are living and flourishing in the world – Faithless, Hopeless, Charityless; let us have at them, dear friends, with might and main. Some there are, and very successful too, mere quacks and fools: and it was to combat and expose such as those, no doubt, that laughter was made. [*Vanity Fair*, ch. 8]

Similarly, in the chapter following Thackeray inserted after his portraits of old Sir Pitt Crawley and his wife passages underlining the fashion in which each of these characters exemplifies the theme of his novel. Of Sir Pitt he wrote:

Vanity Fair – Vanity Fair! Here was a man, who could not spell, and did not care to read – who had the habits and the cunning of a boor: whose aim in life was pettifogging: who never had a taste, or emotion, or enjoyment, but what was sordid and foul; and yet he had rank, and honours, and power, somehow: and was a dignitary of the land, and a pillar of the state. He was high sheriff, and rode in a golden coach. Great ministers and statesmen courted him; and in Vanity Fair he had a higher place than the most brilliant genius or spotless virtue. [ch. 9]

As Thackeray went on from the point where his 1845 narrative ended, he was able to avoid the relatively crude and awkward patchwork of these earlier insertions. He moved with increasing ease from narrative to commentary and back again. His theme sufficiently stated, he no longer found it necessary to insist heavily on its explicit formulation. Nevertheless, he did not lose his guiding vision of the world as 'Vanity Fair', and all his effects were planned to emphasize it. His letters everywhere reveal his concentration upon the ethical issues raised by the action of his novel. In July of 1847, for example, he told his mother:

Of course you are quite right about Vanity Fair and Amelia, it is mentioned in this very number. My object is not to make a perfect character or anything like it. Don't you see how odious all the people are in the book (with the exception of Dobbin) – behind whom all there lies a dark moral I hope. What I want is to make a set of people living without God in the world (only that is a cant phrase) greedy pompous mean perfectly self-satisfied for the most part and at ease about their superior virtue.[21]

And after his novel was completed, he explained to Robert Bell, who had protested against the 'foul atmosphere' of *Vanity Fair*:

If I had put in more fresh air as you call it my object would have been defeated – It is to indicate, in cheerful terms, that we are for the most part an abominably foolish and selfish people 'desperately wicked' and all eager after vanities. . . . I want to leave everybody dissatisfied and unhappy at the end of the story – we ought all to be with our own and all other stories. Good God dont I see (in that may-be cracked and warped looking glass in which I am always looking) my own weaknesses wickednesses lusts follies shortcomings? . . . We must lift up our voices about these and howl to a congregation of fools: so much at least has been my endeavour.[22]

III

Thackeray's contemporaries were profoundly impressed, as we are to-day, by 'the generalizing eye, the penetrative humor, and the genial breadth of sympathy'[23] which enabled him to present convincingly the immense panorama of English life that one finds in *Vanity Fair*. No doubt these qualities in themselves suffice to explain his emergence to popularity after ten years of relative neglect. But Thackeray's novel brought him prestige as well as popularity; and this prestige derived from his capacity to judge the social scene as well as to portray it. Indeed, the conception of the novelist's responsibility which informs *Vanity Fair* was the chief factor in establishing Thackeray's contemporary reputation. It freed him from the diffidence and scoffing aloofness that had previously prevented him from giving his talent free play; and it provided him with an organizing idea, about which to arrange the wealth of impressions that he had accumulated.

The proof that Thackeray's novel earned him a position, not merely as one more accomplished entertainer of the calibre of Ainsworth, Disraeli, or Bulwer-Lytton, but as a great moralist, is not far to seek. Charlotte Brontë wrote, in dedicating the second edition of *Jane Eyre* to Thackeray:

There is a man in our own days whose words are not framed for delicate ears; who, to my thinking, comes before the great ones of society, much as the son of Imlah came before the throned Kings of Judah and Israel; and who speaks truth as deep, with a power as prophet-like and as vital. . . . I see in him an intellect profounder and more unique than his contemporaries have yet recognized; because I regard him as the first social regenerator of the day – as the very master of that working corps who would restore to rectitude the warped system of things.[24]

To-day these phrases sound almost ludicrously overstrained. But we are deficient in historical understanding if we dismiss them as merely Miss Brontë's excited way. There is abundant corroborative testimony to the powerful effect of Thackeray's novel upon its first readers, from which I cite the recollections of John Cordy Jeaffreson:

Men read those much-abused yellow pamphlets that came out month after month; and strong men, men not given to emotion, least of all to religious excitement, laid them down with tearful eyes and full hearts; and they were not a few who prayed earnestly to the Almighty for mercy and help, and rose from their knees with a determination to be men of charity.[25]

The early reviews of *Vanity Fair* everywhere reveal sluggish consciences stirred by the evidence of social corruption that Thackeray had amassed and interpreted. Harriet Martineau left *Vanity Fair* unfinished, unable to go on from 'the moral disgust it occasions';[26] Miss Rigby, who persisted, declared in the *Quarterly Review* that it was 'one of the most distressing books we have read for many a long year'.[27] John Forster in *The Examiner* was appalled by its 'exhalations of human folly and wickedness'.[28] Robert Bell in *Fraser's Magazine* found it a 'revolting reflex of society', which forced its readers 'to look into the depths of a loathsome truth'. Hogarth's 'Gin Lane' did not seem to him a far-fetched comparison.[29] An anonymous reviewer in a magazine published on the continent, where the lessons of the revolutionary year 1848 loomed large for all to read, went further still. Observing that *Vanity Fair* portrays 'naked and prosaic actuality which is often hideous of aspect but always true to life', he asked anxiously: 'Is it advisable to raise so ruthlessly the veil which hides the rottenness pervading modern society?'[30]

IV

To inquire why Thackeray's contemporaries took *Vanity Fair* and its author so seriously is to ask in effect what was his intellectual position in his age. A modest and unassertive man, Thackeray did not regard himself as a prophet. In the words 'I have no head above my eyes',[31] he once emphatically disclaimed any capacity for abstract thought. But conceivably the very fact that his unsystematic mind found expression in attitudes rather than in theories made his opinions the more acceptable to his Victorian readers. They found in him a teacher who provided a loose but temporarily tenable synthesis of ultimately irreconcilable social standards.

This point can best be illustrated by comparing his view of fashionable society, the epitome of the small class in whose interest England was then organized and governed, with that of two fellow novelists, Disraeli and Dickens. A quarter of a century before *Vanity Fair* was written, members of the upper world hardly troubled to justify their monopoly of privilege. They displayed instead a superb disdain of conflicting interests neatly summed up in Lord Melbourne's remark that he liked the Garter, because 'there was no damned merit about it'. Consider, for example, Lord Orford's reply to an invitation to become President of the Norwich Bible Society in 1824:

Sir, – I am surprised and annoyed by the contents of your letter. *Surprised*, because my well-known character should have exempted me

from such an application; and *annoyed* because it compels me to have
even this communication with you.
I have long been addicted to the gaming table. I have lately taken to
the Turf. I fear I frequently blaspheme. But I have never distributed
religious tracts. All this was known to you and your society. Notwith-
standing which you think me a fit person to be your President. God
forgive your hypocrisy.[32]

Disraeli adopted without reserve the aristocratic attitude illustrated in the letter of this Regency grandee. Like Lockhart he
thought that there was no greater pleasure than 'the calm
contemplation of that grand spectacle denominated "the upper
world". It is infinitely the best of theatres, the acting is
incomparably the first, the actresses the prettiest.'[33] To him
society was opportunity, the embodiment of the career open to
the talents.

Disraeli's picture of fashionable society in *Coningsby* is cool and
detached, devoid of emotional colouring or moral implications.
Here is a characteristic vignette of Lord Monmouth, modelled
upon the same Marquess of Hertford whom Thackeray was later
to portray as Lord Steyne:

Lord Monmouth beheld his grandson. His comprehensive and penetrating glance took in every point with a flash. There stood before him
one of the handsomest youths he had ever seen, with a mien as graceful
as his countenance was captivating; and his whole air breathing that
freshness and ingenuousness which none so much appreciates as the
used man of the world. And this was his child; the only one of his blood
to whom he had been kind. It would be exaggeration to say that Lord
Monmouth's heart was touched; but his good-nature effervesced, and
his fine taste was deeply gratified. He perceived in an instant such a
relation might be a valuable adherent; an irresistible candidate for
future elections: a brilliant tool to work out the Dukedom. All these
impressions and ideas, and many more, passed through the quick brain
of Lord Monmouth ere the sound of Coningsby's words had seemed to
cease, and long before the surrounding guests had recovered from the
surprise which they had occasioned them, and which did not diminish,
when Lord Monmouth, advancing, placed his arms round Coningsby
with a dignity of affection that would have become Louis XIV, and
then, in the high manner of the old Court, kissed him on each cheek.[34]

Disraeli is delighted by the scene and by the actors in it. Without illusions as to Monmouth's moral worth, he yet savours all the refinements of his character, and is at pains to communicate them with delicacy. 'It would be exaggeration to say that Lord Monmouth's heart was touched; but his good nature effervesced and his fine taste was deeply gratified.' The sentence is that of an artist who loves his subject.

In Dickens's *Little Dorrit* we find the reverse of the medal. Dickens's radicalism had been counterbalanced in his early books by a pervasive optimism; as late as *David Copperfield* the edge of his social criticism was blunted by farce. When Mrs. Waterbrook announces over the dinner table that if she has a weakness, it is Blood, Dickens intends us to be amused, not indignant. By the time that he wrote *Little Dorrit*, however, he meant mischief. The book is an attack on 'the Society business'[35] as the organizing principle of the Victorian social hierarchy. Dickens shows society bowing and scraping before 'the great and wonderful Merdle', a financier whose vast operations have raised him suddenly from obscurity to celebrity. Early in the story Dickens describes a dinner party given by the great man:

There were magnates from the Court and magnates from the City, magnates from the Commons and magnates from the Lords, magnates from the bench and magnates from the bar, Bishop magnates, Treasury magnates, Horse Guard magnates, Admiralty magnates – all the magnates that keep us going, and sometimes trip us up.

'I am told', said Bishop magnate to Horse Guards, 'that Mr. Merdle has made another enormous hit. They say a hundred thousand pounds.'

Horse Guards had heard two.

Treasury had heard three.

Bar, handling his persuasive double eye-glass, was by no means clear but that it might be four. It was one of those happy strokes of calculation and combination, the result of which it was difficult to estimate. It was one of those instances of a comprehensive grasp, associated with habitual luck and characteristic boldness, of which an age presented us but few. . . .

Admiralty said Mr. Merdle was a wonderful man. Treasury said he was a new power in the country, and would be able to buy up the whole

House of Commons. Bishop said he was glad to think that this wealth
flowed into the coffers of a gentleman who was always disposed to
maintain the best interests of Society.[36]

Everyone is delighted with Merdle's success, everyone expands in
its presence, except the great man himself, who is haunted by an
undefined *malaise,* by a complaint for which his physician can
find no cure. Not until Merdle has cut his throat in his bath near
the end of the novel does Dickens reveal what has troubled this
idol of 'Society'.

The late Mr. Merdle's complaint had been, simply, Forgery and
Robbery. He, the uncouth object of such widespread adulation, the
sitter at great men's feasts, the roc's egg of great ladies' assemblies, the
subduer of exclusiveness, the leveller of pride, the patron of patrons, the
bargain driver with a Minister for Lordships of the Circumlocution
Office, the recipient of more acknowledgment within some ten or fifteen
years, at most, than had been bestowed in England upon all peaceful,
public benefactors, and upon all the leaders of all the Arts and Sciences,
with all their works to testify for them, during two centuries at
least – he, the shining wonder, the new constellation to be followed by
the wise men bringing gifts, until it stopped over certain carrion at the
bottom of a bath and disappeared – was simply the greatest Forger and
the greatest Thief that ever cheated the gallows.[37]

The same society which delighted Disraeli bored and disgusted
Dickens. Too impatient to analyse it in detail, to explore its
refinements, he summed it up in terms of types and general
impressions, judged it and dismissed it.

In *Vanity Fair* Thackeray steers a middle course between two
extremes. Equally repugnant to him were Disraeli's amoral
acceptance of the *status quo* and Dickens's destructive radicalism.
His response to high life was ambivalent, his picture of it oblique.
He was fascinated by the aristocratic outlook – no attitude is
more often explored in his books – but he could not identify
himself with it in the manner of Disraeli, for he recognized that it
had become an anachronism in a prevailingly middle-class
world. In describing fashionable society he took refuge in irony,
which permitted him to convey at once his attraction and his

repulsion, or in a professed ignorance of its ways, which made it necessary for him to rely for information on what other persons, not always reliable witnesses, had told him.

The masterly chapter entitled 'Gaunt House', for example, is composed chiefly of gossip about Lord Steyne and his family communicated by sardonic old Tom Eaves, 'who has no part in this history', says Thackeray, 'except that he knew all the great folks in London, and the stories and mysteries of each family' [ch. 47]. To complete Eaves's revelations we are accommodated with a cross-section of London opinion as to the propriety of attending Lord Steyne's entertainments:

'Lord Steyne is really too bad', Lady Slingstone said, 'but everybody goes, and of course I shall see that my girls come to no harm.' 'His lordship is a man to whom I owe much, everything in life,' said the Right Reverend Doctor Trail, thinking that the archbishop was rather shaky; and Mrs. Trail and the young ladies would as soon have missed going to church as to one of his lordship's parties. 'His morals are bad,' said little Lord Southdown to his sister, who meekly expostulated, having heard terrific legends from her mamma with respect to the doings at Gaunt House; 'but hang it, he's got the best dry sillery in Europe!' And as for Sir Pitt Crawley, Bart. – Sir Pitt that pattern of decorum, Sir Pitt who had led off at missionary meetings, – he never for one moment thought of not going too. 'Where you see such persons as the Bishop of Ealing and the Countess of Slingstone, you may be pretty sure, Jane,' the baronet would say, 'that *we* cannot be wrong. The great rank and station of Lord Steyne put him in a position to command people in our station in life. The Lord Lieutenant of a county, my dear, is a respectable man.' [ch. 47]

Adopting the guise of 'Rumour painted full of tongues', Thackeray presents Lord Steyne and Gaunt House in perspective, with no less wit and delicacy than Disraeli displays in portraying Lord Monmouth, with no more attempt at palliation than Dickens employs in describing Merdle.

The resulting picture of high society was precisely what the intelligent Victorian reader desired. He still had, in Gladstone's phrase, 'a sneaking kindness for a lord'; but he had lost his assurance in the essential rightness of the aristocratic system.

Thackeray satisfied both his taste and his conscience. 'Thackeray's *Vanity Fair* is pathetic in its name, and in his use of the name,' Emerson wrote; 'an admission it is from a man of fashion in the London of 1850 that poor old Puritan Bunyan was right in his perception of the London of 1650. And yet now in Thackeray is the added wisdom, or skepticism, that, though this be really so, he must yet live in tolerance of, and practically in homage and obedience to, these illusions.'[38]

What comment on the validity of Gide's formula that 'the moral issue for the artist is not that he should present an idea that is useful but that he should present an idea well' is suggested by the account which I have given of Thackeray's acceptance of moral obligation towards his readers and of the consequences of this acceptance in his career? The hazards latent in Thackeray's conflicting views became only too evident in his later work. In 1908, when Galsworthy published *Fraternity*, Conrad wrote to him of the novel:

before all it is the work of a moralist . . . a humanitarian moralist. . . . This fact which you cannot help, and which may lead you yet to become the Idol of the Public – if I may so express myself – arises as the greatest danger in the way of your art. It may prevent the concentration of effort in one simple direction – because your art will always be trying to assert itself against the impulse of your moral feelings.[39]

In the eighteen-fifties Thackeray's critics increasingly urged similar counsels upon him, but he was as incapable as Galsworthy of following such advice. And indeed, *The Virginians*, *Lovel the Widower* and *Philip* – whatever their other merits – oppress the reader by their tired rehearsal of moral commonplaces. In these stories the figure that Thackeray cuts as a moralist almost inclines one to regard Gide's statement as axiomatic.

But a consideration of Thackeray's finer work redresses the balance. To reread *Vanity Fair*, *Pendennis*, *Esmond* and *The Newcomes* is to understand why Henry James placed Thackeray among the novelists whom he thought of 'primarily as great consciences and great minds',[40] why James Hannay admired in him 'the broad sagacity, sharp insight, large and tolerant liberality, which marked him as one who was a sage as well as a story-teller, and whose stories were valuable because he was a sage'.[41] In *Vanity Fair* above all Thackeray's acceptance of the novelist's responsibility was a liberating decision that immeasurably deepened his capacity for social judgment. The moral fervour which fills *Vanity Fair* with the urgency of a fresh revelation gives it a unity and intensity attained by few novels of comparable scope. Confronted by the complexity of contemporary life and by general disagreement regarding ethical presuppositions, the modern writer must no doubt leave the task of moral judgment to his readers; but he suffers as a novelist by doing so.

> SOURCE: from *Essays by Divers Hands: Being Transactions of the Royal Society of Literature in the United Kingdom*, New Series, XXV (Oxford, 1950) 342–56

NOTES

[Notes in the original have been reorganised and renumbered, with chapter-references to *Vanity Fair* inserted in the text.]

1. Quoted by François Mauriac, *God and Mammon* (London, 1936) p. 58.

2. 'Felix Culpa', *Commonweal*, XLVIII (16 July 1948) 323.

3. *Cornhill Magazine*, XIII (Jan 1866) 48.

4. *The Letters and Private Papers of William Makepeace Thackeray*, ed. Gordon N. Ray, 4 vols (Cambridge, Mass., 1945–6) vol. II, p. 258. Cited hereafter as *Letters*.

5. *Letters*, vol. II, p. 312, note.

6. *Letters and Memorials of Jane Welsh Carlyle*, ed. James Anthony Froude, 3 vols (London, 1883) vol. II, p. 3.

7. *Letters*, vol. II, p. 333.

8. 'Thackeray', *Macmillan's Magazine*, IX (Feb 1864) 356.

9. *Letters Literary and Theological* (London, 1881) p. 93.

10. Rowland Grey, 'Thackeray and France (With an Unpublished Thackeray Letter)', *Englishwoman*, XXXVII (May 1918) 112–13.

11. *Letters*, vol. II, p. 316.

12. *Horae Subsecivae, Third Series* (Edinburgh, 1884) p. 180.

13. 'Lever's St. Patrick's Eve – Comic Politics', *Morning Chronicle*, 3 Apr 1845.

14. *Letters*, vol. II, p. 54.

15. *Works*, ed. George Saintsbury, 17 vols (London, 1908) vol. V, 91–2.

16. *Works*, vol. IX, p. 493.

17. *Letters*, vol. II, p. 282.

18. *Letters*, vol. II, p. 197.

19. *Letters*, vol. II, p. 210.

20. *Letters*, vol. II, p. 255.

21. *Letters*, vol. II, p. 309. [See Part One above – Ed.]

22. *Letters*, vol. II, pp. 423–4.

23. H. D. Traill, *The New Fiction and Other Essays on Literary Subjects* (London, 1897) p. 169.

24. *Jane Eyre*, 2 vols (Oxford, 1931) vol. I, pp. ix–x.

25. *Novels and Novelists from Elizabeth to Victoria*, 2 vols (London, 1858) vol. II, p. 279.

26. *Autobiography*, ed. Maria Webster, 2 vols (Boston, 1877) vol. II, p. 60.

27. 'Vanity Fair – and *Jane Eyre*', *Quarterly Review* LXXXIV (Dec 1848) 155. [See Part One above – Ed.]

28. 'Vanity Fair', *The Examiner*, 22 July 1848, 468. [See Part One above – Ed.]

29. 'Vanity Fair', *Fraser's Magazine*, XXXVIII (Sep 1848) 321–2. [See Part One above – Ed.]

30. Quoted from the *Magazin für die Litteratur des Auslandes* in the Readers' Classics edition of *Vanity Fair* (Bath, 1919) p. 61.

31. Reported by George Curtis, *Harper's Magazine*, VIII (May 1854) 840.

32. Quoted by Sir Algernon West, *Recollections*, 2 vols (London, 1899) vol. I, pp. 26–7.

33. Quoted by Andrew Lang, *The Life and Letters of John Gibson Lockhart*, 2 vols (London, 1897) vol. II, pp. 82–3.

34. *Coningsby*, Bk IV, ch. 6.

35. *Letters of Charles Dickens*, ed. Walter Dexter, 3 vols (London, 1938) vol. II, p. 766.

36. *Little Dorrit*, Bk I, ch. 21.

37. Ibid., Bk II, ch. 25.

38. *Journals*, ed. E. W. Emerson and W. E. Forbes, 10 vols (London, 1913) vol. VIII, pp. 113–14.

39. Quoted by H. V. Marrot, *Life and Letters of John Galsworthy* (London, 1935) p. 229.

40. *French Poets and Novelists* (London, 1878) p. 113.

41. *Brief Memoir of the Late Mr. Thackeray* (Edinburgh, 1864) p. 22.

Dorothy Van Ghent

'THE "OMNISCIENT AUTHOR" CONVENTION AND THE "COMPOSITIONAL CENTRE" FUNCTION' (1953)

Almost exactly a century separates *Tom Jones* from *Vanity Fair*; but with *Vanity Fair*, so far as technical developments in the novel are concerned, it is as if there had been none. We are in the story telling convention of the 'omniscient author' sanctioned by Fielding's great example, but with a damaging difference that is due, not so much to an inherent inadequacy of that convention itself, as the spiritual incoherency of another age. It is true that the technique of omniscient authorship can allow a relaxed garrulity – what James called 'the terrible fluidity of self-revelation' – for if the author can enter the story in his own voice, there is nothing to keep him from talking. After discussing Becky's adolescent designs on Jos Sedley, and her visions of shawls and necklaces and aristocratic company which she imagines will be the rewards of marriage with Jos, Thackeray comments, 'Charming Alnaschar visions! it is the happy privilege of youth to construct you, and many a fanciful young creature besides Rebecca Sharp has indulged in these delightful day-dreams ere now!' [ch. 3]. The comment is both inane and distracting – distracting our attention from the tense mental operations of Becky and turning it upon the momentarily flaccid mentality of her author. The effect is one of rather surprised irritation, as it is again when, having described Jos's wardrobe, his pains in dressing, his vanity and shyness, Thackeray remarks, 'If Miss Rebecca can get the better of *him*, and at her first entrance into life, she is a young person of no ordinary cleverness' [ch. 3]. What we feel is that two orders of reality are clumsily getting in each other's way: the order of imaginative reality, where Becky lives, and the order of historical reality, where William Makepeace Thackeray lives. The fault becomes more striking in the following unforgivable parenthesis. Jos has just presented Amelia with flowers. ' "Thank you, dear Joseph," said Amelia, quite ready to kiss her brother, if he were so minded. (And I think for a kiss from such a dear creature as Amelia, I would purchase all Mr. Lee's conservatories out of hand.)' [ch. 4] The picture of Thackeray himself kissing Amelia pulls Amelia quite out of the created world of *Vanity Fair* and drops her into some shapeless limbo of Thackerayan sentiment where she loses all aesthetic orientation.

Nevertheless, the conventions employed in a work of art cannot fairly be judged by themselves; they can be judged only as instrumental to a vision. The time in which Thackeray wrote was, compared with Fielding's time, itself looser in what we might call cultural composition; its values were less integrated in a common philosophical 'style' or tenor of mind. In *Tom Jones*, the convention of the author's appearance in his book as 'gregarious eye', stage manager, and moralist, is a strategy that is used with a highly formal regularity of rhythm, and it animates every turn of Fielding's language, as the ironic life of the language. Most important, the convention had benefited by an age's practice of and belief in form, form in manners and rhetoric and politics and philosophy – that is, by an age's coherently structured world view. The set of feelings and ideas of which Fielding acts as vehicle, when he makes his personal appearances in his book, is a set of feelings and ideas with the stamp of spiritual consistency upon them. They do not afflict us with a sense of confused perspectives between the author's person and his work, his opinions and his creation, as do Thackeray's. Whereas Thackeray seems merely to be victimized or tricked by his adopted convention into a clumsy mishandling of perspectives, Fielding manipulates the same convention deliberately to produce displacements of perspective as an organic element of composition. This is not to say that Fielding's creative perceptions are, on the whole, more penetrating and profound than

Thackeray's; indeed, Thackeray's seem to reach a good deal deeper into the difficulties, compromises, and darkness of the human estate; but Fielding's have the organizing power to make an ancient oral convention of storytelling an appropriate instrument of his vision, whereas the same convention – actually one that is most sympathetic to Thackeray's gift of easy, perspicacious, ranging talk – becomes a personal convenience for relaxation of aesthetic control, *even a means to counterfeit* his creative vision.

Becky ruminates, 'I think I could be a good woman if I had five thousand a year', and adds with a sigh, 'Heigho! I wish I could exchange my position in society, and all my relations, for a snug sum in the Three per Cent. Consols' [ch. 41]. Here she is as true to herself psychologically as is Moll Flanders; but she is more complex than Moll, and we know perfectly that, at this promising stage in her career, the sigh is only a casual fantasy – arising chiefly out of boredom with the tedious business of cultivating the good graces of people much less intelligent than herself – and that if the 'snug sum' were offered, she would not really exchange her prospects for it, for her temperament is not at present to be satisfied with snugness. There are to be pearl necklaces, presentation at court,' a *succès fou* at Gaunt House. But Thackeray interprets for us: 'It may, perhaps, have struck her that to have been honest and humble, to have done her duty, and to have marched straightforward on her way, would have brought her as near happiness as that path by which she was striving to attain it' [ch. 41].

This is a doctrine with which, in principle, we have no cause either to agree or disagree; a novel is not made of doctrines and principles, but of concretely imagined life, and whatever moral principle may be honestly adduced from that life must be intrinsic to it, concretely qualitative within it. *Vanity Fair* is strong with life, but in those concretions where it is alive there is nothing to suggest that to be 'honest and humble' can possibly bring happiness. Becky is the happiest person in the book; she is alive from beginning to end, alive in intelligence and activity and *joie de vivre*, whether she is throwing Dr. Johnson's dictionary out of a coach window, in superb scorn of the humiliations of the poor, or exercising her adulterous charm on General Tufto, whether she is prancing to court to be made an 'honest woman' (in stolen lace), or hiding a cognac bottle in a sordid bed. From Becky's delighted exercise in being alive, we can learn nothing about the happiness to be derived from humble dutifulness. On the other hand, from Amelia's humble dutifulness we can learn nothing that convinces us doctrinally that happiness lies in such a way of life. For it is not only that the brisk gait and vivid allure of Becky's egoistic and aggressive way of life make Amelia look tepid, tear sodden, and compromised: this effect would not occur if the book were soundly structured, if its compositional center (what James called the 'commanding centre' of the composition) were entirely firm and clear.

The actually functioning compositional center of *Vanity Fair* is that node or intersection of extensive social and spiritual relationships constituted by Becky's activities: her relationships with a multitude of individuals – Jos and Amelia and George, old Sir Pitt and Rawdon and Miss Crawley and the Bute Crawleys and the Pitt Crawleys, Lady Bareacres, Lord Steyne, and so on – and, through these individuals, her relationships with large and significant blocks of a civilization: with the middle-class Sedley block, that block which is in the process of physical destruction because of its lack of shrewdness in an acquisitive culture; with the other middle-class Osborne block, that block which has displaced the Sedley block through its own acquisitive shrewdness and through the necessarily accompanying denial of the compassionate and sympathetic human impulses; with the aristocratic Crawley block, in all its complexity of impotence and mad self-destruction, and (in young Sir Pitt, with the 'gooseberry eyes') canny self-renovation through connivance with the economy and morality of the dominant middle class; with the ambiguous Steyne block, that is above the economic strife and therefore free of conventional moral concerns, but in its social freedom, 'stained' deeply in nerves and blood. (In the names he gives people, Thackeray plays – like many novelists – on punning suggestion, as he does in the name of the crawling Crawleys, 'raw-done' Rawdon, Sharp, Steyne, O'Dowd, etc.) This social relationship, concretized through

Becky's relationship with individuals, is the hub of the book's meanings, its 'compositional center'. But beside this violently whirling and excited center is another, a weak and unavailing epicenter, where Amelia weeps and suffers and wins – wins Dobbin and solvency and neighborhood prestige and a good middle-class house with varnished staircases. Organized around the two centres are two plots, which have as little essentially to do with each other as Thackeray's creative imagination had to do with his sentimental, morally fearful reflections. He cannot bear to allow the wonderfully animated vision of Becky's world to speak for itself, for its meaning is too frightening; he must add to it a complementary world – Amelia's – to act as its judge and corrector. One thinks, in comparison, of Balzac, who was writing almost contemporaneously. Balzac was both as skeptical and as sentimental as Thackeray, but he was a passionate rationalist as well, and a much bolder dramatic formalist. In Balzac, the weak and the suffering and the pure in heart do not win. They have no pretensions to effective moral dynamism in the evil Balzacian world, which uses them as illustrative examples of the impotence of an 'honest and humble' way of life.

As the convention of the omniscient author allows Thackeray to keep up a maladroit 'sound track' of personal interpolations, so it also collaborates with his confusion as to where the compositional center of his book lies; for though the Becky-world and the Amelia-world, having no common motivation, confront each other with closed entrances, so to speak, yet the author is able, by abuse of his rights of omniscience, to move facilely through these closed doors. We assume that, in Thackeray's plan, the compositional center of the book was to be the moral valence between the two worlds. But there is no valence between them, nothing in either to produce a positive effect of significance on the other. The only effect is negative: the Amelia-plot pales into a morally immature fantasy beside the vivid life of the Becky-plot. For Becky is the great morally meaningful figure, the moral symbol, in the book, and beside her there is room and meaning for Amelia only as victim – certainly not as 'success figure'. The word 'moral', which we have used rather frequently in these studies, needs perhaps a somewhat closer attention here. Becky is not virtuous, and in speaking of her as a morally significant figure, we cannot possibly confuse her moral meaning with the meaning of 'virtue'. She is a morally meaningful figure because she symbolizes the morality of her world at its greatest intensity and magnitude. The greediness that has only a reduced, personal meaning in Mrs. Bute Crawley, as she nags and blunders at old Miss Crawley's deathbed, acquires, through Becky's far more intelligent and courageous greed – as she encounters international techniques for the satisfaction of greed with her own subtle and knowing and superior techniques – an extensive social meaning. The corruption that, in old Sir Pitt, has meaning at most for the senility of a caste, becomes, in Becky's prostitution and treason and murderousness, the moral meaning of a culture. For Becky's activities are designed with intelligent discrimination and lively intuition, and they are carried through not only with unflagging will power but with joy as well. By representing her world at its highest energetic potential, by alchemizing all its evil but stupid and confused or formless impulses into brilliantly controlled intention, she endows her world with meaning. The meaning is such as to inspire horror; but the very fact that we conceive this horror intellectually and objectively is an acknowledgement of Becky's morally symbolic stature.

There is a French criticism of the English novel, that, in the English novel's characteristic concern with the social scene, it fails to explore 'the deeper layers of personality'. One understands the motivation of this criticism, if one compares representative French and English novels of approximately the same periods, although the criticism itself does not seem to be well thought out. *The Pilgrim's Progress* is populated with social 'types', sparsely limned sketches that isolate certain traits, whereas, almost contemporaneously, Madame de Lafayette's *La Princesse de Clèves* is concentrated upon a depth illumination of the tortured psyche of a delicate woman who, in a loveless marriage, is moved by an illicit passion. Even *Clarissa Harlowe*, which is commonly thought of as an exhaustive representation of a young woman's emotions, is, because of its mythical qualities, rather more of a vision into the social soul than into that of a credible individual; and the difference is brought out by comparison with the almost

contemporaneous *Manon Lescaut*, by the Abbé Prévost, in which
the subject has certain affinities with that of *Clarissa* (except that
it is the girl, here, who is the libertine, and the young man who is
the afflicted one), but which is again – like so many French
novels – a concentrated depth drawing of personal psychology
rather than a social vision. One could pursue a number of other
examples in the same way. But the difference is a relative
difference only. For the 'deeper layers of personality' are
meaningless unless they can be related, at least by inference, to
aspects of life that have some social generality; while social life is
meaningless unless it finds embodiment in individuals. A more
significant difference between classical French novels and classical English novels is one of method. The English novel has tended
traditionally to symbolize certain phases of personality through
the concrete image (Christian as the 'man in rags' with a burden
on his back; the Philosopher Square standing among Molly's
'other female utensils' when the curtain falls in the bedroom;
Clarissa, with streaming eyes and disheveled bosom, prostrating
herself before Lovelace; Jaggers washing his hands or Miss
Havisham beside the rotten bridecake); while the French novel
has tended traditionally to a discursive analysis of feeling and
motive, as has the French drama. Image and analysis are merely
two different ways of mirroring what goes on in the soul. The
methods are never exclusive; and we find such significant
exceptions to the general tendency as Flaubert's *Madame Bovary*,
where the image dominates, and Conrad's *Lord Jim*, where
analysis dominates.

Let us illustrate, from *Vanity Fair*, the method of the image and
what it is able to imply as to the 'deeper layers of personality'.
Characteristically, in this book, the social concern is paramount.
We have spoken of the various 'blocks' of this civilization, some
slipping into rubble by the crush of the others or by internal
decay, some thrusting themselves up by the neighboring default-
ment. But governing all the movements is one ethos of aggressive
egoism, articulated through the acquisition of cash and through
the prestige fantasies born of cash. Becky herself is a member of
no particular class and confined to no particular 'block'.
(Significantly, she is the daughter of a Bohemian artist and a

French music-hall singer.) She is more mobile than any of the other characters, because of her freedom from caste, and thus is able to enter into a great variety of class relationships: this is the peculiar novelistic virtue of the picara and picaro, and the enduring source of virility of the picaresque form – the protagonist's freedom of movement. Still acting under the same ethos as that governing the whole civilization, Becky is able to represent its tendencies without class pretenses. Thus Becky, like Moll Flanders, though a strongly individualized character, is the type of a whole civilization, a small-scale model of a world, a microcosm in which the social macrocosm is subtilized and intensified and made significant. With this predominantly social bearing of the novel, the characters – even Becky – tend to be depicted in a relatively 'external' way: that is, there is relatively little discussion of the nuances of their feelings and their motivations; they are not self-analytical characters, as characters in French novels tend to be, nor do they spend much time in deliberate analysis of each other; they appear to us physically, in action; and – with some generalized interpretive help from the author himself (whose interpretations, as we have noted, we cannot always trust) – we enter into their motives and states of feeling by our own intuition. Examples are manifold. There is Becky's meeting of George's eyes in the mirror as she and Amelia, Jos and George, are leaving for Vauxhall: a flashing, accidental illumination of his vanity and vulnerability – and though here might be an excellent opportunity for Becky to engage in psychological speculations and deliberations, little of the kind occurs. There is the physical flash, the illumination by image only, and Becky has George's number. And yet later, when George and Amelia, Becky and Rawdon, meet on their honeymoon trips at Brighton, and Becky with almost unconscious slyness encourages George to make love to her, the early image of the meeting of eyes in a mirror plays on the reader's understanding of motivation, as it does again when we see Becky in overt sexual aggressiveness at the Brussels ball. There has been no need of discursive analysis of motive; the image does the work.

Or – another instance of the work of the image – there is Jos, in his obesity and his neckcloths and his gorgeous waistcoats. We should not expect Jos to analyze himself, nor anyone else to have an interest in analyzing what he feels, for he is below the level of what is rationally interesting; and yet, from the physical picture alone, we are made intuitively aware of deeply disturbed 'layers of personality' in Jos. He is one of the most complicated psychological portraits in the book (more complicated, for instance, than that of another voluptuary, the Marquis of Steyne, who has more refined opportunities than Jos and a better head), extremely unpleasant, with suggestions of impalpable submerged perversities, pathetic, with a pathos that is at the same time an outrage to our feeling for what is humanly cognizable in pathos – for Jos is a glandularly suffering animal, with the 'human' so hidden in his tortured fat that we feel it to be obscene, while we must still recognize it as human. Jos offering his neck to Isidor's razor . . . is a complex image of a kind of fear so muddied, an image of a psychological state so profoundly irrational, that we react to it with an impulse of horrified laughter – the intuitive horror having no other outlet than in a sense of the absurd. At the same time that these physical images of Jos flash to the mind's eye an impression of something deep and possible in individual personality, they are made by Thackeray to represent to the social reason an extremely significant phase of a culture. We see in Jos's obesity the sickness of a culture, the sickness due to spiritual gourmandism, or, in simpler but still metaphorical words, to 'overeating'; in his shyness of women, the repressions and abnormalities of a sick culture; in his stupidity and febrile conceit, the intellectual numbing and tubercular euphoria of a culture. Thus the physical image, here, mirrors most fearful depths of the personal and, at the same time, most threatening perspectives of the social life.

We shall cite a few more illustrations of this method of the 'image', as Thackeray uses it, keeping in mind its double significance, its significance for personal psychology (the 'deeper layers of personality') and its social significance. But in preparation for these particular citations, we should speak of one singularly important theme of *Vanity Fair*, and that is a theme which we shall call the theme of the 'fathers'. In the eighteenth-century novels that we have read, the 'father' has appeared in a

light that is rather different from the light that is thrown on the
'father' in nineteenth-century novels. . . .

We see, in the notion of the father in eighteenth-century
literature, a reflection of social trust: of trust in and reliance upon
and devotion to a general social system of values – that coherent
'world view' of the eighteenth century that we have spoken of
earlier in this essay. For, under our anciently inherited patriar-
chal organization of the family, an organization that inevitably
extended itself into political organization and philosophic organization, the 'father-imago' has acquired vast symbolic extension
beyond domestic life and into general social life: our 'fathers' are
not only our individual fathers but all those who have come
before us – society as it has determined our conditions of
existence and the problems we have to confront. *Vanity Fair*, with
its panorama of western European international society as
backdrop to the heroine's activities, is full of 'fathers', sick fathers,
guilty fathers. . . .

It is significant of the vital intuitiveness of Thackeray's *Vanity
Fair* that the theme of the 'fathers' should have such importance:
in this book, an immensely impressive female, herself quite
fatherless, manages to articulate in her career the most meaningful social aspects of the 'father' theme. We need, in this view of the
book, to free ourselves from the narrower Freudian aspects of the
theme and to think in terms of Thackeray's broad social
perspective, where the 'fathers' are such variants as Mr. Sedley,
Mr. Osborne, old Sir Pitt, even the Marquis of Steyne: in other
words, such variants as to include all the older, authoritative, and
determinative aspects of society.

And now, with this general notion of the significance of the
theme of parental authority, we can consider what Thackeray
manages to get out of the 'image' of old Mr. Osborne and his
daughters coming down the stairs, in their evening ritual, to
dinner.

The obedient bell in the lower regions began ringing the announcement
of the meal. The tolling over, the head of the family thrust his hands into
the great tail-pockets of his great blue coat and brass buttons, and
without waiting for a further announcement, strode downstairs alone,

scowling over his shoulder at the four females.

'What's the matter now, my dear?' asked one of the other, as they rose and tripped gingerly behind the sire.

'I suppose the funds are falling', whispered Miss Wirt; and so, trembling and in silence, this hushed female company followed their dark leader.   [ch. 13]

In the lines just before this there is one other, inconspicuous, touch: in the drawing room where they are waiting for dinner is a chronometer 'surmounted by a cheerful brass group of the sacrifice of Iphigenia'. The depths which are suggested by this picture, but quite as if accidentally, are the depths of Greek tragedy and, still further back, of Freud's dim, subhuman, imagined 'primitive horde': the 'dark leader' with his 'hushed female company', and the ridiculous but furious Victorian clock 'cheerfully' symbolizing the whole. Antiquity's dark brooding over the monstrous nature of man is made to take on, in this incidental image of a family's going to dinner, the unwholesomeness and perversity that have been added to man's classical monstrosity by 'falling funds', a drop in the stock market.

There is the recurrent incident in the hall outside the bedroom where old Miss Crawley is sick, Becky tending her, everyone – including Becky – waiting for and speculating on the 'reversionary spoils'.

Captain Rawdon got an extension of leave on his aunt's illness, and remained dutifully at home. He was always in her ante-chamber. (She lay sick in the state bedroom into which you entered by the little blue saloon.) His father was always meeting him there; or if he came down the corridor ever so quietly, his father's door was sure to open, the hyaena face of the old gentleman to glare out. What was it set one to watch the other so? A generous rivalry, no doubt, as to which should be most attentive to the dear sufferer in the state bedroom. Rebecca used to come out and comfort both of them – or one or the other of them rather.   [ch. 14]

Short and unemphasized as the passage is (outside of one ironic line, it consists only of an image, the image of Rawdon opening a door and looking into the corridor, of the old man's 'hyaena face'

instantly looking out from an opposite door, of Becky coming
down the hall to 'comfort' them), it contains a pregnant and
disturbing meaning, both for personal psychology and for social
psychology. Later, when Becky will attempt to inform Sir Pitt
about her clandestine marriage, but without telling him the
name of her husband, he will be uproariously amused; but as soon
as she tells him the name – his son, Rawdon – he goes mad with
inexplicable fury. We look back mentally to the incidents in the
hall outside Miss Crawley's sickroom, where son and father glare
at each other and where Becky comes to comfort them *separately*,
holding each in suspense as to her amorous favor. And we look
forward also to that horrible line in Becky's letter to Rawdon
(after the disclosure to Sir Pitt), where she says, 'I might have
been somebody's mamma, instead of – Oh, I tremble, I tremble. . . .' What is contained here is probably the most excruciat-
ingly primitive father – son battle in literature, with one of the
most sensitively feminine but perversely sentimental reflections
upon it. How are we to say, in such a case, whether what we are
observing is the 'deeper layers of personality' or the social scene?

And then there is the description of the turmoil surrounding
old Sir Pitt's death. It consists of a succession of images: Miss
Horrocks fitting in ribbons through 'the halls of their fathers';
again Miss Horrocks 'of the guilty ribbons, with a wild air, trying
at the presses and escritoires with a bunch of keys', [ch. 39] while
upstairs they are 'trying to bleed' Sir Pitt (the 'trying to' suggests
unknown but repulsive derangements); the servant girl screaming and making faces at him in private while he whimpers. The
cumulation of these images, scattered and casual as they are,
makes the face of a gorgon of destiny. The personal and social
idea of the 'father' (an idea which is inextricably both personal
and social) is made the nasty companion of the ribbon-fitting
Miss Horrocks; when Sir Pitt gives the family pearls to Lady Jane
('Pretty pearls – never gave'em to the ironmonger's daughter'),
marital relationships, with all they mean for the security created
for us by our elders, are referred back retrospectively to Sir Pitt's
chronic tipsiness and Lady Crawley's worsted knitting—an
'enormous interminable piece of knitting' – 'She worked that
worsted day and night. . . . She had not character enough to

take to drinking' [ch. 9]; drawers are tried while the 'father' is bled; and finally – so great is the prestige of this 'father' and baronet – the servant girl has full amplitude to scream obscenities and make faces at him, for he has turned into 'a whimpering old idiot put in and out of bed and cleaned and fed like a baby'.

The burden of Thackeray's intuition into personal psychology and its social meaning falls on images like these, and they are innumerable in *Vanity Fair*. But the greatness of *Vanity Fair* is not in scattered images, sensitive as these are. They are all gathered up in Becky Sharp. Becky does for Jos, murderously, at the end; and what she does to Jos is only cancerously implicit in himself and the civilization that has made him; she is the darkness – shining obsidianly in an intelligent personality – in old Mr. Osborne's dense sadism against his daughters and his corruption of the meaning of paternal responsibility toward his son; she manipulates the insane father – son conflict between Sir Pitt and Rawdon; and she is the 'guilty ribbons' of Miss Horrocks (instead of a servant's ribbons she has a courtesan's pearls) and at the same time the whimpering idiocy of the dying Sir Pitt (paralleling his repulsive attack of mortality on Jos) – or she is at once all the imperatively aggressive, insanely euphoric impulses of a morally sick civilization, and an individual condensation of that civilization. We question whether we would understand her at all, or be charmed by her buoyancy or appalled by her destructiveness, if her impulses were not memorabilia of our own and her civilization our heritage.

SOURCE: extracts from *The English Novel: Form and Function* (New York, 1953) pp.139–52 (paperback edition pp.171–8†, 181–2, 183–6).

Kathleen Tillotson

'THE DEBATABLE LAND BETWEEN THE MIDDLE CLASSES AND THE ARISTOCRACY' (1954)

. . . Thackeray turns away . . . from heroes and heroines, from the conventional ending, from the 'professional parts of novels'. And he evades the contemporary categories: *Vanity Fair* is not a novel of low life (its lowest level is the apartments at Fulham, or – unexpectedly – the elder Sir Pitt's *ménage* in Great Gaunt Street), nor of high life (the highest level is the ball at Gaunt House, which would contain some surprises for the devotees of Mrs. Gore),[1] it is not a military novel, despite Waterloo, nor a domestic novel, despite the number of family scenes. It is not historical, although it is a novel about the past; the period in which it is set is robbed of its usual glamour, and the past is strangely interpenetrated by the present. Thackeray's preface, 'Before the Curtain', illustrates his almost malicious way of teasing expectation:

There are scenes of all sorts; some dreadful combats, some grand and lofty horse-riding, some scenes of high life, some of very middling indeed: some love-making for the sentimental, and some light comic business; the whole accompanied by appropriate scenery, and brilliantly illuminated by the Author's own candles.

He promises variety; but he also gives unity, and not only by the continuous presence of the 'Author's own candles'. The principles of organization in *Vanity Fair* must next be considered: the positive truth which Thackeray substitutes for the conventions of fiction.

By choosing as his field 'the debatable land between the middle classes and the aristocracy'[2] he takes a social area which, though less extensive than Dickens's, gives him considerable vertical range. All the characters are seen in relation to 'society', living in it or on it; for each character he defines the rung on the ladder, the place on the slippery slope, the rocky ledge where they hang by finger-tips. None are unplaced; which means that the 'other nation' is excluded – it was not beyond his ken, but he chose to ignore it here.

There is less scope for oddity than in Dickens's world, for Vanity Fair is a world in which it is important to conform. Those who give up the pretence of conforming, like Sir Pitt Crawley or Lord Steyne, show that Thackeray can provide his own grotesques, with only the monstrosity which actual life provides. Specific comparison with Dickens illustrates Thackeray's different attitude to reality: the observed reality is often the same, but Thackeray mines into it, where Dickens makes it a springboard into fantasy. Even in his names Thackeray wishes 'to convey the sentiment of reality', Dickens's may be actual, but they are chosen for their oddity and comic appropriateness, while Thackeray masks his satire in plausibility, preferring a subtle suggestiveness; as in 'Steyne', with its pun and its relation to Regency Brighton; or the contrast, rich in association, of the liquid and romantic 'Amelia Sedley' with the hinted racial astuteness of 'Rebecca Sharp'.

Thackeray's characters exist in a denser context than perhaps any characters in fiction. They are aware of past time; they draw on childhood memories.

. . . am I much better to do now in the world than I was when I was the poor painter's daughter, and wheedled the grocer round the corner for sugar and tea? Suppose I had married Francis who was so fond of me. . . .   [ch. 41]

It is the only time we ever hear of 'Francis'. In the shadow, just beyond every character, but ready to catch the spotlight for a single instant when needed, seem to be all the people the character has ever met. Here is the sole appearance of Edward Dale:

the junior of the house, who purchased the spoons for the firm, was, in fact, very sweet upon Amelia, and offered for her in spite of all. He married Miss Louisa Cutts (daughter of Higham and Cutts, the eminent corn-factors) with a handsome fortune in 1820; and is now living in splendour, and with a numerous family, at his elegant villa, Muswell Hill. [ch. 17]

Odd corners of their houses, or possessions, may similarly light up at a touch. Their ancestries and family histories may be given; the baptismal names of the Crawley ancestors, according well with their surname, epitomize the political vanities of two centuries. And no single paragraph about Lord Steyne tell us more about him and his society, or about vanity in high places, than that list of titles and honours in his 'obituary':

the Most Honourable George Gustavus, Marquis of Steyne, Earl of Gaunt and of Gaunt Castle, in the Peerage of Ireland, Viscount Hellborough, Baron Pitchley and Grillsby, a Knight of the Most Noble Order of the Garter, of the Golden Fleece of Spain, of the Russian Order of Saint Nicholas of the First Class, of the Turkish Order of the Crescent, First Lord of the Powder Closet and Groom of the Back Stairs, Colonel of the Gaunt or Regent's Own Regiment of Militia, a Trustee of the British Museum, an Elder Brother of the Trinity House, a Governor of the White Friars, and D.C.L. . . . . [ch. 44]

Such fullness of documentation, never introduced heavily, but ready to be drawn on where it is needed, is significant of Thackeray's emphasis on character in its social relations. This has been noted by all his critics, and best defined by Brownell:

Thackeray's personages are never portrayed in isolation. They are a part of the *milieu* in which they exist, and which has itself therefore much more distinction and relief than an environment which is merely a framework. How they regard each other, how they feel toward and what they think of each other, the mutuality of their very numerous and vital relations, furnishes an important strand in the texture of the story in which they figure. Their activities are modified by the air they breathe in common. Their conduct is controlled, their ideas affected, even their desires and ambitions dictated, by the general ideas of the society that includes them.[3]

But it would be wrong to see Thackeray as a fatalist about character. That Becky believes she might have been a good woman on five thousand a year is itself part of her character ('Becky consoled herself . . .)'[ch. 41]; some virtues may be accidental, but 'circumstance only brings out the latent defect or quality, and does not create it'.[4] Thackeray is not optimistic enough about human nature (less so, for example, than George Eliot) to have much belief in the power of people to change themselves: 'We alter very little. . . . Our mental changes are like our grey hairs and our wrinkles – but the fulfilment of the plan of mortal growth and decay' [*Pendennis*, ch. 59]. His characters are so mixed, so often on a moral borderland, so subject to time, and also so gradually unfolded – often with unpredictable detail – that they do not give the impression of being static. But they are not shown as evolving, nor do they undergo much inward conflict; and so the unity given to a novel by dominating or developing characters is not found. Only one of Thackeray's novels – *Pendennis* – is even formally built upon the fortunes of a single character; and Arthur Pendennis is less an interesting individual than a nineteenth-century variant of Everyman.

Without recourse to obvious devices, without a hero or heroine or any single central figure, without any 'inward' study of development in character, Thackeray nevertheless makes us feel *Vanity Fair* a unity. This has sometimes been underestimated, and the novel apologized for as loose, rambling, and casual, though admitted to be rich and comprehensive: the apology may even lay the blame on the serial form. But the serial novel, serially written, is . . . really the less likely to be loose and rambling; only some degree of forethought makes such writing even possible; and the reader's interest, spread over a year and a half, will not be held unless there is a genuine continuity and a firm centre of interest. It is a contention of this whole study that both novelists and critics of this time were interested in 'unity'; we may recall that Lytton claimed that 'composition' should be recognized in novels as in paintings, and *Fraser's* critic of 1851 says firmly: 'One of the great achievements . . . in the art of the novelist is unity. If we cannot get that, the next best thing is progress.' A more reputable critical view, one indeed that is insidiously tempting, is that Thackeray's formal purpose is a 'picture' of society. This view, so persuasively set forth in Lubbock's *Craft of Fiction*, does admit of composition, even if 'picture' is extended to 'panorama'; but it accounts only for a part of *Vanity Fair*. For it allows too little for our fascinated sense of progression; too little also for Thackeray the moralist.

The clear and obvious line of progression in the novel is surely also, when closely considered, the chief of its unities: that is, the converging and diverging, parallel and contrasting fortunes of the two girls, Rebecca Sharp and Amelia Sedley.[5] In narrative terms, the basis of the contrast is simple (the moral contrast, on the other hand, is ironic and complex); it is that Rebecca attempts actively to shape her own fortunes, while Amelia passively accepts hers. They began with 'the world before them', on their last day at Minerva House Academy in Chiswick Mall. Their manner of leaving Miss Pinkerton's differentiates them at the outset in character as well as social status. Rebecca is nineteen and Amelia sixteen, but Rebecca has never been a child (Thackeray refers early to her 'dismal precocity') and Amelia is never to grow up. But throughout the first number (chs 1 – 4) their similarity as well as difference is emphasized; both are occupied with the 'vanity' of husband-hunting (the title of chapter 2 is 'In which Miss Sharp and Miss Sedley prepare to open the campaign'); Rebecca is laying her snares for Jos Sedley, Amelia sighing and smiling at George Osborne. In the closing number, after seventeen years, Amelia at last consents to forget George, and Rebecca at last has Jos inescapably in her toils. Throughout the narrative a balance of interest between Amelia and Rebecca is steadily maintained; in every number there is something of both, and when they are apart the juxtaposition of chapters defining the progress in their histories still forms a pattern. In Number Five (chs 15 – 18) Rebecca is thrown out of favour with the Crawleys when her marriage to Rawdon is revealed; Mr. Sedley has failed in business and George Osborne's defection is threatened, but there is a hopeful turn at the end to bring Amelia's marriage into sight and match the close of

Number Four. In Number Fourteen (chs 47 – 50) there is a
simple contrast between the zenith of Becky's fortunes (presented
at Court, dining at Gaunt House) and the nadir of Amelia's (in
poverty, and parted from her son). In Number Sixteen comes
Becky's 'fall', set beside the first hint of Amelia's 'rise', the
number closing with Dobbin's return from India (ch. 56). There
are also the subtler running contrasts of Becky's treatment of her
son Rawdon, Amelia's of George: subtle, because Thackeray is
critical both of heartless neglect and passionate possessiveness. Or
the likeness within difference of Amelia's stupid fidelity to her
husband's memory, and Becky's stupid infidelity to Rawdon.
Each is an egoist; Thackeray's comment when Dobbin leaves
Amelia is pointed: 'She didn't wish to marry him, but she wished
to keep him. She wished to give him nothing, but that he should
give her all. It is a bargain not unfrequently levied in love' (ch.
66). Outside its context, the second of these sentences would be
taken as describing Becky.

But the structural ironies are clearest when the two histories
converge and entangle: '[Becky] was thinking in her heart, "It
was George Osborne who prevented my marriage". – And she
loved George Osborne accordingly' (ch. 6). Her small revenge of
malicious teasing in chapter 14 (where these words are echoed) is
the prelude to her triumph at Brussels:

[George] was carrying on a desperate flirtation with Mrs. Crawley.
He . . . passed his evenings in the Crawleys' company; losing money to
the husband and flattering himself that the wife was dying in love for
him. It is very likely that this worthy couple never absolutely conspired,
and agreed together in so many words: the one to cajole the young
gentleman, whilst the other won his money at cards: but they
understood each other perfectly well. . . . [ch. 29]

At the ball on the night before Waterloo she receives his note
'coiled like a snake among the flowers' – a note whose substance
is not divulged until the closing number. The next day she visits
the half-suspecting Amelia:

Amelia . . . drew back her hand, and trembled all over. 'Why are *you* here, Rebecca?' she said, still looking at her solemnly, with her large eyes. These glances troubled her visitor.

'She must have seen him give me the letter at the ball', Rebecca thought.

But Amelia's accusations are in general terms, and are so answered:

'Amelia, I protest before God, I have done my husband no wrong', Rebecca said, turning from her.

'Have you done *me* no wrong, Rebecca? You did not succeed, but you tried. Ask your heart if you did not?'

She knows nothing, Rebecca thought.   [ch. 31]

The number ends with George Osborne's death on the battlefield; from this mid-point in the novel proceed Amelia's simple subsequent fortunes – ten years of widowhood sentimentally faithful to a mythical memory, and resistance to Dobbin's suit. The two converge again when Amelia, abroad with Jos and Dobbin, meets Rebecca, now disgraced and outside the social pale, but resilient as ever. She renews her designs on Jos, and when Dobbin, at last despairing of Amelia, returns to England, finds Amelia in her way. She reproaches her for refusing Dobbin:

'I tried – I tried my best, indeed I did, Rebecca,' said Amelia deprecatingly, 'but I couldn't forget – '; and she finished her sentence by looking up at the portrait.

'Couldn't forget *him*!' cried out Becky, 'that selfish humbug, that low-bred cockney dandy, that padded booby, who had neither wit, nor manners, nor heart. . . . He never cared for you. He used to sneer about you to me, time after time; and made love to me the week after he married you.'

'It's false! it's false! Rebecca', cried out Amelia, starting up.

'Look there, you fool,' Becky said, still with provoking good-humour, and taking a little paper out of her belt, she opened it and flung it into Emmy's lap. 'You know his handwriting. He wrote that to me – wanted me to run away with him – gave it me under your nose, the day before he was shot – and served him right!' Becky repeated.   [ch. 67]

Apparently then the wheel comes full circle: Becky ending as she

began, as Amelia's friend. But Thackeray has one more surprise
in store: the revelation is not decisive, for Amelia has already
relented and written to recall Dobbin. The inner necessity of the
scene is rather to leave no sham unexposed, and to keep our
moral attitude to the two 'heroines' complicated to the last. For
Becky's is the true view of the case, and her action righteous,
though from mixed motives. But Amelia's actions, although
muddleheaded, are to the last motivated by love.

'Anyone who mistakes [Amelia] for a simple character has
missed *Vanity Fair*.'[6] The mistake has been common, and has in
modern times taken the particularly silly form of regarding
Amelia as the straight representation of an ideal now outmoded.
But even apart from Thackeray's own view, writ large in phrase
after phrase, his contemporaries did not unanimously applaud
Amelia. Some went even too far in the other direction: 'No
woman resents Rebecca . . . but every woman resents his selfish
and inane Amelia.'[7] (It was perhaps more gratifying to the
woman of the eighteen-forties, and certainly rarer, to see herself
presented in fiction as a clever rogue than as an amiable fool.) If
Thackeray has an ideal in mind, then Amelia and Becky are both
far (though not equally far) removed from it; of the disproportion
between heart and brain possible to the feminine character they
provide extreme instances. Some readers may be more legitimately misled by the necessary difference in treatment. The
active Becky can be displayed, where the suffering, yielding
Amelia must be described. The tone of the description is
deliberately ambiguous, seeming often sentimentally protective,
but with enough impatience breaking through to show that the
author wishes to confuse and make fun of the sentimental reader.
It is not necessary to attribute confusion to Thackeray himself;
there is room with such a character for genuine indulgence as
well as impatience. Besides, he has an ulterior, 'literary' motive in
Amelia: Becky is a wholly new kind of heroine, Amelia the old
kind ironically exposed. It is possible that Amelia may sometimes
be imperfectly disengaged from 'the unwritten part' of his novels,
not quite free from her moorings in his own emotional life;[8]
whereas Becky swims free in the pure element of art.[9] Becky is one
of those characters – like Chaucer's Pardoner – who can fully

engage our aesthetic sympathies while defying most of our moral
ones; Thackeray is not less a moralist for allowing us to enjoy her
as a spectacle, for his judgement of her is firm. Her attraction is
partly that of the triumphant knave in a world of knaves and
fools; enjoyment is not complicated by pity for the less successful
knaves, like the younger Sir Pitt, nor yet for the fools, like Jos
Sedley or even Briggs; these belong to the world of satirical
comedy, where we have the freedom of feeling that 'fools are
responsible for their folly'. The comic inventiveness of these
triumphs provides some of the most brilliant flashes of the book:

She listened with the tenderest kindly interest, sitting by him, and
hemming a shirt for her dear little boy. Whenever Mrs. Rawdon wished
to be particularly humble and virtuous, this little shirt used to come out
of her work-box. It had got to be too small for Rawdon long before it
was finished, though.   [ch. 44]

'How I have been waiting for you! Stop! not yet – in one minute you
shall come in.' In that instant she put a rouge-pot, a brandy-bottle, and
a plate of broken meat into her bed. . . .
   ' . . . I had but one child, one darling, one hope, one joy . . . and
they . . . tore it from me'; and she put her hand to her heart with a
passionate gesture of despair, burying her face for a moment on the bed.
   The brandy-bottle inside clinked up against the plate which held the
cold sausage.   [ch. 65]

But Thackeray does not go too far in enlisting the reader's
pleasure on the side of wickedness. For this he had criticized
Bulwer and Ainsworth: 'Don't let us have any juggling and
thimble-rigging with virtue and vice, so that, at the end of three
volumes, the bewildered reader shall not know which is
which' [*Catherine*, ch. 1]. For this he was even, unjustly, criticized
himself: 'Sin is fire; and Mr. Thackeray makes fireworks of it.'[10]
But his judgement of Becky never falters, and it is made plain to
the reader through one character in particular: Rawdon Crawley. The words in the 'discovery' scene are pointed: 'I am
innocent', says Becky. 'Was she guilty or not?' asks Thackeray,
and apparently leaves it an open question. But the technical
question is not the most relevant one: her essential guilt rests in

Rawdon's simple accusation: 'You might have spared me £100, Becky; I have always shared with you.' The words take us back to the night before Waterloo, with Rawdon making his last dispositions – 'my duelling pistols in rosewood case (same which I shot Captain Marker)'; and Becky stands condemned of cold-hearted treachery.

The relation of these two is one of the main sources of 'progression' in the novel, and is worth tracing. 'Rawdon's marriage', says Thackeray, 'was one of the honestest actions which we shall have to record in any portion of that gentleman's biography.' Unlike George Osborne (the contrast is firmly indicated) he married for love; which puts him at an initial disadvantage with Becky, who married him in hopes of his aunt's money. 'Is his case a rare one? and don't we see every day in the world many an honest Hercules at the apron-strings of Omphale, and great whiskered Samsons prostrate in Dalilah's lap?' [ch. 16]

Becky's contempt is masked at first: '"If he had but a little more brains," she thought to herself, "I might make something of him"; but she never let him perceive the opinion she had of him . . .' [ch. 17]. But not masked for long; not when Miss Crawley's favour seems again within reach: '"You fool! you ought to have gone in, and never come out again," Rebecca said. "Don't call me names", said the big guardsman, sulkily, "Perhaps I *was* a fool, Becky, but you shouldn't say so" ' [ch. 25].

Their relation is fully and picturesquely defined in the farewell scene before Waterloo; but its deterioration is also hinted, in the narrative that so lightly sketches the 'three or four years' which follow [chs 34, 36, 37]. At first, Rawdon's illusions are still intact; 'He believed in his wife as much as the French soldiers in Napoleon'; and with as little grounds. We are left to infer that, his aunt having died and left him only £100, Rawdon is no longer an investment worth nursing. Becky is flying at higher game. The scene that marks the change is of the kind that lights up far more than itself: the evening scene in Curzon Street, Becky in the centre of a party of gentlemen including Lord Steyne. (It is our first introduction to Lord Steyne; Thackeray's method is to make us feel that he has been there a long time.) Rawdon is 'sitting silent without the circle', engaged in 'shearing a Southdown'.

The closing words mark the grouping as typical:

'How is Mrs. Crawley's husband,' Lord Steyne used to say by way of a good day when they met; and indeed that was now his avocation in life. He was Colonel Crawley no more. He was Mrs. Crawley's husband. . . .

'Hang it, I ain't clever enough for her – I know it. She won't miss me,' he used to say: and he was right, his wife did not miss him.

Rebecca was fond of her husband. She was always perfectly good-humoured and kind to him. She did not even show her scorn much for him; perhaps she liked him the better for being a fool. He was her upper servant and *maître d'hôtel.* [ch. 37]

Two years later he is 'more and more isolated every day . . . beat and cowed into laziness and submission. Dalilah had imprisoned him and cut his hair off, too' [ch. 45].

The 'discovery' scene is led up to with great skill; Rawdon's arrest is sprung on the reader as on Rawdon himself, and only then does Thackeray wind back over past events to show how Lord Steyne with Becky's connivance had previously got rid of young Rawdon and the 'sheepdog' Briggs – 'And so two of Rawdon's out-sentinels were in the hands of the enemy'.[11] It is as near as he comes to saying that the arrest was framed.

There is a moral comment in the fact that Becky's downfall comes through the relations that she most despised; it is the innocent and stupid who confound her. She calculates brilliantly, but, like Iago, not quite brilliantly enough. Her neglect of her son disturbed Rawdon. When she kissed the child at Queen's Crawley she had not thought that he might say, 'You never kiss me at home, mother.' Lady Jane 'never felt quite the same to Becky after that remark'. And Lady Jane's simple kindness defeats Becky's calculation, when she releases Rawdon from the spunging-house in time for him to find Lord Steyne at Curzon Street. This is Becky's true nemesis. Contempt for other people is necessary to successful villainy; but within it lie the seeds of its own defeat. The walls of egoism rise, in the end, too high. By suggesting all this, Thackeray does more than condemn Becky; he gives a less pessimistic moral direction to his story. Goodness is not wholly ineffectual.

These, then, are some of the ways in which Thackeray gives shape and purpose to his great pictorial mass; but the most important way has been often undervalued by later readers, because misunderstood. The whole is 'brilliantly illuminated by the Author's own candles'; Thackeray is constantly present, commenting on the action. Only in this novel is it undisguised. Elsewhere he partly identifies himself with a character – Pendennis, or Esmond; or uses a character as narrator – Pendennis in *The Newcomes* and *Philip*, with Clive and Philip as further 'projections' within the story. (The latter device, caught, he admitted, from the despised Lytton, was purposeful: 'I shall be able to talk more at ease than in my own person.')[12] In *Vanity Fair* there is no disguise; the author is present, with a varying range of visibility. He talks to us, about the story and characters, or about something it reminds him of;[13] he is frankly the manufacturer of the narrative ('there are some terrific chapters coming presently'); he is the 'producer' of particular characters (especially of Amelia, who can do so little for herself); he is by turns the responsible, omniscient narrator ('for novelists have the privilege of knowing everything' [ch. 3], the irrespon- sible, baffled spectator ('Was she guilty or not?'), even the mere reporter (himself meeting the characters at Pumpernickel in 1830). Above all he is the moral commentator, the 'preacher in cap and bells', amused, melancholy, hortatory – and constantly barbing his shafts with a *de te fabula*. The atmosphere of his personality – not his private, but his artistic personality – envelopes the story.

Nowadays, apparently, this practice requires defence; and several lines of defence are valid. There is the historical defence. This method was not new or peculiar to Thackeray, save in extent and subtlety. Behind it lies the tradition of Fielding's role of epic poet, with such modifications as the 'comic epic in prose' requires; it is as comedy that Thackeray sees his own novels, and comedy always allows more room for the author. There is also the seeming casualness of Sterne, taking us behind the scenes, showing us the raw material of a novel in process of being worked up. There is also as we have seen the peculiar audience-relation of the serial-writer, reassembling his listeners, responding to their comments with his own. All this helped to make Thackeray's technique easily acceptable in his own time.[14] The average modern reader starts with a prejudice in favour of 'dramatic' presentment; the novel having, since Thackeray's time, foregone many of its advantages in favour of a fancied 'objectivity', and the novelist having dwindled into invisibility. But to press the historical defence might be to admit a limited appeal: or to suggest that he adopted this method unthinkingly. The true justification lies in its appropriateness to his kind of novel.

Thackeray has often been called the novelist of memory; all his stories are seen retrospectively. 'Let us have middle-aged novels', he said in *Rebecca and Rowena*; it is what he gives us, with the light of irony or pathos playing on past fashions and the morning ideals of youth. His commentary is in part a bridge between past and present, suggesting what time changes, what it leaves unchanged; putting past and present alike in a longer perspective. And it is a moral perspective. Thackeray gives us what seems a whole world, densely peopled, varied in scene, with the miscellaneousness and wastage and loose threads of the actual world; but through his comments he makes it plain that he sees the 'tower on the toft' above the 'field full of folk'. The title itself is a comment, the title that came to him in the night 'as if a voice had whispered';[15] it suggests both the observer, and the preacher who 'cries his sermon'. Without Thackeray's own voice, the melancholy and the compassion of his attitude to Vanity Fair might escape us. It is needed merely as relief, from a spectacle that might otherwise be unbearably painful. And not only morally painful, but mentally impoverished. The characters, the best as well as the worst, are almost without ideas; the intellectual atmosphere of the novel is provided by the commentary. 'Can the reader do all this for himself'? If he can, and can do it as well as Thackeray does it for him, he may consider it surplusage.[16]

Thackeray does not escape into commentary from any weakness in presentation; *Vanity Fair* is particularly rich in single scenes which reveal his power of presenting characters and action without comment, through dialogue, grouping, and gesture. Nor is he impulsively allowing his stored reflections to overflow; the effect of casualness in the commentary is as calculated as in

Sterne. The commentary is itself art, selective and economical. Thackeray never tells everything; he leaves much to be read between the lines; the tone of intimate confidence often masks a real reserve. He knows when not to comment directly at all. Much could have been said on the death of George Osborne; this is all that is said: 'No more fighting was heard at Brussels – the pursuit rolled miles away. The darkness came down on the field and city, and Amelia was praying for George, who was lying on his face, dead, with a bullet through his heart' [ch. 32]. It is no simple statement; not only is the immediate reference magnified by the drawing together of Brussels and the battlefield, but its very brevity and the silence surrounding it mark its subject – not the death of one George Osborne, sufficiently shown as odious and contemptible, but Death, sudden, august, and mysterious. But all this is implicit. Yet equally impressive in its own way, and equally enlarged beyond the particular circumstance, is the leisurely commentary on the death of Mr. Sedley [ch. 61], appropriate to a death that is not sudden, but long prepared for, domestic and not dramatic, enmeshed in practical circumstance, and apparently presented as a mere change in habitation. The one method is as essentially part of the novel's texture as the other.

The commentary springs also from Thackeray's wish to 'convey the sentiment of reality'. Through it he openly admits, as no modern novelist dare, *all* the relations of the novelist to his story. The novelist does write what he knows to be 'terrific chapters', he does construct and manipulate his characters, and he is also carried beyond his conscious self ('I have no idea where it all comes from').[17] He remembers, and observes; he is affected, as he writes, by what is happening around him – the 'unwritten parts' of novels. Thackeray's candour about all this is part of his love of truth. Believing in truth, he can afford to admit that what he writes is fiction. And the illusion is not thereby broken. When he calls his characters puppets, it is not their smallness, but their separateness from him, that strikes us; and perhaps his own largeness. 'Thackeray is a Titan . . . [his words] as solemn as an oracle.'[18]

Ah! *Vanitas Vanitatum!* Which of us is happy in this world? which of us has his desire? or, having it, is satisfied? – Come children, let us shut up the box and the puppets, for our play is played out. [ch. 67]

The great picture is not the less great from our final awareness that we and the author stand outside its frame. The words are a recall to life and individual responsibility as the preacher lays his cap and bells aside.

SOURCE: extract from *Novels of the Eighteen-Forties* (Oxford, 1954) pp. 234–56.

NOTES

[Footnotes in the original have been reorganised and renumbered, the chapter-references here being inserted in the text.]

1. Mrs Proctor said, 'He has avoided the two extremes in which so many of our popular writers delight' (*Letters*, ed. Ray, vol. II, p. 313).

2. Review-article by W. C. Roscoe in *National Review* (Jan 1856); collected in *Poems and Essays*, 2 vols (1860).

3. W. C. Brownell, *Victorian Prose Masters* (1901) p. 29. [Extracts from Brownell's appraisal are given in Part Two above – Ed.]

4. *Pendennis*, ch. 59; and cf. *Esmond*, Bk II, ch. 1.

5. The point has of course been made by several critics, from *Fraser's* (Sep 1848) to our own day, but I think with insufficient sense of the subtlety of Thackeray's intentions. [Extracts from Robert Bell's review of 1848 in *Fraser's* are given in Part One above – Ed.]

6. Brownell, *Victorian Prose Masters*, p. 31.

7. Mrs Jameson, as quoted by J. W. Dodds, *Thackeray* (1941) p. 130; Mrs Brookfield, and Thackeray's mother, made similar comments.

8. He told Mrs Brookfield that she was 'a piece of Amelia – My Mother is another half: my poor little wife *y est pour beaucoup*' (30 June 1848; *Letters*, vol. II, p. 394). But it is difficult to take this seriously; the three women can have had little in common with each other or with Amelia except charm and obstinacy. Perhaps there is something of Jane Brookfield's faithfulness to a husband Thackeray was coming to think unworthy of her. But J. Y. T Greig, who has pressed this interpretation furthest (in *Thackeray: A Reconsideration*, 1950), seems to make his bricks of very little straw.

9. There are two possible 'originals' for Becky: Sydney Morgan and Theresa Reviss; but they can have provided no more than the 'germ of the real'.

10. Roscoe, loc. cit. (see note 2 above).

11. Ch. 52. Greig, missing the subtlety of method, remarks that this chapter 'is chronologically misplaced, and was probably an afterthought' (*Thackeray: A Reconsideration*, p. 116).

12. Letter of August 1853 (*Letters*, vol. III, p. 298). There is a hint of it in the use of Tom Eaves in *Vanity Fair*, ch. 47.

13. Sometimes with a journalist's sense for the immediately topical, as in chapter 55: 'Fifine went off in a cab, as we have known more exalted persons of her nation to do under similar circumstances.' This number appeared in April 1848.

14. Contemporary objectors were rare; one was G. H. Lewes, in *The Leader*, 21 Dec 1850, 929.

15. *Letters*, vol. I, p. cxxvi.

16. Brownell, *Victorian Prose Masters*, p. 7; and cf. pp. 9 – 10.

17. *Letters*, vol. III, p. 468, note.

18. Charlotte Brontë, in a letter of 1848. [See extract in Part One above – Ed.]

G. Armour Craig

ON THE STYLE OF *VANITY FAIR* (1958)

... there is still a very material difference of opinion as to the real nature and character of the Measure of Value in this country. My first question, therefore, is, what constitutes this Measure of Value? What is the significance of that word 'a Pound'?
    Sir Robert Peel, speech on the Bank Charter Act (6 May 1844).

Perhaps I might be a heroine still, but I shall never be a good woman, I know.
    Mrs. Gaskell, *Wives and Daughters* (1866).

'Among all our novelists his style is the purest, as to my ears it is also the most harmonious. Sometimes it is disfigured by a slight touch of affectation, by little conceits which smell of the oil; but the language is always lucid.' The judgment is Anthony Trollope's and the lucidity he praises is Thackeray's: 'The reader, without labour, knows what he means, and knows all that he means.'[1] [See Part Two above for other appraisals by Trollope – Ed.] The judgment has been shared by many, perhaps even by Thackeray himself, for he was vigilant in detecting 'fine writing' or 'claptraps' in the work of others,[2] and for himself he insisted that 'this person writing strives to tell the truth. If there is not that, there is nothing.' Yet some reconciling is necessary, for the truth is not always lucid and lucidity may not always be quite true.

There is at any rate a passage in chapter 42 of *Vanity Fair* for Trollope's judgment of which the modern reader – at least this reader – would give a good deal. It describes the life of Jane Osborne keeping house for her father: her sister is now the fashionable Mrs. Frederick Bullock, her brother, disowned by their father for his marriage to Amelia Sedley, has been killed at Waterloo, and Jane now lives in idle spinsterhood in the great glum house in Russell Square.

It was an awful existence. She had to get up of black winter's mornings to make breakfast for her scowling old father, who would have turned the whole house out of doors if his tea had not been ready at half-past eight. She remained silent opposite to him, listening to the urn hissing, and sitting in tremor while the parent read his paper, and consumed his accustomed portion of muffins and tea. At half-past nine he rose and went to the City, and she was almost free till dinner-time, to make visitations in the kitchen and to scold the servants: to drive abroad and descend upon the tradesmen, who were prodigiously respectful: to leave her cards and her papa's at the great glum respectable houses of their City friends; or to sit alone in the large drawing-room, expecting visitors; and working at a huge piece of worsted by the fire, on the sopha, hard by the great Iphigenia clock, which ticked and tolled with mournful loudness in the dreary room. The great glass over the mantelpiece, faced by the other great console glass at the opposite end of the room, increased and multiplied between them the brown holland bag in which the chandelier hung; until you saw these brown holland bags fading away in endless perspectives, and this apartment of Miss Osborne's seemed the centre of a system of drawing-rooms. When she removed the cordovan leather from the grand piano, and ventured to play a few notes on it, it sounded with a mournful sadness, startling the dismal echoes of the house.

Thackeray's prose is seldom better than this. The passage comes from a paragraph that comments on the difference between Jane Osborne's life and that of her sister: 'One can fancy the pangs' with which Jane regularly read about Mrs. Frederick Bullock in the *Morning Post*, particularly the account of her presentation at the Drawing-room. The reader, characteristically, is invited to supply from his own observation the sort of vulgar envy that feeds upon accounts of 'Fashionable Reunions' in the newspaper and to look down on Jane Osborne's suffering as no more than the deprivation of the snobbish pleasures of elegant society. The passage begins, then, easily enough: 'It was an awful existence'. And 'awful' is at first simply a colloquial affectation. It becomes something more, however, as we move into the account of Jane's routine and ascend from the tremors of the breakfast table to the solitude of the drawing room with its covered chandelier 'fading away in endless perspectives': the conversational pitch turns momentarily solemn with the vision of 'this apartment of Miss Osborne's' as 'the centre of a system of drawing-rooms' – including perhaps even that most august of all such apartments where her sister has been received. It would be hard to find this an example of the 'little conceits which smell of the oil', for even here Thackeray does not lose his customary confidential hold upon the reader. The vision is kept close to us by his usual resource: the opposing mirrors 'increased and multiplied between them the brown holland bag in which the chandelier hung; until *you* saw these brown holland bags fading away in endless perspectives'. The 'you' is no doubt as un-obtrusive as an idiom. But it is not inconsistent with Thackeray's constant and fluent address to his reader, an address at its best as easy as idiom. In this very short passage Thackeray has moved from an example of the snobbery he loved to detect to a memorable symbol of the society in which snobbery flourishes. It is a society of endless perspectives, a system of drawing rooms whose center is everywhere, whose circumference is nowhere.

But is this what Thackeray meant? And is it the 'all' that he meant? Certainly the symbol is not characteristic – it is indeed unique in *Vanity Fair*. Usually, or at any rate perhaps too often, Thackeray renders the barren routines of high life in mock genealogies or in the kind of mildly allegorical guest list that follows this passage. We are told that twice a month the solitary dinners of Mr. and Miss Osborne are shared with 'Old Dr. Gulp and his lady from Bloomsbury Square, . . . old Mr. Frowser the attorney, . . . old Colonel Livermore, . . . old Serjeant Toffy, . . . sometimes old Sir Thomas Coffin.' *Vanity Fair*, we recall, began as 'Pen and Pencil Sketches of English Society', as an extension of *The Book Of Snobs*. Yet Thackeray seems to have felt the need of some larger, more inclusive presiding idea. In the early stages of writing the first few numbers he 'ransacked' his brain for another title, and 'Vanity Fair', he said, came to him suddenly in the middle of the night.[4] It seems to have summed up

for him a position from which he could confidently go on with his
'Novel without a Hero', but a position of course very different
from John Bunyan's. The original Vanity Fair as described by
Evangelist is the dwelling place of abominations. But it is after all
only one more obstacle on the road to the Celestial City, and all
such obstacles are rewards in disguise. 'He that shall die there,'
says Evangelist, 'although his death will be unnatural, and his
pain perhaps great, he will yet have the better of his fellow.'
While there are some unnatural and painful deaths in
Thackeray's Fair, there seems to be no act of resistance or
sacrifice by which anyone can get the better of anyone else, and
the irony of the title has no doubt been lively in the minds of
many readers. But Evangelist lays down a more poignantly
ironical prescription: 'he that will go to the [Celestial] City, and
yet not go through this Town [where Vanity Fair is kept], *must
needs go out of the World*.'[5] If there is no Celestial City beyond
Thackeray's Fair, and if there is no hero determined to fight on to
a heavenly peak, it is even more certain that none of Thackeray's
characters shall go out of this world. On every page of *Vanity Fair*
we find description, exposure, comment, from a position much
less elevated and secure than that of an evangelist, yet one from
which we do see into an 'all' as large as a whole society.

Certainly the style of all this commenting and exposing is this-
worldly to a degree that would have puzzled Bunyan as much as
it has troubled some of his descendants. In the preface to *Pendennis*
Thackeray speaks of his work as 'a sort of confidential talk
between reader and writer', and it was the excess of this
conception of himself – 'the little earmark by which he is most
conspicuous' – that Trollope found 'his most besetting sin in
style'. The 'sin' is 'a certain affected familiarity'; Thackeray
'indulges too frequently in little confidences with individual
readers, in which pretended allusions to himself are frequent.
' "What would you do? what would you say now, if you were in
such a position?" he asks.'[6] Yet for Trollope, although this
familiarity might breed occasional contempt, it did not finally
compromise the great virtue of Thackeray's lucidity. 'As I have
said before, the reader always understands his words without an
effort, and receives all that the author has to give.'[7] But to know

what, and to know all, a writer means is to be in his confidence indeed, and it would be a serious lapse of style that his confidence should break down in affectation or something worse.

In 'Before the Curtain', the preface he wrote in 1848 for the completed novel, Thackeray promises his reader 'no other moral than this tag to the present story', that after wandering with him through the Fair, 'When you come home, you sit down, in a sober, contemplative, not uncharitable frame of mind, and apply yourself to your books or your business.' He raises no literary expectations, he promises no carefully graduated feast of human nature, he does not even excuse himself to those who find all Fairs 'immoral' and hence refuse to enter this one. The stern moralists may be quite right in withholding their custom, but those 'of a lazy, or a benevolent, or a sarcastic mood, may perhaps like to step in for half an hour and look at the performance'. This casualness, the queer juxtaposition of 'lazy', 'benevolent', and 'sarcastic', may seem like the very height of good breeding. It does sum up the uncomfortable collocation of responses that any reader must make to some stretches of the novel. But it also promises that this writer will keep us free from violent emotions as we read. It is the guarantee of a special detachment.

Such detachment is often suggested by a coy version of one of Fielding's comic devices. When we witness the departure of Becky and Amelia from Chiswick Mall, the last flurry of farewells is recounted thus: 'Then came the struggle and the parting below. Words refuse to tell it. . . .' The congregation of servants and pupils, the hugging and kissing and crying are such 'as no pen can depict, and as the tender heart would fain pass over' ch. 1). Or, on the morning after the fatal excursion to Vauxhall, Joseph Sedley lies 'groaning in agonies which the pen refuses to describe' (ch. 6) while he suffers the aftermath of rack punch. Becky, disappointed in her attempt to capture Joseph, goes away from the Sedley house to her duties as governess: 'Finally came the parting with Amelia, over which I intend to throw a veil' (ch. 6). Such mild affectations as these amuse a good deal less than their frequency suggests they should, however obliquely they may glance at sentimental explorations of young female affection or the tract-writer's interest in the heavy repentance of the drunkard. But they are the simplest and the least interesting form of a larger kind of detachment.

About other episodes the narrator is more artfully silent. Perhaps the most interesting is the courtship of Rawdon Crawley, which extends over several chapters and is concealed in the narrative of Becky's ministrations to old Miss Crawley. It will be recalled that the success of Becky's attentions to this lady, the old aunt whose wealth is the object of all the Crawleys' envy and scheming, alarms Mrs. Bute Crawley – whose portrait, incidentally, as well as that of her family and of her husband the Rector, make one wonder that Thackeray could have quarreled with Jerrold's anticlericalism.[8] Mrs. Bute's scheming to secure Miss Crawley's money for her own leads her to warn Rawdon that when his stepmother dies, old Sir Pitt will marry Becky. Rawdon's response sets the level of intrigue exactly: ' "By Jove, it's too bad," thought Rawdon, "too bad, by Jove! I do believe the woman wants the poor girl to be ruined, in order that she shouldn't come into the family as Lady Crawley" ' (ch. 14).

He proceeds to the recommended seduction, but is outguessed by the frank and outraged role that Becky adopts when he 'rallie [s] her in his graceful way about his father's attachment'. The game goes on, Miss Crawley recovers from her surfeit under Becky's assiduous care, and shortly news comes that the meek Lady Crawley is dead. Rawdon and his aunt discuss the matter while Becky stands by. 'Rebecca said nothing. She seemed by far the gravest and most impressed of the family. She left the room before Rawdon went away that day; but they met by chance below, as he was going away after taking leave, and had a parley together' (ch. 14). And the next thing we know, old Sir Pitt has come to town and is down on his knees to ask for the hand of Becky. The narrator comments: 'In the course of this history we have never seen her lose her presence of mind; but she did now, and wept some of the most genuine tears that ever fell from her eyes' (ch. 14).

But what does 'genuine' mean here? Or 'they met by chance' in the passage above? Are we to infer that during their 'parley' Becky uses the threat of a proposal from the father to make sure of the son? Are we to infer that the tears are genuine because she has planned too well – the threat she has used to get one husband has turned out to be prophetic, and she might have had the father? Are they tears of rage? of regret? As we move on to the next chapter we certainly find no circumstantial report of when and how Becky and Rawdon are married; instead there is a good deal of indirect veiling of the scene and refusing of the pen. 'How they were married is not of the slightest consequence to anybody.' Perhaps, it is conjectured, they went off one afternoon when Becky was presumed to be visiting Amelia. But the matter is left in uncertainty. On the one hand, 'Who needs to be told, that if a woman has a will, she will assuredly find a way?' And on the other: 'who on earth, after the daily experience we have, can question the probability of a gentleman marrying anybody?' (ch. 16).

The concealment of the circumstances of the marriage may appeal to the lazy, may satisfy the benevolent, and it may give the sarcastic something to work on too. But its most important effect is that the narration here, clustered about with confidential comments and dismissive questions, sets before us a way of knowing the world. It is a way so inferential, so dependent upon unfinished implications, that it comes close to the character of gossip. And a good gossip, while its unfinished sentences and its discreet and indiscreet omissions may keep us from the exhilaration of indignation or rhapsody, can suggest values and insights superior to the vocabulary of the purveyor or the listener. Here, whatever the meaning of that 'by chance' that modifies the meeting of Becky and Rawdon, or whatever the meaning of that 'genuine' that modifies her tears, we can only infer that the marriage is the result neither of grand passion nor of mean seduction. The veiling of the secret here means that we can only accept Becky's marriage as a convenience. Even the grossness of Mrs. Bute's plotting is lost in the shadows.

The questions with which Thackeray disposes of this affair – 'Who needs to be told . . . who can question the probability . . .' – are of course the most conspicuous earmark of his detachment in *Vanity Fair*. There is the issue of who made the first move in Becky's first romance, with the young Reverend Mr. Crisp who came infatuated to tea at Chiswick Mall: after a parenthetical cloud of hints and counter-hints the narrator concludes, 'But who can tell you the real truth of the matter?' (ch. 2). Just as when the pen refuses to tell, the implication here is only coy. But a good many hundred pages later, in what is called 'A Vagabond Chapter' (ch. 64), this kind of coyness can exasperate. It comes in a passage summarizing Becky's career after her fall from polite society in London: 'When she got her money she gambled; when she had gambled it she was put to shifts to live; who knows how or by what means she succeeded? . . . The present historian can give no certain details regarding the event.' The detachment inculcated here is vast and affluent indeed; it is perhaps matched only by the elaborate veiling of the circumstances of Joseph Sedley's death. But the most puzzling questions in the book are those that comment upon its crucial passage.

Every reader of *Vanity Fair* remembers the 'discovery scene' of chapter 53— the scene in which Becky suffers exposure and isolation after her husband and Lord Steyne violently clash. And every student of the novel knows that this scene is a battleground upon which the judgments of a number of Thackeray's critics have collided. Rawdon, having been freed from the spunging house, hurries 'across the streets and the great squares of Vanity Fair, and bursts in upon his wife and Lord Steyne in something less than *flagrante delicto* though ready for embarrassment'.

Steyne was hanging over the sofa on which Becky sate. The wretched woman was in a brilliant full toilette, her arms and all her fingers sparkling with bracelets and rings; and the brilliants on her breast which Steyne had given her. He had her hand in his, and was bowing over to kiss it, when Becky started up with a faint scream as she caught sight of Rawdon's white face. At the next instant she tried a smile, a horrid smile, as if to welcome her husband; and Steyne rose up, grinding his teeth, pale, and with fury in his looks.

He, too, attempted a laugh – and came forward holding out his hand. 'What, come back! How d'ye do, Crawley?' he said, the nerves of his mouth twitching as he tried to grin at the intruder.

There was that in Rawdon's face which caused Becky to fling herself before him. 'I am innocent, Rawdon,' she said; 'before God, I am innocent.' She clung hold of his coat, of his hands; her own were all covered with serpents, and rings, and baubles. 'I am innocent. – Say I am innocent,' she said to Lord Steyne.

He thought a trap had been laid for him, and was as furious with the wife as with the husband. 'You innocent! Damn you!' he screamed out. 'You innocent! Why, every trinket you have on your body is paid for by me. I have given you thousands of pounds which this fellow has spent, and for which he has sold you. Innocent, by – ! You're as innocent as your mother, the ballet-girl, and your husband the bully. Don't think to frighten me as you have done others. Make way, sir, and let me pass'; and Lord Steyne seized up his hat, and, with flame in his eyes, and looking his enemy fiercely in the face, marched upon him, never for a moment doubting that the other would give way.

But Rawdon Crawley springing out, seized him by the neckcloth, until Steyne, almost strangled, writhed, and bent under his arm. 'You lie, you dog!' said Rawdon. 'You lie, you coward and villain!' And he struck the Peer twice over the face with his open hand, and flung him bleeding to the ground. It was all done before Rebecca could interpose. She stood there trembling before him. She admired her husband, strong, brave, and victorious.

'Come here,' he said. – She came up at once.

'Take off those things.' – She began, trembling, pulling the jewels from her arms, and the rings from her shaking fingers, and held them all in a heap, quivering, and looking up at him. 'Throw them down', he said, and she dropped them. He tore the diamond ornament out of her breast, and flung it at Lord Steyne. It cut him on his bald forehead. Steyne wore the scar to his dying day.

The theatricality of the passage – Becky's clinging and quivering, the serpents and baubles on her hands, Rawdon's springing out and his terse manifesto, the flame in the eyes of the wicked nobleman and the lifelong scar on his head – all such features suggest that the creator of Punch's Prize novelists is once again engaged in something like parody.[9] On the other hand it has been asserted that far from a joke, the scene 'is the chief ganglion of the tale; and the discharge of energy from Rawdon's fist is the reward and consolation of the reader'.[10] The most extensive criticism of the scene finds it unprepared for and conveyed by a dramatic technique foreign to Thackeray's genius,[11] but this judgment has in turn been disposed of by another critic who finds Thackeray's usual stamp upon it and some other felicities as well. He suggests that one of these is the way in which 'Steyne wore the scar' echoes 'Steyne wore the star'.[12] By the same sort of reasoning we might infer from 'He tore the diamond ornament out of her breast' that Becky's heart is surpassing hard; and certainly Thackeray tells us that the battle takes the heart out of her. But the one touch upon which Thackeray himself is known to have commented is Becky's response to the sudden burst of energy from Rawdon: 'She stood there trembling before him. She admired her husband, strong, brave, and victorious.' Of this observation Thackeray is reported to have said that it was a touch of genius,[13] and it does consort well with his special genius in the rest of the book.

For although the battle seems to be the expression of outraged honor, it is a collision that misses its main issue and prize. As the resistless masses meet, Becky stands off to one side, and although her admiration is unacceptable or even unknown to Rawdon, and although we are told that her life seems so 'miserable, lonely, and profitless' after Rawdon has silently departed that she even thinks of suicide, there is still a profound irrelevance in this violent scene. Becky's maid comes upon her in her dejection and asks the question that is in every reader's mind: '*Mon Dieu*, madame, what has happened?' And the 'person writing' concludes this crucial chapter with an enlargement of the same question: 'What *had* happened? Was she guilty or not? She said not; but who could tell what was truth which came from those lips; or if that corrupt heart was in this case pure? All her lies and her schemes, all her selfishness and her wiles, all her wit and her genius had come to this bankruptcy.' Becky lies down, the maid goes to the drawing room to gather up the pile of trinkets, and the chapter ends. If Thackeray has not risen to a cruel joke on those readers who find consolation and reward in the discharge of energy from Rawdon, he has at least interrupted their satisfaction.

Lord Steyne's meaning of 'guilty' – 'He thought a trap had been laid for him' by Becky and Rawdon – is of course quite false, though it corroborates the characterization of Steyne as one experienced in double-dealing. 'Guilty' from Rawdon's point of view of course means, as he tells Pitt next day, that 'it was a regular plan between that scoundrel and her' to get him out of the way (ch. 54). And Thackeray goes to as great lengths to make it impossible for us to know that this interpretation is true as he does to conceal the timing and motives of Becky's marriage. To see the entangling and displacing of any clear answer, we need only ask 'guilty of what?' The usual answer is of course 'guilty of adultery' (or guilty of getting ready for it),[14] and Thackeray's silence is commonly attributed to his awareness of the 'squeamishness' of his public. Indeed he himself lends real authority to this account of the matter. In 1840, writing on Fielding, he complains that the world no longer tolerates real satire. 'The same vice exists now, only we don't speak about it; the same things are done, but we don't call them by their names.'[15] And in *Vanity Fair* he complains that he must be silent about some events in Becky's later career because he must satisfy 'the moral world, that has, perhaps, no particular objection to vice, but an insuperable repugnance to hearing vice called by its proper name' (ch. 64). There may well be evidence in Thackeray's personal history to suggest in addition that he was, perhaps even before the separation from his mad wife, evasive and unclear on the subject of sexual behavior. But however complicated the tensions of Thackeray's own emotional experience, and however rigid the scruples of his audience, the answer to the questions with which he comments on this most important episode cannot be a single 'name' or possess any 'proper name'. For he has led us here, however uneasily, with mingled attitudes of parody and outrage, to a startling though incomplete vision of a new social world, a vision exactly proportioned to the irrelevance of the violence we have witnessed.

The words of the passage that command our moral response are precisely those that most clearly approach parody: Becky responds to a nameless 'that' in Rawdon's face by exclaiming 'I am innocent.' If the reader trained in melodrama scoffs at the response and turns Becky into a consummate villain, he will have some trouble getting through the rest of the novel, and it is likely that he will long since have become exasperated with Thackeray's tone, his silences and implications. The same is true, moreover, of the sentimental reader who throws down the volume and declares that Becky has been monstrously wronged and victimized by wicked men in a bad world. But the reader who says, in effect, 'it is impossible to tell whether or of what she is guilty' is exactly in the difficult position of one who accepts Thackeray's narrative as it is given. And what such a reader sees from this position must fill him with wonder if not dismay. For he sees that while he wants to answer these questions, he cannot do so, and he can only conclude that he is looking at a situation before which his moral vocabulary is irrelevant. Becky in her isolation has finally gone out of this world, and it will take a new casuistry to bring her back. Thackeray uses some strong moral words in his comment, it is true: 'who could tell what was truth which came from those lips; or if that corrupt heart was in this case pure?' But while we know that Becky has lied heartily to Steyne, and to his hearty admiration, we cannot know that she is lying to Rawdon when she insists on her innocence. Whatever corruption we may have seen, the question this time is in earnest. The qualities named in the final statement, and especially by its last word, tell us where we are: 'All her lies and her schemes, all her selfishness and her wiles, all her wit and her genius had come to this bankruptcy.' For these are the terms not so much of moral as of financial enterprise, and 'this bankruptcy' is the real touch of genius in the passage. Thackeray's questions and his comment express neither indignation nor sympathy. Rather, they bring before us the terrible irresolution of a society in which market values and moral values are discontinuous and separate. And Thackeray will not – he cannot – support us as we revolt from such a spectacle.

The ghostly paradigm upon which human nature plays in *Vanity Fair* is the credit economy that in Thackeray's own lifetime finally developed from a money economy. Even the constant gambling in Thackeray's Fair, historically appropriate as it may be to his Regency setting (and much of his own early experience as it may reflect), suggests the unpredictability of the system. Distant though the gambler may be from respectability, his luck is only a little less mysterious than the power his winnings confer upon him. However it may be in the most famous conversation recorded in modern literary history, it is all too true in *Vanity Fair* that rich people are different because they have more money.

Thackeray exposed himself to some high-minded criticism from
George Henry Lewes when he published the number containing
Becky's famous reflection, 'I think I could be a good woman if I
had five thousand a year.' For he had commented, 'And who
knows but Rebecca was right in her speculations – and that it
was only a question of money and fortune which made the
difference between her and an honest woman?' (ch. 41). In its
interrogative form the comment is much more precise than the
declaration Thackeray wrote to Lewes. The latter called it
'detestable' to say that 'honesty is only the virtue of abundance'.
Thackeray replied that he meant 'only that he in the possession of
luxuries . . . should be very chary of despising poor Lazarus on
foot, and look very humbly and leniently upon the faults of his
less fortunate brethren'. This is of course no answer; or if it is, it
asks for a curious forbearance towards Becky Sharp. But
Thackeray qualifies at once: 'I am quite aware of the dismal
roguery . . . [which] goes all through the Vanity Fair
story – and God forbid that the world should be like it altogether:
though I fear it is more like it than we like to own.'[16] The likeness
to 'the world' is in the belief that money is magic and in the
frightening awareness, no doubt recently reinforced by the
financial crisis of 1847, that no theory had yet been devised to
control it. Walter Bagehot, in the *Economic Studies* he was
composing in the 1870s, confessed to 'a haze' in the language in
which he described the growth of capital, and he remarked too
with admiration that 'a very great many of the strongest heads in
England spend their minds on little else than on thinking whether
other people will pay their debts'.[17] For him that system was
'marvellous' by which 'an endless succession of slips of written
promises should be turned into money as readily as if they were
precious stones' – so marvelous indeed that it 'would have
seemed incredible in commerce till very recent times.'[18]
Thackeray's attitude, doubtless shaped by the short period he
spent as a bill broker in 1833 – an episode he apparently tried
hard to forget[19] – was not so admiring. His Fair, at any rate, is a
market the movements of which are perplexing in the extreme.

The first mention of the 'guilt' or 'innocence' of Becky's
relations to Lord Steyne comes in a passage about the 'awful

kitchen inquisition' of the servants of Vanity Fair. We are told
that Raggles, the retired butler of Miss Crawley, who owns the
house in Curzon Street where Becky and Rawdon live well on
nothing a year, is ruined by his extension of credit to them. But he
is the victim of something more than the simple excess of
liabilities over assets. The '*Vehmgericht* of the servants'-hall' early
pronounces Becky guilty: 'And I shame to say, she would not
have got credit had they not believed her to be guilty. It was the
sight of the Marquis of Steyne's carriage-lamps at her door,
contemplated by Raggles, burning in the blackness of midnight,
'that kep him up,' as he afterwards said; that, even more than
Rebecca's arts and coaxings' (ch. 44).

The question of guilt here is quite subordinate to the question
of credit, and Raggles is ruined not because he is right about
Becky's guilt but because he believes in a strict correlation
between Becky's moral and financial status. The last of Raggles is
seen at the drunken party of the servants on the morning after the
battle; our last glimpse of him is not as he suffers in ruin but as he
looks at his fellows 'with a wild surprise' upon hearing from Becky
that Rawdon 'has got a good appointment' (ch. 55). It is no
wonder that Thackeray should have said in a letter to his mother
written during the very month when the 'discovery scene'
appeared, 'I can't find the end of the question between property
and labour. We want something almost equal to a Divine Person
to settle it. I mean if there is ever to be an elucidation of the
mystery it is to be solved by a preacher of such novelty and
authority, as will awaken and convince mankind – but O how
and when?[20]

Whatever the fate of the larger question, Thackeray does do
some novel preaching upon bankruptcy in one section of *Vanity
Fair*. John Sedley, we recall, is ruined in the uncertainties
following Napoleon's escape from Elba (ch. 18), and
Thackeray's extended portrait of the 'business and bustle and
mystery of a ruined man' (ch. 20) seems at first sight dispro-
portionate. Of course the bankruptcy accounts for the career of
Amelia, but not for all of it. For old Osborne, who also emerges
from the background just here, is described as behaving towards
his former friend Sedley 'with savageness and scorn'. Our

attitude is shaped precisely by Osborne's insisting that as a bankrupt Sedley must be wicked – that he is both out of business and out of the circle of decency. 'From a mere sense of consistency, a persecutor is bound to show that the fallen man is a villain – otherwise he, the persecutor, is a wretch himself' (ch. 18). And Osborne is characterized more grossly still by his opposition to Amelia for his son, by his insistence that George marry the rich mulatto Miss Swartz, and by his vast self-righteousness. Osborne is perhaps an inept caricature of the City man who has succumbed completely to the superstitions of money, but he is a new kind of portrait, and one not less complicated than Dickens's portrait of another hard business-man whose adventures were being issued in installments at the same time.

While Thackeray's Mr. Osborne is a crude warning to those who identify bankruptcy and corruption, Dickens's Mr. Dombey is an astonishing testimonial to the degree of violence that must be exerted to link the experience of bankruptcy with moral reform. In the same month, March of 1848,[21] in which they read of the collision between Rawdon and Lord Steyne, readers who followed both authors were shaken by a passage of dreadful violence that describes a collision between Mr. Dombey's manager, Carker, and a railway engine (ch. 55). Dombey witnesses the event and faints at the sight – it is not an 'accident' but the physical embodiment of a terrible obsession. When we next encounter Dombey (ch. 58) he is superintending the bankruptcy of his firm which results from Carker's secret machinations and which he will do nothing to avert. He is alone in the world, for he has driven away his gentle daughter Florence, and he is a 'ruined man'. With gruesome immediacy he thinks of suicide, but just before the knife strikes, his daughter rushes in, a great reconcili-ation and redemption occurs, and Mr. Dombey, no longer worth five thousand or very much of anything a year, is at last a good man. For all his inventive energy Dickens cannot make clear the relation between the departure of Carker from this world and the moral conversion that Mr. Dombey then undergoes. But this number of *Dombey and Son* together with the contemporaneous number of *Vanity Fair* suggests the extreme lengths to which two of the most sensitive minds of the mid-century were driven in their effort to reconcile the mysterious power of finance capitalism with the requirements of private morality. 'Sell yourself' still meant the worst degradation, but the time was approaching when it would become a formula for 'success'.

In *Vanity Fair* at any rate Becky's bankruptcy offers no clearer connection between villainy – or goodness – and loss of credit than does the situation of Old John Sedley that Osborne so ruthlessly categorizes. The thoroughness with which Thackeray has covered his tracks suggests that no single transaction, not even payment by adultery, is at issue here. The kind of credit upon which the Crawleys lived so well in London and Paris is beyond the power of any act or value to overtake, for it is the social version of that system in which the perpetual promise to pay is taken for the perpetual fact of payment. 'The truth is, when we say of a gentleman that he lives well on nothing a year, we use the word "nothing" to signify something unknown' (ch. 36). It may be that Rawdon and Becky are 'wicked', but their wickedness will not account for their credit as they pursue the fashionable life. Just as the war that so mysteriously yet inevitably ruined John Sedley was, as Thackeray tells us, a lucky accident interrupting the endless double- and triple-dealing among nations (ch. 28), so for Becky an accident interrupts the double-dealing and counter double-dealing of the scramble for social power. The perspectives here are indeed almost endless; they are certainly beyond the limits of innocence or guilt. Even Rawdon, who experiences something like conversion or reform as Becky's career reaches its height, is not quite secure. His one assertion to Becky after the battle is an ironic fulfillment of Steyne's accusation: 'You might have spared me a hundred pounds, Becky, out of all this – I have always shared with you' (ch. 53).[22] And the last words he speaks in the novel are as ambiguous as any question from the narrator: ' "She has kep money concealed from me these ten years", he said. "She swore, last night only, she had none from Steyne. She knew it was all up, directly I found it. If she's not guilty, Pitt, she's as bad as guilty, and I'll never see her again, never" ' (ch. 55). It is hardly possible to find the outrage of manly honor in these exactly struck last words. The distinction between 'guilty' and 'as bad as guilty' would be the final viciousness if it were not the final irrelevance.

But, again, is this what Thackeray means, and is it the *all* that he means? We can believe so only by acknowledging that the easy confidence between reader and writer promised at the beginning has been renounced, for we are here outside the domain of laziness, benevolence, or sarcasm. If the renunciation were the deliberate act of a supreme ironist who turns and rends us for our naive acceptance of his confidential detachment, Thackeray would indeed have created a masterpiece. But in the crucial scene and in portions of the chapters that lead to it Thackeray has exposed us to violent emotions that no politeness can conceal. The enmity between Little Rawdy and Lord Steyne, for example, is an extension of Becky's neglect of her child that erupts into physical violence: Becky boxes his ears for listening to her on the stairs as she entertains Lord Steyne (ch. 44). The child indeed makes his first speaking appearance in the same chapter as that in which Lord Steyne also first appears, grinning 'hideously, his little eyes leering towards Rebecca' (ch. 37). The juxtaposition is emphasized when little Rawdon is apostrophized: 'O thou poor lonely little benighted boy! Mother is the name for God in the lips and hearts of little children; and here was one who was worshipping a stone.'

The appeal is no mere instance of competing with the creator of little Paul Dombey, as everyone who has read Thackeray's letters to his own mother will know. It is an appeal similar to many others in the narrative of Amelia, although there Thackeray is more characteristically reticent. When Amelia and her mother are reunited after her marriage, though Thackeray begins by referring to 'How the floodgates were opened,' he adds, 'Let us respect Amelia and her mamma whispering and whimpering and laughing and crying in the parlour and the twilight.' And when Amelia retreats to meditate in 'the little room' with its 'little white bed' in her old home, Thackeray desists: 'Have we a right to repeat or to overhear her prayers? These, brother, are secrets, and out of the domain of Vanity Fair, in which our story lies' (ch. 26).

Even – especially – if we construe this scene and its secrets as an expression of Amelia's first awareness that she is to be a mother herself, it still involves relationships and sentiments outside the 'domain' that Thackeray so thoroughly explored. It is a domain bounded by the 'politeness' invoked in that early address to the reader in which the narrator promises 'to love and shake by the hand' his 'good and kindly' characters, 'to laugh confidentially in the reader's sleeve' at the 'silly' ones, but 'to abuse in the strongest terms that politeness admits of' all those who are 'wicked and heartless' (ch. 8). Such terms of abuse for the wicked and love for the good are for the most part so polite that we accept them with all the detachment guaranteed by the Manager of the Performance. But the limits of this detachment – its very bankruptcy – can be shown only as we glimpse the howling wilderness outside, where the secrets of private feelings are violently confused with public forces of huge and mysterious dimensions, and where there is neither lucidity nor truth.

What Thackeray does then exhibit within the domain of the Fair is the impossibility of self-knowledge and, in the fullest sense, dramatic change. The most intimate experiences of the self, whether in prayer or in love, in disappointment or in outrage, must be kept outside. Becky's 'I am innocent' is no more an articulation of the truth than it is the lucid exposure of a lie. But to put us where we cannot know 'What *had* happened' and to face us with the bewildering irrelevance of our polite detachment, Thackeray was driven to an extreme that no style of his could control. He could not be clear without being untruthful, and he could not be truthful without being obscure. He tried to recover himself, it is true, in the subsequent chapters by returning to the conception of Becky that most saves his book. The most interesting feature of her characterization is not that she begins from the ambiguous social position of the orphan and governess – ' "I don't trust them governesses, Pinner," says the Sedley housekeeper with enormous assurance, "they're neither one thing nor t'other. They give themselves the hairs and hupstarts of ladies, and their wages is no better than you nor me" ' (ch. 6). Thackeray is concerned with much more than the favorite Victorian example of social mobility. The greater truth about Becky is that she is a mimic, that she trades on the difference between fantasy and society, between the role and the fact. But the truth of endless mimicry is much too large for the domain of the lucid. It is larger than any drawing room, park, or square of Vanity Fair, and it could be forced in only by an act of violence that darkened lucidity and concealed truth. The casuistry upon which *Vanity Fair* rests is unique, and the responses of many thousands of readers for a hundred years to this much-read book must constitute one of the most erratic subterranean currents of our moral history.

SOURCE: essay in *Style in Prose Fiction: English Institute Essays*, ed. Harold C. Martin (New York, 1958); reprinted in *Thackeray: A Collection of Critical Essays*, ed. A. Welsh (Englewood Cliffs, N.J., 1968) pp. 229–47.

NOTES

[Notes in the original have been reorganised and renumbered, with chapter-references inserted in the text.]

1. *An Autobiography*, ed. Frederick Page (London, 1950) p. 244.
2. See, for example, his review of 'A New Spirit Of The Age', *Works*, ed. Saintsbury, vol. VI, p. 424; or some advice on 'finewriting' in *Letters*, ed. Ray, vol. II, p. 192.
3. Preface to *Pendennis*.
4. Gordon N. Ray, *Thackeray: The Uses of Adversity: 1811 – 1846* (New York, 1955) pp. 384 – 5.
5. *The Pilgrim's Progress*, ed. Edmund Venables, rev. Mabel Peacock (Oxford, 1925) pp. 82 ff.
6. Anthony Trollope, *Thackeray* (London, 1879) pp. 197 – 8.
7. Ibid., p. 198.
8. See Ray, *Uses of Adversity*, pp. 370 – 1.
9. As has been suggested by Kathleen Tillotson, in *Novels of the Eighteen-Forties* (Oxford, 1954) pp. 233 – 4.
10. Robert Louis Stevenson, 'A Gossip on Romance', *Memories and Portraits* (New York, 1910) p. 239 (vol. 17 of the Biographical Edition of the *Works*). Stevenson's judgement is endorsed by Professor Ray in *Uses of Adversity*, p. 410.
11. Percy Lubbock, *The Craft of Fiction* (London, 1954) pp. 101 ff.

Lubbock's argument has been criticised by Professor Ray, in *Uses of Adversity*, pp. 409 – 10, and by Geoffrey Tillotson, in *Thackeray the Novelist* (Cambridge, 1954) pp. 82 ff.

12. G. Tillotson, *Thackeray the Novelist*, p. 84.

13. See Ray, *Uses of Adversity*, p. 500, note 19; and *Letters*, vol. II, p. 352, note.

14. See, for example, Ray, *Uses of Adversity*, p. 502, note 14.

15. *Works*, vol. III, p. 385.

16. *Letters* vol. II, pp. 353 – 4.

17. *The Works and Life of Walter Bagehot*, ed. Mrs Russell Barrington, 10 vols (London, 1915) vol. VII, pp. 248, 131.

18. Ibid., p. 251.

19. See *Uses of Adversity*, pp. 159 – 60.

20. *Letters*, vol. II, p. 356.

21. See K. Tillotson, *Novels of the Eighteen-Forties*, p. 318.

22. For a quite different interpretation, see K. Tillotson, *Novels of the Eighteen-Forties*, pp. 248–51. [See above, pp. 136–7–Ed.]

A. E. Dyson

AN IRONY AGAINST HEROES (1966)

. . . *Vanity Fair* is surely one of the world's most devious novels, devious in its characterisation, its irony, its explicit moralising, its exuberance, its tone. Few novels demand more continuing alertness from the reader, or offer more intellectual and moral stimulation in return. In part, at least, this deviousness can be seen to relate to Thackeray's own life. As Gordon Ray has shown in his admirable biography, Thackeray knew Vanity Fair from the inside, with all the insight of a man engaged in its ways, yet deeply ill at ease. One remembers his complex dissatisfactions with his lot. He regretted his nationality, thinking that he would have written better in some other language – an illusion which his own achievement surely exposes, even if we invoke no other names for the defence. He regretted his century, imagining that he would have been more at home in the eighteenth: but would Swift and Sterne have disgusted him as they sometimes did if this were true? He regretted his occasional poverty, and the restless bohemianism which followed the tragedy of his married life, but this was the very material of his art: without such experiences, he might have remained a clever and savage journalist to the end of his days.

Such dissatisfactions led to the iconoclasm of his earlier days, but they paved the way, too, for his compassion. He said himself, on one occasion, that he was created with 'a sense of the ugly, the odd, of the meanly false, of the desperately wicked'. The intensity with which he always responded to the human comedy pushed him towards a more radical criticism of society than perhaps he intended. He acquired, as Walter Bagehot noted, a heightened sense of human inequalities, of the diversity of criticism to which

the unprotected and poor are especially exposed. One sees how
readily his temperamental restlessness responded to the restlessness of Vanity Fair itself – to its noise and bustle, its surface
gaiety, its instinctive cruelty, its truthlessness and faithlessness, its
occasional courage and resilience, its desolating lack of heart's
ease.

Such considerations lead us very naturally towards
Thackeray's pervasive ambivalence of tone. Where does he stand
in relationship to his characters, and to their world? Does he
come to them chiefly as friend or foe? The explicit indications of
attitude, which are numerous enough, and to some readers
offensive, do not take us very far. In the opening
pages – beautifully and hauntingly written, like so much that is
to follow them – he presents himself as a puppet-master, the sole
creator of his characters, and their destiny. By the laws of art, this
is self-evidently true: all writers do invent their characters, and
decide what their fate is to be. By the laws of great art, however, it
is a half-truth at best. The greater the writer, the more likely he is
to find other laws taking a hand; to find as Richardson did in
Clarissa, and Tolstoy in *Anna Karenina*, that he cannot deal with
his own characters as simply as he may wish. *Vanity Fair* turns out
to be a novel where the puppet-master is, after all, bound by the
iron discipline of his own greatness. The characters come alive,
and their creator cannot blacken or praise them superficially
without his readers detecting and resenting the lie; they come
alive in the real world of human morality, where every
complexity of sensitive response must be allowed for, whether the
creator fully approves of such complexity or not. As E. M.
Forster has pointed out, Becky Sharp is an outstanding example
of a 'round' character; she defies any rule of characterisation that
simple logic might prescribe, and becomes as familiar and
unpredictable as if we had known her all our lives. Thackeray, of
course, knew when his characters came alive as well as we do, and
his role of puppet-master is only one of the various *personae* he
adopts. Sometimes, he claims the puppet-master's privilege of
knowing his characters' secret thoughts, and telling us what these
are. But at other times he is reticent, as one would be in life; we
are never shown Amelia's deepest moments of grief, though we

know the torment they must be. And very occasionally – though on particularly important occasions, as it turns out – he throws open the enigma of life itself as part of his art: who *can* be sure when Becky is telling the truth?

The reader of *Vanity Fair* soon finds other evidence to belie the notion that artifice and contrivance are all. To an unusual degree we have the sense of a real world going on all round the main characters, full of diversity and colour, full of characters who appear and disappear, enacting at the edge of our consciousness the same patterns of sin and anxiety which hold the centre of the stage. This use of surrounding detail and seeming irrelevance to reinforce the main structure of the book reminds us of Sterne; as, to a lesser extent, does the fluidity of the time-scale that Thackeray adopts. Though there is nothing as obviously eccentric as the digressions and flash-backs of *Tristram Shandy*, we find that Thackeray's narrative does shift backwards and forwards in time in a way not always easy to chart. The effect is of a 'real world' into which the novelist's memory dips rather than of an artificial world which he creates as he goes along. Later in the novel, Thackeray represents himself as a man who learns of all the main events by hearsay. The omniscient narrator, the preacher in cap-and-bells, gives way to this further *persona*, middle-aged, curious and detached.

To learn caution about Thackeray's role as puppet-master is to learn caution about the explicit moral judgements of which the novel is full. Some modern critics have blamed Thackeray for saying too much, but this is surely a naïve misunderstanding of his technique. The tradition of commenting upon characters goes back at least to Fielding, but even in *Tom Jones* we are kept continuously on the alert. Are we really to admire Master Blifil's honesty as we are told we should, and to look forward to the hanging of Tom at the end? Fielding adopts the pose of a conventional moralist as a challenge, forcing us to match our personal wits and sense of values against his own. In *Vanity Fair* Thackeray pursues a similar strategy, with ironic overtones even subtler in their range. We are reminded of Fielding's influence in the knowing, man-of-the world asides; in the ferocity, the gusto almost, with which various kinds of hypocrisy are exposed. There is even something of Sterne in Thackeray's willingness to act the fool, to claim the cap-and-bells as his own. But the prevailing tone of *Vanity Fair*, is very different from Fielding's, and *a fortiori* from Sterne's. There is a lack of warmth about it in certain moods: if Thackeray had invented Tom Jones he would surely have found his hero more difficult than Fielding did to forgive, while Uncle Toby one cannot imagine him inventing at all. For though Thackeray's iconoclasm is in part exuberant, it also has a tinge of bitterness; it is nearer than Fielding and Sterne ever are to despair. Very readily the teasing and flamboyance give way, at moments of strain, to the tone of the preacher, no longer in cap-and-bells, but solemn and prophetic now in his own right. The title of the novel is taken from Bunyan, and though Thackeray has nothing of Bunyan's clear-cut doctrine to depend upon, he shares the occasional mood of a Wisdom writer; religious judgements are inescapably present, though not directly expressed. In the introductory note 'Before the Curtain', we are warned of the melancholy induced by Vanity Fair – a melancholy which gives rise to, and shades into, compassion for the suffering and transience of man. Behind the ostensible warmth of tone, which we can never rely on, there is warmth of a deeper and costlier kind. We are involved in the fate of the characters we laugh at, not distanced from them; what happens to them in the end we really must know.

Obviously, then, Thackeray's tone is a complex affair; its local nuances can never be isolated from the whole. We are always left wondering what to make of it, whether it really is as simple, or as moderately simple, as it is dressed out to seem. There is the rather arch playfulness, for instance, that surrounds both Becky and Amelia: is this simply a sentimental evasiveness on Thackeray's part, or does it serve some more devious end? On the surface, the archness is tender towards Amelia, sharp (like her name) towards Becky; yet its eventual effect is to diminish Amelia, while making Becky appear interesting, and even great. Around Amelia, Thackeray deliberately creates a cloying tone, apparently in order to confirm the complacency of his readers, yet really to create in them a growing unease: what *are* these virtues we are being so cosily invited to admire? How *can* we respond with this degree of whimsy to an adult? Around Becky, however, the same tone plays with very different effect. Throughout the novel, she is referred to as 'our little schemer', very much as one might speak of a naughty but not wholly unsympathetic child. In the period when her fortunes are at low ebb, and she sinks to being an extremely seedy (though still resilient) adventuress, Thackeray writes about her almost in the tone of *The Rose And The Ring*:

So our little wanderer went about setting up her tent in various cities of Europe, as restless as Ulysses or Bampfylde Moore Carew. Her taste for disrespectability grew more and more remarkable. She became a perfect Bohemian ere long, herding with people whom it would make your hair stand on end to meet.

The effect of this is so odd that one is tempted to regard such archness here, if not elsewhere, as an aesthetic flaw. The implication is presumably that Becky lived for a time as a courtesan, yet the tone seems designed to deflect attention away from the actual fact. We have only to imagine Shakespeare writing about Cleopatra as a little schemer whose plots would make our hair stand on end to see how far from serious the passage is.

Nevertheless, too much can be made of such blemishes; certainly they exist in the novel, but they should not blind us to the extreme subtlety of the ironic strategy as a whole. I have mentioned the archness of tone at the start because modern readers are especially likely to need guidance on this: they will be alienated by it more immediately than most Victorians would have been, but they may fail to realise that usually, if not always, this is precisely what Thackeray intends. In what follows, I shall assume that he is one of the most sophisticated of our ironists, and that nearly every effect is very exactly and maturely contrived.

When we look more closely at Thackeray's leading actors, his subtlety soon begins to emerge. Criticism of their personal characters comes very easily to him – too easily, we are immediately forced to suspect. There are Becky's lies and Sir Pitt's meanness, Mr Osborne's anger and Mrs Bute's

treachery – all very wicked, surely?, as the author takes every
opportunity to assert. Such comment is, we sense, a very surface
affair; a kind of thin ice, on which we are too effusively invited to
skate. Social and religious comments are less explicitly stated, yet
they are certainly implied, and with mounting insistence as the
full pressure of the novel comes to be felt. It occurs to us, after a
time, that these deeper implications may run counter to the
simpler personal ones that are paraded on the surface; that things
may be very much less simple than they seem. Consider, for
example, the contrast between Becky and Amelia, around which
so much of the action is built. The destinies of the two girls are
clearly to be intertwined, the one a conventional heroine (though
Thackeray denies her the name), the other a villainess specially
designed to make our hair stand on end. As Amelia withdraws
from school into her world of money and privilege, Becky is
thrown out into the battle of life, with nothing but her wits on her
side. We see the girls both trying to catch husbands, the one aided
by her mother's socially acceptable stratagems and a good
dowry, the other almost fatally handicapped by the lack of these
things. At Waterloo we see them with the husbands they have
eventually won, Becky triumphant now because of her inborn
resilience, Amelia beginning to sink under the deeper handicap
of her inner nature – her lack of any real intelligence or talent, or
of the courage and will-power needed when life turns sour.
Towards the end of the novel there are further reversals, and the
two girls, both older and sadder, both soiled by life, neither much
wiser, work out the underlying logic of their lives. Becky has to
live now without the husband she has loved in her way, Amelia
has to live with the second husband she has accepted just slightly
too late. During the action the two women are compared in a
great many ways. We see them both as mothers, Amelia too
indulgent, as we would expect, Becky too detached. At times,
Becky seems a very false friend to Amelia; she behaves very badly
at Waterloo, and becomes one of the many people that Amelia
has to fear. The actual harm she does is less, however, than it
appears; there is no planned malice in it, since this is not a sin she
has it in her to commit, and George's character would be the
same whatever she did. There is also an evening of accounts later

on: if Becky rather contemptuously harms Amelia by flirting
with her husband before Waterloo, she equally contemptuously
does her a good turn as the novel is nearing its end. The second
act – the use of George's old letter to disillusion Amelia about his
memory – is as finely ambivalent as many of the other decisive
actions in the book. At one earlier point Becky has reflected that
she could crush Amelia by producing George's letter, but she has
had too much casual good-nature to put this to the test. When she
eventually does produce the letter it is in order to help Amelia,
yet her emotions must have included a certain triumph; her
motives must have been characteristically mixed.

In the contrast between Becky and Amelia, the moral
characters of the two girls are always involved. At a very deep
level, Thackeray is critical of them both. The notion that his
attitude to either can be taken at face value can survive only for a
reader of the most superficial kind. In a letter written to his
mother in July 1847 Thackeray had this to say about Amelia (no
doubt slightly overstating the truth):

My object is not to make a perfect character or anything like it. Don't
you see how odious all the people are in the book (with the exception of
Dobbin) – behind whom all there lies a dark moral I hope. What I
want is to make a set of people living without God in the world (only
that is a cant phrase) greedy, pompous, mean perfectly self-satisfied for
the most part and at ease about their superior virtue.

Just after the novel was finished, he told Robert Bell in another
letter: 'I want to leave everybody dissatisfied and unhappy at the
end of the story – we ought all to be with our own and all other
stories.'

Undoubtedly in making these comments Thackeray was
sincere, but like all critical comments they are necessarily less
subtle than the force of the novel as a whole. For the moment, I
should like to concentrate a little on the strategy of characterisation which underlies such intentions. On the face of it, Amelia
is the virtuous girl of the two, sweet and gentle, though with a
helplessness that soon begins to cloy. 'The charming sweet thing'
is a first impression most people have of her, modulating to 'the

poor sweet thing' fairly soon. At school she has many friends among the girls, but when the battle of life is entered upon nearly all women, including her mother, come to view her with contempt. To men she remains an object of courteous attention, but hardly an obvious choice (except to Dobbin, who loves her) as a wife. Thackeray himself appears to sympathise with her, and he does in fact establish her tenderness as the virtue it is. But adverse judgements, often rather slyly foisted off on 'the world', begin to mount. Her love of George is imperceptive and self-indulgent. She blinds herself to his faults and (more seriously perhaps) refuses to see that he does not love her; duty and dignity are thrown overboard in the pursuit. When she wins George, she has little wit or liveliness to offer in return for the sacrifice which he sees himself as having made. As the novel progresses her future is increasingly overshadowed by fears, and we sense that she is destined to be a casualty in the battle of life.

Her virtues also turn out to be more tainted than they at first appear. Her great claim to virtue is the passiveness of self-sacrifice, yet is self-sacrifice, as she practises it, not an insidious self-indulgence in disguise? As a mother she is weakly and harmfully indulgent, as a daughter she fails her parents in their years of need. When George is alive, her love for him is self-willed and self-regarding; when he is dead, the myth of her marriage becomes an evasion of Dobbin's love.

Becky, in contrast, is ostensibly bad, yet her heroic qualities shine out against Amelia's faults. She is sparkling, clever and resilient; from her earliest years she has had to live by her wits, and if the world is against her, is this not mainly because she inherited neither status nor wealth? Her anti-social qualities are at least as much the effect of the world's dealings with her as their cause. Thackeray goes out of his way to blacken her character in his opening pages, as though he entirely shares the standards by which she is judged. As she flings Dr Johnson's 'Dixonary' at the feet of good, silly Miss Jemima, we see her convulsed with hatred and rage; when the coach moves off, 'the young lady's counten-ance, which had before worn an almost livid look of hatred, assumed a smile that perhaps was scarcely more agreeable'. During her stay at the Sedleys' she is accused of envy and covetousness, malice and pride; it seems as though all the deadly sins must be laid at her door. We hear of the time when she was caught 'stealing jam' at eight years of age, as if faults which would be venial in a well-to-do child must be accounted mortal in her.

As the action of the novel unfolds, it is true that her sins become more substantial. She wounds Amelia, ruins Raggles, plays fast and loose with a great many friends and admirers, treats her husband (as she does everyone else) with good-natured contempt, though after her fashion she loves him. Her thoughtlessness as a mother is hard to forgive; when Thackeray says 'she had no soft maternal heart, this unlucky girl' for once he is not exaggerating the truth. She lives always as a parasite and sometimes, if we take the hints, as a harlot. At the end, it is even suggested that she becomes a murderess – and though this is only malicious gossip and almost certainly untrue, Thackeray's 'Who *can* tell?' echoes uncomfortably in our ears.

Despite all this, it is clear that Thackeray overstates the conventional case against Becky knowingly and deliberately, as the case against Tom Jones was overstated by Fielding. When we ask how we come to detect this, and in any way at all to be on Becky's side, the answer takes us nearer to the heart of the book. In one sense, it may be simply that Becky's courage and resilience are admirable in themselves, whether they are applied for good or ill; in this familiar sense Thackeray may be of his heroine's party without knowing it – or more likely, knowing it slightly better than he would wish. Another possibility is that our sympathy with Becky is sentimental or indulgent and little more. Some critics, indeed, have written as though this were true of Thackeray himself: his 'sentimentality' can be dissociated, they suggest from his 'irony', and regarded as a balance on the other side. When bitter censoriousness has brought Becky down, good-natured sentimentality brings her up again; tears and laughter alternate like April weather, and the author is simply a creature of his moods. Such a view is, I am suggesting, extremely superficial, but where Becky is concerned there may be a particular reason why it appeals. Criminals always *are* easier to sympathise with from a distance, in literature as in life; Becky is

undeniably a character more easy to forgive when she is safely
contained in the pages of a book.

None of this, however, does more than scratch the surface of
the problem, for surely we do admire Becky, and legitimately,
however glad we are to be outside the range of her wiles? The fact
is that she *belongs* to Vanity Fair, both as its true reflection, and as
its victim; for both of which reasons, she very resoundingly serves
it right. Like Jonson's Volpone, she is a fitting scourge for the
world which created her – fitting aesthetically, in the way of
poetic justice, and fitting morally, in that much of her evil is
effective only against those who share her taint. Dobbin is largely
immune to her, since he is neither a trifler, a hypocrite nor a snob.
The other characters are all vulnerable in one or other of these
ways, and we notice that those who judge her most harshly are
frequently the ones who have least earned such a right.

The right to judge is, of course, the crux, for Vanity Fair is a
social place, and no critique of individual characters can be
conducted in a void. What Thackeray comes near to suggesting,
like Bunyan before him, is that a society based upon privilege and
money is rotten in some fundamental sense. The very concepts of
Christian morality become, in such a context, an evasion; an
attempt to visit upon the underprivileged and the unprotected
sins which more properly belong to society at large. In a world of
class and privilege, the simple ideas of 'lying' and 'stealing', when
applied by the haves to have-nots, will clearly not do. An ideal
validity they may have, but in the world as we know it they are
turned into a mockery of themselves. How far Thackeray was
aware of these implications, or wished to be aware of them, it is
hard to say. In the novel, he places both his readers and himself in
Vanity Fair. We are all tainted with the Crawley hypocrisy,
whether of Mrs Bute or Miss Crawley, of Sir Pitt or of Becky
herself. Exactly here, however (and surely this is intended, too?),
a further temptation is put in our way. To be all tarred with the
same brush, and to be brought to realise that we are, can be a
relief as well as a challenge. Need we really do more than the next
man in the way of penance, if we have done no more than he in
the way of guilt? To judge ourselves guilty, and read on, is less
uncomfortable than setting about a wonderful mending of the

world. All satirists suffer from this possible evasion of their challenge, but some perhaps suffer less than others – and a few might be tempted to take the same escape route themselves. In 1848, the year of Revolution as well as the year of *Vanity Fair*, Thackeray confessed himself a Republican but not a Chartist. He had no wish to be associated with the hated 'levellers', yet his picture of society is remarkably in tune with theirs. The poison of 'snobbery' had always fascinated him, but whereas his earlier satire was boisterous and comic, the satire of *Vanity Fair* reaches more unerringly towards the roots. The Bute Crawleys are supposed to be Christian, but their plots against Rawdon and Becky are evil in a purely competitive sense. Miss Crawley imagines herself to be a liberal and a Republican, but she is as parasitic as Becky herself (they are truly birds of a feather), though at the other end of the moneyed scale. Almost every sin in Vanity Fair can be traced, beyond personal weakness, to the fundamental laws of money and class; to fawn upon the rich and kick the poor is a Christian law of the land. The poison in Vanity Fair infects the bottom rungs of the social ladder as well as the top: Mrs Sedley's servants join in the hunt against Becky when she has fallen from grace, her own servants turn against her when Rawdon has stormed off and they sense that her social position is at an end. The poor have more than their chains to lose in Vanity Fair, they have their opportunities for hurting one another as well. If Thackeray went less far than the Marxists in political analysis of the scene he depicts, it may have been (to give him the benefit of the doubt) because his view of human nature was correspondingly gloomier than theirs.

The whole institution of marriage is bound up with these attitudes, as Thackeray is also concerned to bring home. When Mrs Sedley is shocked by Becky's stratagems, after her husband has explained them to her, her shock is not to do with prudery but with class. How dare a hired governess of dubious parentage 'look up to such a magnificent personage as the collector of Boggley Wollah?' The cruel realism of this becomes still more detestable when it mingles with conscious snobbery and insensitivity – as it does in George Osborne, when he also conspires against Becky's attempts to steer quietly to port in

Joseph Sedley's arms. Thackeray's savagery in such passages has been sometimes overlooked, one suspects, by readers who deplore his 'prudery' without realising how realistic about sex he can also be. He was reticent about physical love, as all Victorians were, but in *Vanity Fair* there are franknesses that can shock us even now. Becky, for instance, is not a sensual woman at all; given wealth and social position, she would have managed without sexual adventures fairly well. She is willing to marry Joseph Sedley for all his absurdity; and our very revulsion from this, if we experience revulsion, may be only a sentimental lack of realism about marriage of our own. In Vanity Fair, as Thackeray depicts it, sex is as little reverenced or respected as anything else. On the one hand, it is a subject for endless gossip and malice; a common frailty in which we are all likely to be caught out unless we take sufficient care (but if we are caught Heaven help us, since Vanity Fair is understanding but in no way forgiving about those who fall by the way). And on the other hand, it is a powerful asset to a mother looking round for a good catch for her daughter. Though the weaklings of the world like Amelia may think only of love, a mother will think rather of physical attractiveness and charm. These are the true assets she has to trade with in the marriage market – assets almost as substantial as the dowry itself, though who doubts that money speaks a little louder in the end?

In all such matters Thackeray reports faithfully and even ferociously what the world is like, with a directness that speaks very strikingly across a hundred years of sexual emancipation to ourselves. He is willing to show how far from being pure-minded young soldiers are when they joke together, courteous though their attentions to an Amelia may be; he is willing to depict the cynicism of Mr Osborne, who will readily see George amuse himself with any woman he fancies, as long as he is not mad enough to want to make her his wife. Boys will be boys, says Mr Osborne in effect, but 'unless I see Amelia's ten thousand down, you don't marry her' . . . 'And that's flat'. A modern reader is often tempted, I think, to treat this as bitter satire, rather than as the very minimal realism which it is. What Thackeray is saying, surely, is that the Flesh has very little chance indeed of triumphing when the time comes for it to do battle with the World.

Our sympathy with Becky, to return to this, is so closely connected with, as to be almost inseparable from, the context of Thackeray's social realism. Even while conventional judgements are being made against her, a social background is movingly, if less noisily, sketched. We hear of 'the dismal precocity of poverty' without surprise. In the contrast with Amelia, it is at once apparent that whereas the one girl is cushioned, the other must fight to survive. Their quest for a husband is similar, but Becky, with no mother to help her, must risk the insults and misunderstandings attendant upon doing everything for herself. And this, really, is why we are on her side: not because we idealise her ruthless scheming, or foolishly imagine that we should get along rather well with her ourselves, but because we see the need for what she does. In a society using Christian values almost wholly perversely, resilience and energy are forced to know themselves, in a Becky, as conventional sins. For this reason too we forgive her, for we see how little right society has to judge her as it does. She is indeed its reflection, and interesting to us largely because she has the courage and energy, though so heavily handicapped, to play its game. We notice that though she employs hypocrisy, she is never taken in by it herself; she does not make her sin a virtue, and is to this degree preferable to those who do. She is never revengeful or consciously hard-hearted; she is able (a really saving grace) to laugh at herself exactly as though she were someone else.

Reflecting upon this, we see the deeper purposes Thackeray must have in mind. To a much larger extent than we would expect, Becky's judgements on people are the novelist's own. When she writes a letter to Amelia, for instance, mocking the uncouth and canting inmates of Queen's Crawley, Thackeray assures us that it is the wicked Becky speaking, and not himself: 'Otherwise you might fancy that it was I who was sneering . . . I who laughed . . . whereas the laughter comes from one who has no reverence except for prosperity, and no eye for anything beyond success.' [ch. 8] But this dissociation of himself from Becky is largely false, and the irony is of the two-edged kind we find throughout. Given that Thackeray himself judges with compassion, and that this quality is one that Becky, by the nature of things, does not have, the judgements she makes of Queen's Crawley are substantially the same as his own. Because she sees the standards by which the world actually lives in such sharp contrast with the standards by which it professes to live, she can judge as well as exploit it in its chosen terms. For, indeed, she belongs to Vanity Fair herself, and reform, whether for herself or for it, is very far from her thought. She glories in the world's game with all the superior energy and intelligence that she can command. It may even be fair, if one thinks in these terms, that the comparatively innocent should have to suffer along with the rest. Old Raggles might seem an innocent victim, but is he not as corrupt and open to punishment as anyone else? By thrift he assembles his nest-egg, and by trust he loses it; yet his trust is tainted with snobbery, the mark of Vanity Fair is on it for us to see.

The obverse of this is that Becky's character rises in our esteem as that of her victims sinks. How could her gaiety and courage have expressed themselves in any more worthy way? Had she been born to position or power, she would have risen nobly to the role. ' "It isn't difficult to be a gentleman's wife," Rebecca thought. "I think I could be a good woman if I had five thousand a year." ' And so, as the world judges, she could have been. Who would more charmingly distribute charity than a privileged Becky, or more graciously accept in return the world's esteem? She could have been a Queen, we are told, if she had been born to it; and it is apparent enough that she could.

Lacking, however, these natural advantages, Becky knows that the appearance of respectability and wealth must be sought for instead. And since Vanity Fair is as much pleased with the appearance as with the reality, until such time as the discrepancy is seen through and the hunt can begin, Becky has all her intuitive understanding of its values on her side. The appearance can be maintained, it is true, only by exceptional effort; the world's homage is bought at a price, and those who cannot pay cash must know how to charm, and flatter, and amuse. For long periods Becky creates and maintains the required appearance; her resourcefulness and gaiety seem never-ending, though she knows (as Lord Steyne brutally confirms to her) that she is living in a house built of straw. And she lifts Rawdon up to apparent affluence and comfort with herself. Though others suffer as she does so, and have to suffer, she is a good wife to Rawdon from the first. It is not the least of the novel's ironies that she loses her husband without really deserving to (though the circumstances leading up to this are surrounded with characteristic enigma); and that this last rebuff is the bitterest of all, the rebuff she needs most courage to survive.

At this point in the novel we surely pity her; and our attitude has by now become a most searching moral comment upon ourselves. Of course we have to judge as well as pity, but have we, as readers, earned the right to judge? Have we even any pity that rings true, or that Becky will need or be prepared to accept if it does? Again and again Thackeray reminds us that we, too, belong to Vanity Fair. To condemn Becky easily is *a fortiori* to condemn ourselves; how are we to make any judgement without resorting to hypocrisies deeper and more shameful than her own? The imaginative power of Thackeray's vision forces the reality of this dilemma upon us: some further dimension must be sought before we can be sure that we have the right. Should it be the religious dimension, perhaps, to which the word 'vanity' directs us? Or the political one, to which the whole analysis of class and money appears to point?

As I have already insisted, we can by no means be sure how far Thackeray would have committed himself in such ways. He was no religious mystic, though he catches the profound melancholy of the contemplative; nor was he a political agitator, though the moral of *Vanity Fair* might have seemed obvious to Karl Marx. Most of his explicit comments reinforce the notion that he is criticising human individuals rather than the structure of society as a whole, yet the novel's pattern, I have tried to show, prevents us from leaving the matter comfortably at this.

Perhaps Thackeray never did decide how far the poison at work in Vanity Fair is a social sin, which decisive social action might remove, and how far it is a personal flaw, an ineradicable vanity in the heart of man. The lack of a clear-cut answer may account in part for his restlessness, which we always sense behind the apparently easy elegance of the style. Religious and political solutions can, however, be a form of glibness themselves. Can we expect Thackeray to offer a clearer answer to such problems than we have worked out for ourselves? For at least a hundred years now the Western mind has been discovering enigmas and doubts. In extending our understanding and compassion, Thackeray does the work a novelist is chiefly concerned to do.

This brings us to the novel's true greatness, to its claim to be one of the undoubtedly major novels that we have. It was Charlotte Brontë, one of Thackeray's earliest admirers, who said:

It is 'sentiment' in my sense of the term – sentiment jealously hidden, but genuine, which extracts the venom from that formidable Thackeray, and converts what might be corrosive poison into purifying elixir.

If Thackeray did not cherish in his large heart deep feeling for his kind, he would delight to exterminate: as it is, I believe, he wishes only to reform.

The 'deep feeling' and 'corrosive poison' are not opposites, but simply different sides of a unified response to life. We sense the capacity for the former in Thackeray's great sonorous phrases about vanity: 'Yes, this is Vanity Fair; not a moral place certainly; nor a merry one, though very noisy'; we sense it in the sympathy we are made to feel for nearly all of the characters, even when – and perhaps especially when – we have also seen them at their worst. Mr Osborne's selfishness and tyranny are strongly realised, yet his suffering when George dies is none the less powerful and real. Thackeray is able to make us feel pity for a man like ourselves even as we probe the bitter impurities of grief:'And it is hard to say which pang it was tore the proud father's heart more keenly – that his son should have gone out of the reach of forgiveness, or that the apology which his own pride expected should have escaped him' [ch. 35]. Mr Sedley also becomes, in his ruin, a broken and pathetic figure; even Miss Crawley comes to an end which we feel to be worse than she deserves.

The most remarkable example of Thackeray's compassion,

however, is surely to be found in his dealings with Amelia. The strategy of her characterisation is at least as subtle as Becky's, though there are somewhat different ends in view. In writing of Amelia earlier, I stressed the main intention of Thackeray's irony: he tries to trap us into an easy and arch indulgence towards her in order to shatter this, later, with a very damaging moral critique. But this is half the story only, and not the half that matters most. It is in keeping with the subtlety we expect from a major novelist that our disillusionment with Amelia should contain a further trap of its own. The swing from simple indulgence to simple censure is easy to make; too easy if morality is to be very much more than a game. By shifting the tone of his irony in various puzzling ways, Thackeray invites us not only to see the causes of judgement, but to probe their validity. With Amelia as with Becky, in fact, we are made to look beyond conventional judgements to that true situation – more costly to contemplate – which we so often miss. When Thackeray rebukes our easy sentimentality towards Amelia, he is clearing the way not for cynicism, but for pity of a truer kind. Cynicism indeed is not the opposite to sentimentality but its twin, another kind of shallowness which we too easily swing towards when rebuked. We discover that though sentimental indulgence is a travesty of compassion, clear-sighted judgement ought to be simply a stepping-stone on the way. What Thackeray makes us see is that Amelia is an incurably neurotic woman, destined to unhappiness whether things go well with her or ill. The contrast between herself and Becky is to some degree a contrast between robust mental health and mental defeat. Becky survives even the gravest hardships and rebuffs, Amelia remains fearful even when she achieves, or seems to achieve, her heart's desire. The comments Thackeray makes upon her are always delicately poised. Soon after her marriage – far too soon – we read: 'Her heart tried to persist in asserting that George Osborne was worthy and faithful, though she knew otherwise' (ch. 29).

Amelia's 'knowledge' is really, of course, a fear: it is the presentiment of evil which always besets her, as a measure, perhaps, of her own inadequacy. It is also, however, a justified fear; one senses that she is the kind of person whose fears create situations in which they are most likely to be fulfilled. Though her fears are described as knowledge, moreover, and though para- noia converts fears into 'knowledge' in this way, this is not a knowledge by which she chooses to live. Her fears are true, in a manner which only culpable self-deception could fail to see, yet after George's death Amelia suppresses them, building instead a myth of his absolute devotion by which to live. This, in turn, becomes a mode of evasion, both of her responsibilities as a daughter and as a mother, and of the ever-present challenge of Dobbin's love. The suggestions clustering around this situation are typical of Thackeray's complex sense of reality. Even apart from the obvious weakness of Amelia's conduct, its underlying selfishness is relentlessly exposed. She never really considers Dobbin, or anyone else apart from herself – and this despite the fact that self-sacrifice is the virtue always attributed to her, the virtue that she would claim for herself. Further ironies open out from such perceptions. Is Dobbin's fidelity to the living but unresponsive Amelia entirely different from Amelia's fidelity to the dead George? Might not Dobbin's love, unbeknown to Amelia, be the one experience that could have quietened her fears and given her peace?

Our awareness of these cross-currents is beautifully stage- managed; and represents one of Thackeray's most interesting challenges to ourselves. The material for censoriousness is offered in abundance, but is censoriousness the most human response we can make? Not, surely, if we think of life as it is, with all its perversities; with all its intolerable perplexities and burdens, especially for the lonely and weak. Most of the judgements just suggested against Amelia are touched with glibness: true in a sense they may be, but the whole truth is a bigger and more saddening affair. The kind of love Amelia lavishes on George may be excessive, but had he been worthy of it, the situation could have been transformed. If Amelia had had the good luck to fall in love with Dobbin, her particular virtues might have been productive, not sour, her lack of intelligence and talent might have mattered scarcely at all. One might blame her, perhaps, for preferring George's good looks to Dobbin's plainness (and indeed if there is a sensualist in the book, Amelia rather than Becky fills the role). But life is like that after all; since we cannot fall in love to order, can Amelia's evasiveness about Dobbin be wholly and honestly blamed? It may also be that certain types of tenderness, of self-sacrifice and reticence, can take root only in such soil as Amelia provides. When Mr Sedley on his death-bed repents of the harshness he and his wife have shown towards Amelia, he may be recognising a true flaw in their treatment of her (surely he is), and not simply indulging a last nostalgia in the moment of death.

We rush too easily into censoriousness when reading novels, as Thackeray well knew; the luxury of catching fictional characters out in errors can be very readily mistaken for unusual moral maturity in ourselves. Compassion is better than censure, in literature as in life; by involving us as he does with his characters, Thackeray makes this more than usually plain. It is just when we want to judge most harshly that he allows his stress to fall another way – on the perversity of circumstances and the shortness of time, on the need for forgiveness which embraces us all. The most memorable moments in the novel are those when this insight comes to the surface, and the deep currents of feeling crystallise in phrases we are never likely to forget. The tormented striving, the enigma, the restlessness give way to a grander sense of human solitude and need. Things go wrong for this character or that beyond any deserving, and we see him confronting the world bewildered and alone. There is the poignant moment just before Waterloo, when George comes in late to Amelia after his flirtation with Becky, to be with her, as it turns out, for the last time: 'Two fair arms closed tenderly round his neck as he stooped down. "I am awake, George," the poor child said, with a sob fit to break the little heart that nestled so closely by his own' [ch. 29]. And there are other moments, no less pure and heart-rending, that we remember: Mr Sedley's confession to his wife of his loss of money, in words as desolating as they are brief: ' "We're ruined, Mary. We've got the world to begin over again, dear" ' [ch. 18]; and little Rawdon Crawley's reaction when the mother whom he once idolised boxes his ears before Lord Steyne:

'It is not because it hurts me,' little Rawdon gasped

out – 'only – only'– sobs and tears wound up the sentence in a storm. It was the little boy's heart that was bleeding. 'Why mayn't I hear her singing? Why don't she ever sing to me – as she does to that bald-headed man with the large teeth?' [ch. 44].

We remember, too, Becky's own reflections, characteristically tough, yet hardly less poignant for that, when during her later wanderings she thinks again of the husband she has lost:

'If *he'd* been here,' she said, 'these cowards would never have dared to insult me.' She thought about 'him' with great sadness, and perhaps longing – about his honest, stupid, constant kindness and fidelity, his never-ceasing obedience, his good-humour; his bravery and courage. Very likely she cried, for she was particularly lively, and had put on a little extra rouge when she came down to dinner. [ch. 64].

To all of us in Vanity Fair, the weak and the strong, the proud and the humble, the good and the bad, there come such moments, when after the bustle and gaiety, the hoping and working, the striving and fearing, we find ourselves downcast and alone. At such moments, in Thackeray's depiction of them, all the irony and cynicism, the hatred of worldliness and scorn of fools, gives way to this note of a deeper compassion:

Ah! *Vanitas Vanitatum!* which of us is happy in this world? Which of us has his desire? or, having it, is satisfied? – , Come, children, let us shut up the box and the puppets, for our play is played out. [ch. 67].

SOURCE: extract from *The Crazy Fabric: Essays in Irony* (London, 1966) pp. 76–95.

Ioan M. Williams

'THE ROLE OF THE NARRATOR'
(1968)

Interpretation of *Vanity Fair* depends on an understanding of the relationship between Thackeray (as author), the narrator, and the events and characters of the story. The mistake of confusing Thackeray with his narrator is an elementary one, but one that can be made by quite sophisticated critics. Dorothy Van Ghent, in *The English Novel: Form and Function* (1953) [an extract from which is included in this selection – Ed.], is a good example, objecting to the idea of Thackeray himself intruding in the novel and pulling the characters out of the fictional world by speaking of them in relationship to himself. That the narrator and Thackeray are not to be identified is obvious from the facts which we learn about him in the course of his narration – that he was young fifty years ago, that this boyhood occurred twenty-five years ago, and that he has a wealthy maiden aunt and a wife called Julia!

In which case, several questions remain: for what purpose did Thackeray create him and put his personality between the reader and the story, and to what extent does he represent the official voice of the author? These questions are of central importance and must be answered before criticism as pointed as that of Dorothy Van Ghent can be answered and full understanding of the novel achieved.

REALISATION IN 'VANITY FAIR'

With regard to the most basic criticism which Dorothy Van Ghent puts forward and which has frequently been made – that the narrator interferes between the reader and the created world of the characters – the obvious and easy answer is that the narrator is as much a part of the created world as Becky Sharp or Rawdon Crawley. If he is not Thackeray himself, who is he but a character? Thackeray took care, towards the end of the novel, to put the narrator into the world which he was describing by making him give an account of his original meeting with the people whose story he has been telling. Elsewhere, outside the novel, he insisted on the importance of realisation and vivid representation with an emphasis worthy of his critics. Thus, he wrote to David Masson to the effect that Art is not Art *rather than* Nature, insisting that 'the Art of Novels is to represent Nature; to convey as strongly as possible the sentiment of reality'. Indeed, the very critics who have objected to his 'spoiling' the impression of life have done so on the grounds that what is spoilt is a quality of realisation seldom exceeded by other novelists. In his own day Thackeray was said to have done more for the establishment of realism in the novel than any other writer; it is ironic that he should since have been criticised for destroying what he created.

The narrator – who, after all, is as finely realised as Becky Sharp! – is a part of the created world of *Vanity Fair*, but his relationship with the reader is different from that of the other characters who stand at a farther remove. By virtue of his vivid realisation Thackeray created two dimensions, putting the narrator in a position from which he can withdraw out of sight and hearing at important moments in the story, taking the liberty at times of stepping forward to join the puppets, at others of stepping back and joining us.

THE LONG-EARED NARRATOR

The question of what Thackeray intended to effect by creating this intrusive narrator is bound up with the other question of why he chose, in the preface and throughout the novel, to stress the fact that the characters were puppets in a puppet show which was being played in a world which was not the world of the narrator and the contemporary reader. The answer to both questions is to be found in the work of Thomas Carlyle.

The cover of the original parts of *Vanity Fair* bore a design [reproduced in Part Three above – Ed.] of a narrator, in motley and a long-eared cap, standing on an upturned tub and addressing an audience as long-eared as himself. Both Kathleen Tillotson and Thackeray's biographer, Gordon Ray, have pointed out that this design is a reference to a passage in Carlyle's essay 'On Biography', published in *Fraser's Magazine* in 1832. Carlyle attacked the emptiness of contemporary novels but qualified his attack by saying that even the worst of them might contain something:

Of no given book, not even a Fashionable Novel, can you predicate with certainty that its vacuity is absolute; that there are not other vacuities which shall partially replenish themselves therefrom, and esteem it a *plenum*. How knowest thou, may the distressed Novelwright exclaim, that I, here where I sit, am the Foolishest of existing mortals; that this my Long-ear of a Fictitious Biography shall not find one and the other, into whose still longer ears it may be the means, under Providence, of instilling somewhat? We answer None knows, none can certainly know: therefore, write on, worthy Brother, even as thou canst, even as it has been given thee.

Thackeray refers to this passage again in chapter 8 of *Vanity Fair* when he is speaking of the 'humbugs and falsenesses and pretensions' which abound in Vanity Fair and about which even he, the long-eared narrator of a novel, must be truthful.

THE MEANING OF VANITY

It does not seem to have been suggested that there is more behind Thackeray's reference to Carlyle's essay than a mock-modest protest of his own seriousness of purpose. But in Carlyle's essay on J. W. Croker's edition of Boswell's *Life of Johnson*, to which the essay 'On Biography' was meant to serve as a preface, there is a passage which suggests a much deeper relationship than this. In this passage Carlyle speaks of great men and contrasts them with ordinary people:

. . . while others hovered and swam along, in the grand Vanity Fair of
the world, blinded by the mere Shows of things, these saw into the
Things themselves, and could walk as men having an eternal lode star
and with their feet on the sure paths. Thus was there a *Reality* in their
existence; something of a perennial character; in virtue of which indeed
it is that the memory of them is perennial. Whoso belongs only to his
own age, and reverences only *its* gilt Popinjays or soot-smeared Mumbo
jumbos, must needs die with it: though he have been crowned seven
times in the Capitol . . . there was nothing universal, nothing eternal in
him; he must fade away, even as the Popinjay-gildings and Scarecrow-
apparel, which he could not see through.   (Carlyle, 'Boswell's *Life of
Johnson*', 1832.)

Thackeray told us that the title of *Vanity Fair* came to him during
the night with no warning and no apparent associations, but it is
not necessary that we should attempt to prove that a passage
which he must have read was in his mind when he wrote the
novel. The important thing is that this passage from Carlyle
suggests the most basic intention that Thackeray had in writing
Vanity Fair.

'Vanity' in this novel is not to be taken as having simply a
biblical reference such as that which we see in Bunyan's *Pilgrim's
Progress* where the idea of the Fair originated. The word refers to
a concept fundamentally allied to that which is involved in the
passage from Carlyle – it suggests that those who seek it are
fundamentally godless and are living their lives without
directing their energies in a fruitful way. According to Carlyle's
interpretation of life, Amelia would be a creature who was
seeking after Vanity because she worshipped something unreal,
and Dobbin would be so because he sought for happiness and
expected to find it by means of another human being.

This leads to the explanation of why Thackeray spoke of his
characters as puppets rather than as men and women – because
according to the attitude to life which his reading of Carlyle had
helped him to, none of the characters acquire the status of human
beings; all are puppets in a very real sense, driven by their own
desires rather than purposefully seeking an object worthy of the
devotion of complete men and women. From time to time certain
of them realise the direction in which they are being impelled and

have sufficient strength of character, to alter their course. For others an essential poverty of nature makes it impossible to do anything but hover and swim along on the tide of their own desires. . . .

In *Vanity Fair* we are not always conscious of the narrator, but there is never any attempt made to make us forget that he is in charge of the story. The great scenes are delivered as 'great scenes', are part of the showmanship of the narrator and something in which he takes a proper pride. He is even aware of – and makes sure that we are aware of – the periodic climaxes which the novel owes to the fact of its being published in parts. He plays with the reader's involvement and curiosity, commenting on various ways of relating the events and sometimes deliberately holding back information or giving it before, in the 'normal' course of events, it would have become due. Throughout the novel there is a tension between our sense that the story is going on before us, in its own present tense, and our sense that only the telling is going on before us, the story having occurred in the past.

This tension was the result of Thackeray's most basic intention in writing the novel. He wanted to create the impression that while the present of the characters and their actions was real and substantial, yet it was, in another sense, unreal and insubstantial. The miseries of the characters are very real to them, but according to the terminology found in the work of Carlyle to which Thackeray refers us they are no more than shadows, their world no more than an empty show. Sedley's pathetic attempts to restore himself; Amelia's grief for George; Osborne's frustrated love; Becky's dilemma of being forced by her own desires to seek something which cannot satisfy her: all these things are the result of a basic failure in the characters who inhabit Vanity Fair to free themselves from the domination of their own desires and to adjust themselves to reality. Consequently Thackeray put the narrator between the characters and the reader and used him just as he used other devices of style and construction to create his novel, a glittering, shifting and yet ultimately most solid masterpiece.

SOURCE: extracts from *Thackeray* (London, 1968) pp. 67– 71, 75–6.

Edgar F. Harden

THE DISCIPLINE AND SIGNIFICANCE OF FORM IN *VANITY FAIR* (1967)

Almost all critics of *Vanity Fair* have assumed that Thackeray's novel had no very carefully worked out structure and have been content to make rather general comments on the form of the novel: it was loosely improvised along the line of a contrast between Becky and Amelia. J. Y. T. Greig, for example, believes that Thackeray not only lacked Fielding's ability to work out a highly detailed plot but also suffered from the additional handicap of being forced to compose hurriedly for monthly serialization. To Greig, '*Vanity Fair* is unified and shapely up to and including the episodes of Brussels and the Battle of Waterloo: for although it contains two heroines, the adventures and sufferings of the one are causally related to the adventures and sufferings of the other. It becomes unified and shapely again after chapter 43 (Pumpernickel), and for the same reason. But in between – roughly 300 pages – the plot of the first and last sections of the book is suspended, and the unity of the novel disappears.'[1]

These statements raise a number of issues that invite special comment. In the first place, a causal relationship between the adventures and sufferings of Becky and those of Amelia is almost totally nonexistent prior to the reunion of the married couples in Brighton (ch. 22). Up to that point, the adventures of the two girls had led them to Russell Square and agreeable hours with Jos and George, but after that, the sole causal relationship had occurred when Amelia's position as George's fiancée caused him snobbishly to prevent Becky's entering the family by marrying Jos; George's deliberate attempt to embarrass the suffering Vauxhall carouser on the morning after caused Jos's headlong flight to Cheltenham (ch. 6). Between chapters 6 and 25, there is no causal connection whatever between the two plots. Furthermore, though Becky's later success in gaining entry to the household of Jos and Amelia indeed isolates Amelia (ch. 66) and places her in jeopardy (ch. 67), there are few other effects; Thackeray is at pains to show that Amelia wrote the crucial letter to Dobbin before Becky urged her to do so and produced George's note.

Indeed, there is no necessity for an intimate causal relationship between the two plots of any novel, especially this one. The thematic significance of *Vanity Fair* depends not on any such causal relationship but on parallels among the lives of its characters. The novel's structure shows careful planning and an intricate linking of details. Furthermore, such phenomena as the exigencies of serial publication and Thackeray's tardiness, which critics like Greig so easily assume to be causes of poor artistry, require further study and interpretation. Almost alone among critics of Thackeray, Mrs. Tillotson has argued that 'the serial novel, serially written, is . . . really the less likely to be loose and rambling.'[2] While acknowledging that Thackeray's continuing journalistic efforts required considerable time, and remembering that his labors for each monthly part included the creation of drawings for two steel engravings and a number of woodcuts, one might also suggest that Thackeray's frequent struggles at the end of the month can justly be seen not simply as the result of indolence and the cause of poor workmanship, but perhaps equally as evidence of agonizing efforts to write a well-ordered serial novel.

Since we have little surviving evidence of Thackeray's practices in composing *Vanity Fair*, except for the manuscript in the Morgan Library that preserves twelve of the first thirteen chapters, we must turn to the printed text and study it primarily as a serial publication. When we do, we discover evidence that revises our opinion of Thackeray's method and permits a deeper awareness of the relationship between theme and structure in *Vanity Fair*. So far, the two chief studies of unity in Thackeray have been by Geoffrey Tillotson and Myron Taube. Tillotson believes that although none of Thackeray's novels reveals the wonders of plot construction found in *Tom Jones*, 'Thackeray had it in him to have made a big intricate unity.'[3] In writing *Vanity Fair*, Thackeray very possibly had no more than a sketch of the general plot, which he fleshed out as he went along (hence, for example, the repeated postponement of Waterloo), but as Gordon Ray has shown, he did know his direction long in advance.[4] The question then becomes one of method: exactly how did he go about organizing the novel?

Tillotson asserts that in Thackeray's novels the reader finds 'continuity' (p. 20), a oneness of subject, form, and manner, while Taube explains[5] that *Vanity Fair* abandons the traditional unity of plot and instead finds coherence in a new principle: the contrast of characters and their actions. Each monthly number concentrates on revealing the characters and does so by providing us with a complete set of contrasts. Except for the misleading assertion that the contrasts come 'complete' (p. 131) in each number, these statements are true, though they still leave the novel with only an intermittent regularity. Taube has emphasized the pairings *within* individual numbers, but further examination of the work leads to a more radical discovery. Although it has been claimed that Thackeray's novel lacks the kind of design that keeps the reader aware of its overall unity,[6] the fundamental argument of this paper is the exact reverse. *Vanity Fair* has a thorough-going pattern that specifically pairs and groups successive installments, carefully linking one serial part to another with multiple and rhythmic connections. As the original subtitle implies, sketch is matched with sketch, portrait with portrait, and action with action.

We do not know exactly when Thackeray began planning or writing *Vanity Fair*; we can merely observe that the surviving fragment of text in the Morgan manuscript appears to have been started by early 1845, about two years prior to the beginning of serial publication. Some time before 8 May a portion of the novel had been submitted to Henry Colburn with inconclusive results, but Thackeray had found a publisher by January 1846; the novel's appearance was subsequently deferred from May of that year until January 1847. The point is that after the original period of incubation Thackeray had a considerable length of time for further thought, during which he found a new principle of design. Although Thackeray's manuscript in the Morgan Library shows numerous revisions, one stands out: the writing and insertion of chapter 5, 'Dobbin of Ours', into an older version of the text. This addition was crucial, for thereby Thackeray committed himself to the pattern of the novel as we now have it.[7] Chapter 5 makes a vital connection with chapter 1 and so begins the symmetrical arrangement of monthly parts that represents Thackeray's most interesting contribution to the form of the serial novel. The outline (see Appendix) indicates this structure. Though the schema has a cumulative weight, such an extreme condensation of materials limits the conclusiveness of the arguments. The outline, therefore, is intended to serve as a guide through the complicated detail; its implications will be discussed below.

The parallel structure of the first two numbers has been recognized, though not in a sufficiently exact way. Professor and Mrs. Tillotson, for example, offer thematic justification for chapter 5 and briefly explain how the structure of the new number recalls that of its predecessor by balancing Swishtail's against Miss Pinkerton's and showing how the schoolboy relations and snobberies extend into the adult world (p. xix). One might add that the prominent mock-heroic tone[8] also enforces the parallelism between the two chapters, as does the satire on English schools and school life. Yet there are also a number of specific parallels that provoke comparison and contrast. In chapter 1, Amelia's character and popularity contrast with Becky's character and unpopularity; the same antithesis exists in chapter 5 between Cuff and Dobbin. Therefore, in comparing the two underdogs, we see the pointed difference between Becky and Dobbin, which is further developed in these two chapters and later. In chapter 1, when Miss Pinkerton is bidding farewell to Amelia, Becky enters and disrupts the parting; in chapter 5, when Cuff is beating George, Dobbin intervenes to defend the victim. The first climax in chapter 1 consists of a battle between Becky and her mock-heroic opponent, Miss Pinkerton; the

Dobbin – Cuff engagement obviously recalls that incident, not only by being another battle, but because both Becky and Dobbin are struggling against domineering bullies after having had an indecisive encounter with their rivals previously. Becky's 'little battle' with Miss Pinkerton is fought for baser motives, of course, and with crueller weapons. She gains her object-ive – freedom – and then insults Miss Pinkerton amusingly but also gratuitously, snobbishly, and with malice.

This characterization of Becky is reinforced in the second climax and its parallels: after Becky sweepingly rejects Miss Jemima's generous if simple-minded present of the dictionary, events in chapter 5 twice serve to contrast with her gesture. Cuff magnanimously offers assistance to Dobbin, who blushingly accepts it; as an indirect result, Dobbin receives a prize-book in Becky's 'mother-tongue' and generously responds by giving a tuck-out for the whole school. The only section[9] of either chapter that does not fit into a joint pattern is the ending of chapter 5, which carries forward from the conclusion of the first number the movement towards Vauxhall. The final important fact to observe, however, is that Thackeray has begun a practice he will repeat: a suspension of chronological development allows him not only to offer information retrospectively but to present material in a sequence parallel to that of an earlier number. Almost the whole of chapter 5 manifests this practice.

The middle of the first number, chapters 2 and 3, might be entitled 'The Opening of the Campaign Against Joseph Sedley'; its counterpart, chapter 6, relates the close of that campaign. We begin with two coach rides, one to Russell Square and one to Vauxhall, and then slip into two retrospective sections: the narrator's unfavorable account of Becky's past, including her attempts on the Reverend Mr. Crisp, and, in chapter 6, a survey of foolishly favorable attitudes towards a match between Becky and Jos. After arriving in Russell Square and touring the Sedley house, Amelia gives Becky presents and important information about Jos's financial and bachelor status; the section ends as Becky silently vows to catch Jos. After the arrival at Vauxhall in chapter 6, Becky also goes on a tour, this time with Amelia's brother through the gardens; though Becky encourages Jos all she can, here it is his intention that remains unspoken, and so her vow of chapter 2 remains unfulfilled. The ironic point of this comic pairing seems clear: his blundering is a match for her cunning.

In chapter 3, Mr. Sedley's mocking of Jos's appearance seriously alarms the timid dandy, but when in chapter 6 George more selfishly and elaborately makes fun of Jos's behavior, the effect is even more unsettling. Mr. Sedley's action, though coarse, contrasts favorably with George's conduct, for the young man's motives are as snobbish and pompous as anything in the behavior of his victim. George's mimicry, of course, rasps on the tender nerves of the bacchanalian, who is not mollified as in chapter 3; but left alone to ponder on his ludicrousness. Consequently, while Becky could quickly recover from the embarrassments of curry and chili, Jos finds the aftereffects of rack-punch and mockery more agonizing and enduring: he stays in bed all day and dares not return to Russell Square. Therefore, while chapter 3 ends with only a temporary setback for Becky, who fruitlessly awaits the timid Jos in the drawing-room upstairs, chapter 6 comes to a climax as Amelia watches George approach her father's house while Becky looks out in vain for Jos. In place of the tip-toeing Jos departing from Russell Square in chapter 3, we have Jos's note announcing his departure from London without calling again; it is then Becky who must leave Russell Square permanently.

The concluding chapter of Number Two ironically establishes Sir Pitt Crawley and, to a lesser degree, his younger son as counterparts to Mr. Sedley and Jos. In chapter 4, Jos had arrived at Russell Square to begin a new, if limited, series of adventures with Becky; chapter 7 begins as Becky arrives in Great Gaunt Street for an introduction to a new and considerable series of experiences. The analogies are all comically inverted: here the place at a prosperous table of the coarsely jesting Mr. Sedley, whose notion of placating his victim consists of offering him excellent champagne, is taken by the coarsely jesting Sir Pitt, offering Becky a drop of beer, demanding his pint for carrying her baggage, and finally apportioning out the penurious fare of tripe and onion.

The thunderstorm which keeps the young people indoors in chapter 4 leads to a cheerful evening at Russell Square, as Jos entertains Becky with long stories about India amid the festive accompaniments of music and refreshments, while in chapter 7 Becky spends a much more quiet evening in the dark house on Great Gaunt Street, though she finds entertainment in listening to Sir Pitt's extended confidences. The two numbers end as Jos fails to propose while bound in Becky's green silk skein but prepares himself for Vauxhall by vowing to 'pop the question' there; in chapter 7 after the failure of her campaign against Jos, Becky looks toward a new quarry and prepares for Queen's Crawley by choosing to dream of Rawdon. Apparently a short passage was needed to fill out the second number, since the lament for things past has no counterpart in Number One. Thackeray makes his addition relevant by casting the passage in a melancholy tone and adopting his characteristic point of view, the retrospective vision, which culminates here in the cry: *ubi sunt?* Just as the Gardens in which Jos prepared for an imaginary future with Becky have now passed away, so too the evanescence of Becky's conveyance, as she moves towards her insubstantial future, has been revealed by time.

After indicating his novel's structure by this obvious pairing of the first two monthly numbers, Thackeray went on to elaborate his technique, grouping most of the numbers together in pairs and gathering the rest, on two occasions, into units of three. Unlike most subsequent readers, his original audience did not have the disadvantage of reading an edition that ignored the novel's division into serial parts. Consequently, Thackeray could count on some recognition of *Vanity Fair*'s structure. For the less observant reader, he added overt cross-references between the grouped numbers.

One such obvious link connecting Numbers Three, Four, and Five can be found at the end of chapters 7, 12, and 15, where the narrator comments on his own role. In Number Three, he asks us to recognize the difference between him and his characters so that we may be fully aware of his moral purpose: 'to combat and expose' folly and evil while approving goodness. In Number Four, we are requested to observe the distinction between selfishness and idolatry. While 'shift, self, and poverty' instruct Becky and find their emblem in the orange blossoms of mercenary attachments, and while Amelia is guilty of an extravagant hero-worship, yet if we understand the superiority of the warm-hearted excess over the coldly calculating one, we can adequately sympathize with Amelia's love for George and value 'this blind devotion', for it is directed towards another human being instead of solely towards one's self. At this point the narrator reminds us of his omniscience and his ability to play a dual part, but renounces the betraying role of Iachimo for the approving role of Moonshine, since Amelia's love reflects faith, beauty, and innocence, in contrast to the 'Faithless, Hopeless, Charityless' rogues of chapters 8, 12, and – as we are about to see – 15.

In the corresponding portion of Number Five, the narrator explicitly recalls this passage while talking about Becky: 'If, a few pages back, the present writer claimed the privilege of peeping into Miss Amelia Sedley's bed-room, and understanding with the omniscience of the novelist all the gentle pains and passions which were tossing upon that innocent pillow, why should he not declare himself to be Rebecca's confidante too, master of her secrets, and seal-keeper of that young woman's conscience?' Now, however, he goes on to expose rather than sympathize and approve. Moreover, by recalling the earlier passage, itself connected to the one at the end of chapter 7, in effect he asks us to compare the three of them and to notice how he applies the original purpose (ch. 7) to approve behavior in chapter 12 and to undermine it in chapter 15. Amelia, we are told in chapter 12, has 'not a well-regulated mind'; instead of acting in a well-regulated and, by implication, selfish way, she manifests the genuine feeling that makes selfish, patterned behavior seem empty and worthless. As a result of this tripartite structure, we can now, in chapter 15, understand those passages fully, for we again see the desire to serve one's self by worldly attachment; this time Becky manifests it and the ironic narrator calls such a desire the wish of a 'properly regulated mind'. When Becky regrets that she had to decline such 'a piece of marvellous good fortune' as marriage to Sir Pitt, we see the orange-blossom mentality at work again. Only, this time, instead of sympathizing with its opposite, the narrator emphasizes the shortcomings of selfishness. Becky's hasty choice of the impecunious Rawdon when she might have had the baronet clearly reveals how the calculations of human beings are inevitably limited by the incalculable. Therefore, we are placed in a position to evaluate, as Becky cannot in her eager greed, the improbability of her hope for Rawdon's future and for Miss Crawley's money.

Another example of the narrator's openly calling attention to a parallelism of successive monthly units occurs in Numbers Twelve and Thirteen. The subject is a series of contrasts between the Osborne and Sedley households. Chapter 43 opens with pictures of Osborne's tyranny and unhappiness, while chapter 46 shows us Sedley's dependency and unhappiness. Fred Bullock's mercenary behavior is set off by Clapp's faithful attachment, and Maria's coldness to her father by Amelia's devotion to her son. We then shift to a completely overt parallelism as the narrator recalls Jane Osborne's 'awful existence', caused especially by her father's continuing estrangement from young George and his growing rage at his other grandchildren: 'We have seen how one of George's grandfathers . . ., in his easy chair in Russell Square, daily grew more violent and moody, and how his daughter, with her fine carriage, and her fine horses, and her name on half the public charity lists of the town, was a lonely, miserable, persecuted old maid.' Now, however, Osborne is about to relent towards George, and so towards Jane. The purpose of the narrator's cross-reference, therefore, is to remind us of what prompts Osborne's brooding tyranny and to highlight its reversal: Jane sees young George and tells Osborne at the end of Number Twelve, while at the end of Number Thirteen, Osborne himself sees the boy and Amelia comes to believe that young George's future is properly with his wealthy grandfather. To understand one number fully, we have to retain a consciousness of its paired predecessor.

We are assisted in doing so by Thackeray's illustrations as well as by his text. In numbers Six and Seven, for example, the growth and diminution of George's devotion to Amelia is governed primarily by the presence of other women, as the engraving of Miss Swartz and that of the 'Family Party at Brighton' remind us. Likewise in Number Sixteen, to epitomize young George's life in Osborne's house and to emphasize the epistolary connection to

Numbers Fourteen and Fifteen, Thackeray provides an engraving that depicts the young sybarite taking up a letter from a tray being held out to him. In Numbers Seventeen and Eighteen the happy reunion of Dobbin and Amelia, captured in part by a steel engraving, is matched and developed by their happiness together in Germany, with its engraving, 'A Fine Summer Evening'.

As we make these connections between numbers, we discover that the effects produced by Thackeray's technique are infinitely varied. At one point, for example, the eighth and ninth numbers focus on a series of contrasts between individual characters: Amelia's wifely incompetence and Mrs. O'Dowd's capable preparations; Amelia's melancholy response to marriage and Rawdon's joyous one; and finally, George's collection and then dispersal of his inheritance versus Rawdon's presentation of his effects to Becky and her calculation of their worth. This series ends with a widening of scope: morning approaches as the transports load for departure to Belgium, and it arrives as the regiment marches off to war. At another point, we find the most famous use of pairing: to produce the effect of shocking contrast of events. Number Eight ends with dawn, as the city awakes, and the first major section of the novel is brought to a close with the last (revised) words of Number Nine: 'Darkness came down on the field and city: and Amelia was praying for George, who was lying on his face, dead, with a bullet through his heart.' Thackeray also uses parallels for the purpose of alternating contrasts and comparisons, as he does in connecting Numbers Three, Four, and Five. Pitt's ambition (ch. 9) establishes a value with which we contrast Amelia's love (ch. 13) and compare the selfish ambitions of Becky and Mrs. Bute (ch. 16). Sir Pitt's prosperity then finds lateral counterparts in Osborne's dominance and, ironically, in Miss Crawley's hysteria and Sir Pitt's impotent rage when they discover the identity of Becky's husband.

The development of action may also occur laterally and produce rhythmic sequences. After the new Sir Pitt's familial letter to Rawdon and his check for little Rawdon, we note Becky's delight at the first acknowledgment and then compare her use of the second, which reveals more clearly how financially

'unsafe' her position is. We observe a worsening also in a
succeeding parallel: in chapter 40, Becky frees herself from her
husband's company and attention by securing a 'house-dog',
Briggs; in chapter 44, the servants have come to believe her guilty
of using that liberty to establish an adulterous relationship with
Steyne. The two visits of Becky and Rawdon to Queen's Crawley
continue the pattern: in chapter 41, Becky conciliates both Sir
Pitt and Lady Jane, but she is not so successful with Lady Jane on
her next visit (ch. 45). In chapters 20 and 24, Dobbin arranges
George's marriage in the former and tells Osborne about it in the
corresponding portion of the latter. Whereas George's vanity is
flattered by Amelia's love, his father's vanity is first flattered by
the false expectation of surrender and then balked by the news of
George's marriage. In addition, Sedley's senile anger and empty
prohibition find their more extreme and effective counterparts in
Osborne's violent rage and alteration of his will. Even their facial
appearances suggest each other: Sedley's ghastly expression at
hitting Osborne a blow and Osborne's 'strange look' at having
dealt with George.

One should note especially that the novelist could accomplish
this parallelism only by distorting the narrative sequence, and
that such a distortion suggests the strength of Thackeray's wish to
achieve symmetry and rhythmic progression of the narrative.
Instead of ending Number Six with, say, a condensed version of
chapter 23 culminating in the avenging thunderclap at the door,
Thackeray chooses to end it by shifting to Brighton. Consequently, chapters 23 and 24, which deal with Dobbin's efforts
in London and parallel the structure of chapters 19 and 20,
constitute a flashback. Admittedly, several additional reasons
may be offered to explain this particular distortion, the most
plausible of which seems to be that Thackeray had already
decided on the conclusion of Number Seven and therefore wished
to end Number Six with mention of the move towards Belgium;
repeated evidence also makes clear, however, that doubling back
appears at such times and is conducted in such a way as to
preserve and take advantage of the structural pattern outlined in
this essay.

At one point the narrator calls attention to his maneuver and emphasizes its plausibility: 'Our history is destined in this chapter to go backwards and forwards in a very irresolute manner seemingly, and having conducted our story to to-morrow presently, we shall immediately again have occasion to step back to yesterday, so that the whole of the tale may get a hearing.' Insofar as this narrative retrospection is a comic 'disorder', however, it is a disorder related to the war – in fact, caused by the war:

Although all the little incidents must be heard, yet they must be put off when the great events make their appearance; and surely such a circumstance as that which brought Dobbin to Brighton, viz. the ordering out of the Guards and the line to Belgium, and the mustering of the allied armies in that country under the command of his Grace the Duke of Wellington – such a dignified circumstance as that, I say, was entitled to the *pas* over all minor occurrences whereof this history is composed mainly, and hence a little trifling disarrangement and disorder was excusable and becoming. [ch. 25]

The narrative disorder is only seeming, of course, and has its various effects. Amid the comedy we already have an ironic foreshadowing: when we come to observe the disarrangement and disorder caused by the war, they will be neither 'excusable', 'becoming', nor, ultimately, 'trifling', but they and not the 'dignified' circumstances will, as usual, constitute the novel's subject matter and interest. Consequently, in terms of the narrative structure, 'dignified' circumstances and the events of men's little peacetime pursuits each take their appropriate place; as the mocking tone of the passage indicates, though the former may ostensibly take precedence, the latter will comment on them and reduce their significance at last, as we shall see at the end of Number Seven, for example. The climax of Number Seven balances and undercuts the 'dignified circumstance' which concludes Number Six, for the news of the army being ordered to Belgium finds its ironic structural equivalent in the news of money which sends Becky and Rawdon to London. The mixture of discomfiture and amusement, success and failure, which we see at the end of this portion of the novel suggests also what the war will bring to all these characters, and such appears to be the passage's ultimate purpose.

Looking at *Vanity Fair* from a more distant standpoint, we can see nine blocks of material that fall into groups of four and five, the demarcation coming after the battle of Waterloo. The first block begins with the departure from Chiswick Mall and the opening of the campaign against Jos (Number One); it concludes with the close of the campaign against him and with Becky's subsequent departure from London (Number Two). Block Two commences as Becky establishes herself with Sir Pitt (Number Three) and concludes as Amelia is accepted by George (Number Five). Unsuccessful efforts to conciliate Miss Crawley begin and close the third block, while the fourth moves from England to Waterloo. In short, the first portion of the novel rises to a climax in its middle, which is found in the unique block of three numbers. Actually we find a double climax: first comes the revelation that Becky has a husband; then Number Five, the center of these nine numbers, reveals his identity and triumphantly concludes with Amelia's success in getting a husband, thereby preparing for the climax of Number Nine when she loses him.

This larger movement, first toward the success represented by marriage and then away from it to complete separation, is reversed in the last five-ninths of the novel, and in terms of an elaborate counter-rhythm. This time there is a central block and it consists of the only other unit comprising three numbers; moreover, the symmetry is utterly precise, for the climax occurs in the middle number of the central block, Number Fifteen, when Becky's marriage is permanently disrupted. This event is thus the negative counterpart of Block Two's climax. The novel's concluding movement then develops Amelia's success, as she now finds her second husband. Here is the positive counterpart of Amelia's loss of George at the end of Block Four (Number Nine). Since Becky began the pattern of rejections in chapter 1, it remains in chapter 67 only for Dobbin and Amelia to reject her.[10] In an overall as well as closely detailed sense, therefore, *Vanity Fair* shows thorough 'unity' and 'shapeliness', to adopt the terms and values of Greig and others critical of Thackeray's craftsmanship.

Thackeray never again organized a novel quite so elaborately, and his subsequent works themselves suggest reasons why. Perhaps after mastering the exacting compositional requirements of a novel published in parts, he found the intricacy of *Vanity Fair*'s pattern too demanding; it is certain, however, that the particular method of this work is not nearly so appropriate for his later serial novels because they do not offer the contrasts produced by a continuous double plot. Though his next serial, *Pendennis* (1848–50), is also a novel without a 'hero', it does have one main character and it follows his adventures with a single-mindedness absent from *Vanity Fair*. The same is true in varying degrees of *The Newcomes* (1853–5), each half of *The Virginians* (1857–9), and the late shorter works: *Lovel the Widower* (1860), *Philip* (1861–2), and *Denis Duval* (1864), all three of which appeared in the looser confines of a periodical. We can still see traces of the lateral pattern in *Pendennis*, but not in *The Newcomes* nor in any work written after *Henry Esmond* (1852). *Esmond*, of course, reverts to the older kind of plot mastered by Fielding and remains independent of the demands made by publication in parts; as a regression in this sense, it helps mark a permanent change in Thackeray's writing habits.

Instead, then, of developing an elaborate plot in *Vanity Fair*, Thackeray offers us two loose plots with highly articulated connections. The functions of such a pattern seem apparent. A writer still making the transition from journalism to novel-writing and beginning an ambitious attempt to construct a full, twenty-layered work – according to the standards set by Dickens[11] – apparently needed the restraints imposed by this new form. Although Thackeray had previously written fiction for serialization, he had now to deal with the immense difference between writing for periodical publication in a magazine and for serialization in separate monthly numbers; the difference, in a word, is uniformity in length. As a glance at *Fraser's Magazine* will show, none of Thackeray's fiction before *Vanity Fair* had appeared in equal installments. For example, the installments of

Catherine (1839–40) varied between nine and eighteen pages, those of *A Shabby Genteel Story* (1840), between twelve and sixteen, those of *The Great Hoggarty Diamond* (1841), between eleven and twenty, and those of *Barry Lyndon* (1844), between twelve and twenty pages. Even in *Barry Lyndon*, the work which offers closest parallel as an extended novel, where his apparent goal was one sheet of sixteen pages, he achieved that length only five times out of eleven, missing on the other occasions by one, three, four, four, two, and two pages. Such inconsistency by one contributor, of course, did not much matter to a magazine editor, who needed only to produce an issue of 126 pages, whatever the length of its individual pieces might be.

But the writer of a novel whose parts each had to fill thirty-two pages, a length doubling the former chance of error, now had to be exactly right. If he ran slightly short, he could use woodcuts or a tailpiece to fill up space, but he could not run too short or print a text that ran over. The procedure Thackeray chose enabled him to 'time' his installments, for he had a repetitive sequence. The pattern, however, permitted the novelist considerable latitude. One of its most important functions was to provide useful guidelines for fresh achievement, since the material of one number furnished the basis for its counterpart. The writer had his pattern; he could then work out the major analogies, expanding and supplementing them as he saw fit and as imagination suggested.

Its most immediate usefulness was to the writer himself, but because paired numbers had the same internal rhythm, he could not only 'time' installments while writing them but also expect his audience consciously and unconsciously to make the same lateral connections – even across a month's time, since the number was the unit of memory, and especially because he so obviously paired the first two numbers and made overt cross-references between subsequent groups. Although the physical form of almost all editions puts the reader at a disadvantage by failing to indicate *Vanity Fair*'s part-structure, if he is aware of the serial parts he can appreciate their important function, for besides providing considerable artistic discipline, the pattern of juxtaposition itself reveals the novel's meaning: the thematic effect of detailed parallelism between two or three monthly numbers emerges as the latter regularly recalls and comments on the former, and so provides a comment on itself. More broadly, the structure emphasizes that, in spite of the differences in men and their lives, all the inhabitants of Vanity Fair are ultimately circumscribed by an inescapable pattern of sameness that epitomizes their most fundamental significance.

[For APPENDIX see pp. 205–13–Ed.]

NOTES

1. J. Y. T. Greig, *Thackeray: A Reconsideration* (London and New York, 1950) p. 106. See also such appraisals as Anthony Trollope, *Thackeray* (1879; reprinted 1902) p. 96; Charles Whibley, *William Makepeace Thackeray* (1903) pp. 91–2 [see Part Two of this volume for Trollope and Whibley extracts–Ed.]; George Saintsbury, *A Consideration of Thackeray* (London, 1931) p. 166; and John W. Dodds, *Thackeray: A Critical Portrait* (New York, 1963) p. 110.

2. K. Tillotson, *Novels of the Eighteen-Forties* (Oxford, 1956) pp. 239–40 [See Part Four above–Ed.].

3. G. Tillotson, *Thackeray the Novelist* (London, 1963) p. 12.

4. Gordon N. Ray, *Thackeray: The Uses of Adversity* (New York, 1955) pp. 406–9, 499.

5. Myron Taube, 'Contrast as a Principle of Structure in *Vanity Fair*', XVIII (1963) 119–35.

6. G. Tillotson, *Thackeray the Novelist*, p. 49.

7. For a summary of the evidence covering this two-year period, see Ray, *Uses of Adversity*, pp. 384–7, 494–5; and G. and K. Tillotson's edition of *Vanity Fair* (London and Boston, Mass., 1963), Introduction, pp. xvii–xxi, xxvii–xxix. [The Tillotsons' discussion of this aspect is not included in the extract presented in Part Three above–Ed.].

8. For a discussion of the mock-heroic tone and its function is these two chapters and later, see E. F. Harden, 'The Fields of Mars in *Vanity Fair*', *Tennessee Studies in Literature*, x (1965) 123–32.

9. I use the term 'section' in referring to those portions of each chapter that are marked off by a break in the text. Chapter 5, for example, has

four sections, the last of which is one of the relatively few sections that has no counterpart in a paired number. Though chapter 1 has only two sections, it offers parallels to three sections of chapter 5, just as the three chapters of Number Two pair off with the four chapters of Number One.

10. Contrast the admiring but inaccurate description by Lord David Cecil in *Early Victorian Novelists* (London, 1934) p. 80.

11. See K. Tillotson, *Novels of the Eighteen-Forties*, p. 29; and John Butt and K. Tillotson, *Dickens at Work* (London, 1963) p. 14.

APPENDIX

[In this reproduction of Professor Harden's schema, the numbering convention (roman numerals, lower case) of the original serialised publication is retained, with arabic numbers added in parentheses to facilitate reference to chapter-citations elsewhere in this volume – Ed.]

Number One

i (1)
education at Miss Pinkerton's
Amelia's popularity; Becky's unpopularity
Miss P's parting with Amelia; Becky enters
battle between Miss P and Becky
Miss Jemima kindly gives dictionary; Becky tosses it back

ii (2)
coach ride to Russell Square
retrospect: narrator's unfavorable account of Becky's past

Amelia and Becky tour house; Becky vows to catch Jos

iii (3)
Mr. Sedley mocks Jos's appearance; Jos alarmed
Becky overcome by curry and chili, but rallies
Becky awaits Jos, who leaves Russell Square

iv (4)
Jos arrives at Russell Square
Mr. Sedley coarsely jesting; offer of champagne
a cheerful evening at Russell Square
Jos prepares for Vauxhall: vows to propose to Becky

Number Two

v (5)
education at Dr. Swishtail's
Cuff's popularity; Dobbin's unpopularity
Cuff beating George; Dobbin intervenes
battle between Cuff and Dobbin
{ Cuff is magnanimous; Dobbin accepts help
{ Dobbin receives prize-book; gives tuck-out for school

vi (6)
coach ride to Vauxhall
retrospect: various favorable views of Becky's and Jos's future together

Jos and Becky tour Vauxhall; Jos fails to propose

George mocks Jos's behavior; Jos alarmed
Jos remains in bed, overcome; fails to call
B awaits Jos, whose note announces departure from London

vii (7)
Becky arrives at Great Gaunt Street
Sir P coarsely jesting; offer of beer; request for beer
a quiet evening in gloomy Great Gaunt Street
B prepares for Q's Crawley: chooses to dream of Rawdon

Number Three	Number Four	Number Five
viii (8) Becky settles at Queen's Crawley B's amusement and satire re Crawleys	xii (12) Amelia rejected by fashionable ladies Amelia's timidity and hero-worship	xv (15) Becky offered protection at QC by Sir P Becky's affected modesty re Crawleys
ix (9) Sir Pitt dominant Pitt protects Lady Crawley Pitt's ambition Sir Pitt's prosperity Miss Crawley's monetary security and hence dignity	xiii (13) George dominant Dobbin helps Amelia Amelia's love Osborne's dominance Amelia's doubts, caused by Osborne's mercenary suspicions	xvi (16) Becky dominant Miss Crawley offers Becky protection Becky's ambition; Mrs. Bute's ambition Miss C's hysteria; Sir P's impotent rage Rawdon's monetary doubts; B's confidence
x (10) Becky makes secure her position at Queen's Crawley Rawdon's fortunes vs. Pitt's	George succeeds in getting money from Osborne George's fortunes vs. Sedley's	xvii (17) dispersal of Sedley's effects; Dobbin vs. Becky & Rawdon R's & B's fortunes vs. Mrs. Bute's
xi (11) Mrs. Bute sees threat in Becky's arrival at Queen's Crawley Mrs. Bute promotes Rawdon's interest in Becky B promised as match for father & son	xiv (14) Briggs displaced by Becky's arrival in Park Lane Becky captivates Rawdon, who sees Mrs. Bute's efforts Sir P proposes to B; she already married to son	wviii (18) Europe threatened by Napoleon's landing at Cannes Osborne brutally rejects Sedley and Amelia George proposes to Amelia

Number Six

xix (19)
Mrs. Bute takes command in Park Lane

Mrs. Bute greedily searches out details of Becky's past
Becky & Rawdon appeal to Miss Crawley in the Park

xx (20)
Dobbin arranges George's marriage
George's vanity flattered by Amelia's love

Sedley's senile anger; his *pro forma* prohibition
George respects Amelia as the only lady in O's circle

xxi (21)
Osborne fawns over Miss Swartz
Osborne orders George to secure Miss Swartz
George collects money from Chopper
Geo taken by Amelia's society, offended by Miss Swartz's
George's picture of himself as a noble man of honor
George's oath to marry Amelia

xxii (22)
Osborne's expectations of victory remain unfulfilled
George & Amelia married
Jos's pose deludes him
Becky makes up with George
news of army ordered to Belgium

Number Seven

xxiii (23)
Dobbin becomes George's economic plenipotentiary in London

Dobbin charitably details virtues of George & Amelia
the children pay court to the one with the penny

xxiv (24)
Dobbin tells Osborne of George's marriage
Osborne's vanity flattered by expectation of surrender; balked by George's marriage
Osborne's violent rage; he changes will
Dobbin is the most respected officer in the regiment

xxv (25)
Dobbin attempts to entertain Amelia
letter announcing George is cut off
Becky tells Rawdon to collect from George
George prefers Becky's society to Amelia's
George's picture of himself as a thoughtful husband
Amelia's vow to go to Belgium with George

Mrs. Bute's reign unexpectedly ends
Becky & Briggs reconciled
Becky's letter deludes her
Miss Crawley accepts call from Rawdon
news of money sends Becky & Rawdon to London

Number Eight	Number Nine
xxvi (26) hotel in Cavendish Square; Amelia timid & ignorant effect of marriage on Amelia: melancholy George collects his inheritance & begins its dispersal	xxx (30) O'Dowd's quarters; Mrs. O'D capably serving her husband effect of marriage on Rawdon: happiness Rawdon gives his effects to Becky; she totals her valuables
xxvii (27) George, Amelia, & Jos join the regiment Mrs. O'Dowd in command morning: transports loading for Belgium	Dobbin entrusts Amelia to Jos Amelia helpless morning: regiment marches off to war
xxviii (28) Jos gallantly agrees to escort Amelia abroad Jos gets Belgian servant; Belgian love of commerce Brussels: a perpetual military festival Becky arrives with Tufto; Amelia saddened	xxxi (31) Jos in command at Brussels Isidor's servile greed Brussels: rumors of the war Becky prepares for retreat with Jos; Amelia hostile
xxix (29) Becky's brilliance at opera subdues Amelia & Mrs. O'D	Mrs. O'D replies to B's neglect of Amelia
George's idea of himself as woman-killer Becky triumphs over Amelia at ball; accepts Geo's note George exultant, gambles frantically & wins news that army will march; George returns to quarters George prepares for departure dawn: the city awakes	xxxii (32) Van Cutsum's idea of self as warrior; Jos's as military man B triumphs over Bareacres, rejects note; offers Jos horses Jos frantic, pays immensely news of allied victory at Quatre Bras; Jos remains sound of cannon; Jos flees night: George dead

Number Ten

xxxiii (33)
news of Rawdon's promotion
Becky amuses Miss Crawley with letter from Continent
behavior of Sir Pitt begets scandal
Pitt cultivates Miss Crawley

xxxiv (34)
Pitt & Lady Jane establish themselves with Miss C
Lady Jane artlessly succeeds with Miss Crawley
Pitt's difficulties: Jim as rival; Pitt prevails
B's success in Paris capped by birth of son & heir
Pitt marries & becomes Miss Crawley's heir
Pitt dominated by aunt & mother-in-law

xxxv (35)
George beloved & unforgiven by father
the past: Osborne visits Belgium

Osborne's rigid imperviousness
Osborne's jealous rejection of Amelia and unborn child
Dobbin's devotion
y. George is Amelia's life; Dobbin shut out

Number Eleven

xxxvi (36)
news of Rawdon's quitting Guards & selling out of army
Becky captivates Parisian society
Rawdon's gambling begets unfortunate reputation
Becky deals with Rawdon's creditors

xxxvii (37)
Becky & Rawdon establish themselves with Raggles
B's flippancy in vogue among a certain class in London
Becky's difficulties; Rawdon's threats; Becky prevails
B looks to success in London; sees poss. death of y. Pitt
Pitt inherits Miss C's money; B & R ingratiate themselves
R as Mrs. C's husband; to be replaced by Steyne & companion

y. Rawdon neglected by mother; doted on by father
the future: y. George meets y. Rawdon

xxxviii (38)
Sedley's tottering delusions
Amelia's jealous quarrel with mother over y. George
Dobbin's devotion
y. George is Amelia's life; Dobbin shut out

Number Twelve

xxxix (39)
Mrs. Bute's hypocrisy
Pitt & Lady Jane visit QC; Sir Pitt gives her pearls
Sir Pitt's dotage; Ribbons' delusions
Mrs. Bute takes command on evening of Sir Pitt's stroke

xl (40)
Pitt assumes control of Queen's Crawley
new Sir Pitt's letter to Rawdon
Becky's delight at acknowledgment
Becky's dismissal of y. Rawdon
Becky secures Briggs as moral sheep dog

xli (41)
Becky & Rawdon visit Queen's Crawley

Becky conciliates Sir Pitt and Lady Jane
Jane gives banknote for y. R; Sir P promises education
Sir PCs look forward to seeing R Crawleys in London

xlii (42)
Osborne's tyranny and unhappiness
Bullock's mercenary behavior
Maria's coldness to Osborne
Jane's miserable life vs. Maria's
Osborne ends Jane's relations with Smee
Jane sees y. George & tells Osborne

Number Thirteen

xliii (43)
Lady O'Dowd's tyranny & kindness
Glorvina besieges Dobbin; she gets pink dress
Dobbin's indifference; Glorvina's delusions
Dobbin requests leave on news of Amelia's engagement

xliv (44)
Becky is general-in-chief in Great Gaunt St.
Sir Pitt's check for y. Rawdon
Becky's delight at acknowledgment
Becky's repudiation of y. Rawdon
servants pronounce Becky guilty of adultery

Becky & Rawdon visit Queen's Crawley

xlv (45)
Becky pleases Sir Pitt but not Lady Jane
Sir Pitt gives Rawdon £100
R visits Jane; Sir P visits B; women keep apart

xlvi (46)
Sedley's dependence and unhappiness
Clapp's faithful attachment
Amelia's devotion to y. George
Jane's miserable life vs. Maria's
Osborne accepts Jane's relation with y. George
Osborne sees y. Geo; A believes his future is with O

Number Fourteen	Number Fifteen	Number Sixteen
xlvii (47) Gaunt House & its back door 'natural' oppositions in Steyne family madness of George Gaunt; presentiment haunts Steyne	li (51) Gaunt House & doors it opens for Becky B overcomes inevitable social opposition charades: death, illicit love; illusion & precarious triumphs	liv (54) G. Gaunt St: R enters Sir P's house Mac believes B guilty; seeks reconciliation news about revolution of servants in Mayfair
xlviii (48) B triumphant: presented to King Becky asks Steyne for money to give Briggs & gets it Raggles paid; B puts away rest of money for herself	lii (52) Steyne triumphs: gets place for y. R Steyne amused to discover B's deception but removes Briggs Rawdon becomes attentive to B & stifles doubts	lv (55) B insulted; partly quells rebellion Wenham asserts Steyne's innocence; Mac accepts but returns money Raggles bankrupt; Rawdon goes off to Coventry
xlix (49) Steyne orders invitation to Gaunt House written for Becky & Rawdon Becky ignored by the women; pitied & helped by Steyne's wife	liii (53) Rawdon writes to Becky from spunging-house Rawdon ignored by Becky; pitied & helped by Sir Pitt's wife	lvi (56) y. George fully established in Osborne's house; receives ltrs on silver tray y. George toadied to by schoolmaster & Osborne
l (50) Amelia breaks down re y. Geo under hysterical mother & imprudent father Amelia gives up son; y. George delighted	Becky's pose re Steyne breaks down in front of Rawdon Rawdon leaves Becky; she in state of shock	Amelia bears up under querulous mother & tottering father Dobbin arrives at school with Jos; y. George delighted

Number Seventeen

lvii (57)
lottery of life giving different fates
death of Mrs. Sedley
Dobbin sick but recovers
Jos flattered by D into caring for Amelia & y. George
Dobbin delighted at arriving in England

lviii (58)
disembarkation: Dobbin's journey to London
Dobbin dresses up to see Amelia
Dobbin & Amelia happily reunited
Amelia taken in by y. George

lix (59)
Jos detained at Southampton
Jos conducted to reunion with Sedley
Amelia rejects idea of marriage with Dobbin
Dobbin prompts Jos to establish a fine house

lx (60)
Amelia gets visiting book, page, maid, chariot
Jos goes to court; Amelia stays home

Number Eighteen

lxi (61)
second-floor arch: inevitability of a common fate
death of Sedley
Osborne dies
Jos takes interest in Amelia after inheritance
everyone delighted at departing for Continent

lxii (62)
embarkation: journey to Rotterdam
Jos brings court suit for presentations
Dobbin & Amelia happy together
Amelia educated to see Dobbin's merits

lxiii (63)
Jos decides to stay in Pumpernickel
Jos conducted to audience with Victor Aurelius XVII
Amelia walks a polonaise with Dobbin
vanity prompts Victor Aurelius XIV to build Monplaisir

Becky alone, tattered, losing money
Jos goes gambling & meets Becky

Number Nineteen

lxiv (64)
Becky dispiritedly neglects herself & reputation
Becky gains entrances but is rejected
Becky rejected by Steyne; leaves Rome

lxv (65)
Becky attracts Jos
Dobbin dubious about Becky
reunion between Becky & Amelia

Number Twenty

lxvi (66)
Becky feelingly narrates her misfortunes to Amelia
Amelia decides to accept Becky; Dobbin urges rejection
Amelia refuses to reject Becky; Dobbin breaks away

lxvii (67)
Becky attracts Jos
Becky becomes supporter of Dobbin
reunion between Dobbin & Amelia

SOURCE: essay in *Publications of the Modern Language Association*, LXXXII (1967) 530–41.

Barbara Hardy

RANK AND REVERSAL (1972)

Upper and Lower, Richer and Poorer, Master and Man, Husband and Wife, Rogue and Gull, Prince and Subject, Elder and Younger, Mentor and Pupil: these are some of the social, political and familial pairs into which Thackeray, through social analysis and with dramatic sensibility, groups his characters. To my mind, one source of critical uneasiness[1] about Thackeray's handling of big scenes like the discovery scene in *Vanity Fair* is the separation of Thackeray's art from his social analysis. But I believe his sense of theatre is intricately connected with his classification of social and psychological relations, which he tends to see as part of a power-structure involving class and possessions. He tends also to take great pleasure in the way the social relation works with and also against psychological relations, and such pleasure shows itself in his portrayal of reversals in relationships. At times the reversal involves an insight about particular people in a particular relation to each other, for this is of course fiction, not social typology. But the reversal always concerns a sense of the relative fixity of social roles and relations, though this fixity can be changed or even broken down.

I begin with the famous scene from *Vanity Fair*, which I think needs no defence or apology, only a fuller and closer recognition of its scope and depth in analysis and drama. Thackeray himself drew attention to one detail in the scene when he told James Hannay: 'When I wrote the sentence ['She admired her husband strong, brave, and victorious'], I slapped my fist on the table and said "that is a touch of genius"'.[2]

It is precisely here that Thackeray's power seems most deserving of close scrutiny. There is indeed a sense of moral relief in the spectacle of Rawdon's action, and it involves a pleasure in seeing a favourite but degraded character expand, both morally and physically. Rawdon has long had our approval, for his lovingness, his generosity, his fatherly tenderness, his innocence and his clumsiness. His rakish past, never very clear, has long sunk into a convenient haze, apart from his gambling, and here Becky's manipulation has carried responsibility and blame. In a novel where ascendancy in the pecking order carries such opprobrium – it testifies to the corruption of wit, intelligence, art, and the energies of greed, ambition and social aggression – there is the honourable degree of failure, shared by Rawdon, Briggs, Dobbin and other good innocents. But Thackeray allows us to have our cake and eat it in this reversal of the pecking order, this defeat of Becky and Lord Steyne, this triumph of a virtue sufficiently unideal, unheroic and mixed to attract free approval.

It is a triumph of Thackeray's moral satire that Rawdon's innocence and stupidity should be given this victory. It is a triumph of his psychological insight that the reader's approval should be shared by Becky, sufficiently a woman of her time to enjoy the virile display, even in her husband, and no less for its startling unfamiliarity. Reader's surprise is linked to character's. All this, and more, is felt as a direct consequence of the single physical stroke of Rawdon's 'arrest' of Steyne. This comes after three paragraphs in which Rawdon has said nothing, while Becky and Steyne have screamed, smiled, attempted laughter, tried to grin, protested innocence, denied innocence and so on. Then Rawdon, 'springing out, seized him by the neckcloth, until Steyne, almost strangled, writhed and bent under his arm. "You lie, you dog!" said Rawdon, "You lie, you coward and villain!" ' Rawdon's very inarticulateness, his simple, conventional, military language, has now come into its own, in the face of the failure in wit and art of these two clever overreachers. The sudden spring, the seizing of the neckcloth, and the blows, have the further triumph of reversing Rawdon's own physical arrest and humiliation of the previous night.

However, this kind of release has considerable complexity. It has been prepared for in Rawdon's very slow realization of Becky's betrayal, in his reading of her silence and absence, and last, in the letter where she finally shows how she underestimates his powers of mind. Moreover, the reader suddenly grasps much that has hitherto lain in the background of the soldier's character. Thackeray often knows much more about his characters than he lets on, and both Rawdon and Major Pendennis are abruptly revealed as capable of bravery and various strengths which are perfectly in character with their history as seasoned campaigners. There was always more to Rawdon than the rake and gambler, after all: now his military history, the decency, affection, toughness, generosity and recent nostalgia for youth, all come fully into their own. The dramatic scene here acts as a node for the character. It reflects back on our experience, showing the past to be more consistent and more complex than we knew, while also drawing on its implications for clarity of comprehension now. Once we reflect, it is surprising and yet inevitable that Rawdon should be brave, strong and victorious. Once we reflect, we find that we have been, like Becky, undervaluing the powers of a rather unintelligent and boring man.

Thackeray's touch of genius here is subtle; it is also consistent, typical and absolutely central. Not only does it show up the limitations of Becky's intelligence and artifice, in a way that arrests and challenges our own easy approval and interest, but it also defines her present losses. At the moment – the only moment – of appreciation, she loses Rawdon. Thackeray, for all his celebrated 'intrusiveness', does not say and does not need to say a word about this irony and nemesis. We feel it, in the reversal and the release. Thackeray's conception of drama is dramatic in the way of George Eliot and Henry James, who first put the action 'inside'. In the most memorable scenes of such dramatic triumphs as *Middlemarch* and *The Portrait of a Lady*, what we now admire is the outer envelope of physical scene and its inner psychic contents. Thackeray's method can be panoramic, as Lubbock says, but it can also switch from panorama to inner action. His method can be generalized, narrative, provisional and non-committal, as other critics have said, but it can sharpen and harden into lucid particulars. Chapter 53 of *Vanity Fair* (and other scenes like it) can stand comparison with the best of George Eliot and Henry James.

. . . We see Becky at a loss, not indeed for the first time, but more crucially than before. Then we see her sense of loss and guilt overcome by a feeling of admiration. We see in her resilient and instinctive acknowledgement of Rawdon's strength that brain and art are not the only means to mastery. We also see Steyne at a loss, uncontrolled and afraid, power, wit and irony falling to pieces. We see Rawdon in the ascendant, and not just because he is strong and brave but because the other two are put down morally, hence his commands and Becky's compliance. We also see the strange, sad blend of loss and gain, for Becky and Rawdon, in the terrible discovery. With all this goes that sense of the fascination of people, of their marvellous capacity to surprise and shock, which can accompany or even override profound or shattering crises. Thackeray is a brilliant analyst of ennui, and Becky's losses and punishments are in part defined in terms of ennui and boredom. In this scene, however, and for the first time, she is not bored by her husband. Her admiration for his victorious virility is a conventional sexual and social reaction, and it is on the cards that Thackeray was aware of this. Some of his critics have sentimentalized Becky,[3] but he himself kept a sure grasp of her own conventional little character. Hence her Royalism, and the way it displays itself. She is a climber, not a radical, and her moments of social criticism are merely sporadic.

Thackeray is pointing what he always appears to enjoy showing, a shift in the social and moral hierarchy. Becky is down, Steyne is down, Rawdon is up. Rawdon is in the ascendant in spite of his misery, and in spite of the conventional humiliation of the cuckold's position, which he challenges and overcomes. He is exposing the precariousness of social and intellectual gain, the shiftingness and shiftiness of the mobility and hierarchy of *Vanity Fair*, which in its class gains and its economic gains is fast-moving and chancy, very like a fairground, and very like England at the beginning of the century. But he is also revealing the chanciness of intelligence and wit, which have gained Becky so much hitherto. Some of Thackeray's most interesting revelations about Becky are her limitations, her inefficiencies and her failures, though it must be said that her capacity to put up with failure, to adapt and survive, is of course also an important part of the complex portraiture. Here Becky's discovery of her limitations, and her recognition of unfamiliar powers in another person, form part of a larger pattern of discovery in the novel. Amelia and Dobbin also have to learn the complexity of people by discovering limitation: Amelia has to recognize the limitations of her dead husband, Dobbin the limitations of Amelia herself; their personal revelation scene, where Dobbin tells Amelia that she is not worthy of his love, is another quieter and more inward-looking instance of Thackeray's concern with displacement and reversal.

Thackeray can lean as heavily as he likes on the externals – the dress, jewels, clothes, furniture, lights, movement – because at the centre of all the brilliant outer scene is his absolute confidence about people's feeling and thinking life. All the same, it would be shallow not to recognize his mastery of the social envelope. Becky has staged this scene, has arranged the lights, dressed the part, smothered herself with jewels, got rid of servants and husband, all the unwanted characters, like the clever producer and actress that she is, and the point can scarcely be missed when we recollect that the previous big scene showed the charades at Gaunt House, or that the intervening chapter 52 showed the squalor of the sponging-house. The objects are aggressively present in the social significance, both as unwholesome prizes, 'her own were all covered with serpents, and rings, and baubles', and as spoils of war: 'She began, trembling, pulling the jewels from her arms, and the rings from her shaking fingers, and held them all in a heap, quivering and looking up at him. "Throw them down," he said.' The objects remain significant to the end, after Rawdon's investigation of her desk, after her sense that she is left, dishevelled, 'dresses and feathers, scarfs and trinkets, a heap of tumbled vanities lying in a wreck', right up to the last enigmatic detail (not explained and complete until the next chapter) of the maid gathering up the trinkets from the floor. People are related to the objects, presents, trophies, spoils, ornaments, sleights, deceits, vanities, and Thackeray has his eye on the envelope, on the object, room, house. He is the kind of social novelist who knows the price and the value of everything. But he knows more than this. In the next chapter of *Vanity Fair*, in another scene of social reversal, the servants and rightful owners take possession of the drawing-room, the maraschino, the cream-dish, the little gilt glass and the beautiful chintz sofa. But Thackeray's marvellous eye for the social scene must not blind us to his interest in the mind and the feelings. The servants take over the spoils desperately, wretchedly and fearfully. His power as a novelist shifts our interest rapidly from the objects to the human response of Becky and her not very revolutionary victims. At his best, in these first major novels, it is a shift from outer to inner life which provides tension and elucidation. Thackeray strikes one as a Jamesian novelist in the complete sense of the term; he has the kind of mind on which nothing is lost – brooch, ring, banknote, painted face, emotional and intellectual activity.

In chapters 53 and 54 the characters are all shocked, and the reader is too, as always in Thackeray at his best. (It is one of the great losses in *The Newcomes* that shocks and surprises come singly, slightly and almost predictably, as, for instance, in the revelation of Clive's marriage or the lost will, or Rosey's death.) But in chapter 54 the reader may not only share Becky's earlier sense of Rawdon's limitation, but may well also have trouble with Thackeray's rendering of the 'problem' of technical adultery. I remember seeing a production of Pirandello's *As You Desire Me*, after which the audience went off still asking the question, *Was* it her, then? – a question which it had been the play's purpose to annihilate. I feel a similar sense of frustration and understanding when critics[4] continue to show interest in the answer Thackeray refused to give, to his question, 'What *had* happened? Was she guilty or not?' Thackeray has several good reasons for not answering, and for suggesting that this question and that of Becky's truthfulness on this one point are quite irrelevant. It is meaningless in the case of such large and proven corruption. We have been observing her lies for fifty chapters by now, and Thackeray is interested in truth and lies rather than in chastity, fidelity and adultery. Once again, his moral sense seems ahead of its time, and judging from much critical discussion, in some ways ahead of ours. Rawdon says, 'If she's not guilty, she's as bad as guilty', a remark which some critics have, most oddly, found shocking. G. Armour Craig,[5] for instance, observes the

'viciousness' of Rawdon's comment and concludes that the
avoidance of an answer is a necessary but deplorable evasion on
Thackeray's part. I conclude, rather, that it is grounded on a
larger and more profound sense of value than that of sexual
ethics. Thackeray is pointing to Becky's manipulation and
betrayal of Rawdon, to the mean self-interest partly grasped in
Rawdon's 'I always shared with you'. The reader has seen her
meanness and treachery extend far beyond the secret hoarding to
her pretence, to Lord Steyne, that Rawdon forced her to extort
money. Hence the full irony of Steyne's reference to Rawdon as a
'bully'. The reader is in a better position to appreciate Steyne's
misconception and the accuracy of Rawdon's 'as good as
guilty' – Becky has manipulated not only Rawdon but his
reputation, and in ways which make the question of her actual
adultery appear thinly technical. Disloyalty, deceit and the
destruction of reputation, Thackeray is saying, are worse than
adultery. Critics who fail to see this are perilously close to Becky,
who is also unable to appreciate the finer points of morality, even
if she is telling the truth when she says 'I am innocent'. It is
Rawdon who is intuitively right about the moral position, and
seeing his superior moral intelligence is another pleasure in our
experience of enlightenment. Rawdon is shown as having an
emotional and moral range that we had not appreciated, and the
step forward in our understanding is both a realistic enhancing of
character, and a process in the moral dynamics of the novel.
What I have spoken of as the uncomfortable appraisal of what we
had in common with Becky is entirely typical of Thackeray's art.
He wants to make the reader uncomfortable, and succeeds.

A generalized sense that morality is more complex than we had
thought comes through the particularity of learning that these
people are less simple than we thought. In this process, the
reading of a novel is not all that different from the intelligent
experience of life. In *Vanity Fair*, the process partly depends on
flexible and agile movement of satire. We look directly and
critically at simplifications of judgment. Becky has seen Rawdon
as a caricature, manageable, stupid, compliant, and disposed of
him as such. She finds that he is rather different. But note how far
Thackeray is from producing heroic surprises. It is true that we

see that Rawdon's energy and honour are admirably alive, but if
we start to admire him too fervently, we shall almost certainly be
further disconcerted when he accepts the governorship. No
heroics here, but a tough sense of revenge and survival. Likewise,
in the scene where Rawdon asks Pitt to look after his child,
Thackeray allows us in a certain fashion to enjoy the feeling of
brotherly love and loyalty, especially refreshing after the exhi-
bition of extreme cynicism and betrayal. But only after a fashion.
Pitt first reveals his anxiety about money, and only when that
priority is settled does he feel free to engage in a sincere enough
show of brotherly feeling. Thackeray does not suggest that there
is no such thing as disinterestedness, but he does say that
disinterestedness is easier in certain circumstances than in others.
As soon as Rawdon says 'It's not money I want', Pitt is able to
show 'genuine alarm', 'commiseration', 'cordiality', and to show
himself as 'much affected'. Thackeray's treatment of discovery is
dependent on such a strong grasp of the complexity of the human
passions and mind, on his refusal to create caricature, except for
his most shadowy nonce characters. And although the characters
whose complexity we most discern and enjoy are the major ones,
Becky, Amelia, Dobbin and George, even lesser characters like
Pitt and Lady Jane reflect the same deep insight.

It is not only the reader who enjoys the human show. Becky,
most remarkably, also enjoys and appreciates the surprises of
human nature, and on many occasions Thackeray manages to
draw with one stroke her appreciation of her own complexity and
that of nature. Like Pitt, she is also hardly ever capable of
disinterestedness. It is, for instance, noticeable that her enjoyment of Rawdon's virility is quickly followed by her feeling that
she may still be able to keep something back from him. (In this
case, money and knowledge.) Often what she appreciates is
bound up with her own self-love, as when she enjoys her technical
defeat at the hands of the gentle and compliant Lady Jane
(another reversal in the social and psychic order) because she
realizes that Jane's attack is a jealous one and therefore very
flattering. But she is not fully sensitive to Lady Jane's moral
disgust, which proceeds not only from jealousy but from her
maternal disapproval of Becky's hypocrisy and harshness about

little Rawdon. As ever, Thackeray is immensely subtle. Becky is
not good at appreciating real disinterestedness and does not read
Jane with total accuracy. The same subtlety emerges in the scene
towards the end when Becky magnanimously (but not wholly
unindulgently) produces the letter George hid in her bouquet
long ago, and uses it in order to persuade Amelia to give up the
false idol and send for Dobbin. When Amelia adds a further
surprise to the scene by admitting that she has already done this,
Becky enjoys the disclosure with her usual appreciative gusto:
'Becky screamed with laughter – "*Un biglietto*," she sang out
with Rosina, "*eccolo qua!*" – the whole house echoed with her
shrill singing.' Her perception of Amelia's unexpected and
untypical action modulates cleverly from the earlier
touch – 'soothed and kissed her – a rare mark of sympathy with
Mrs Becky' – so that we are back in the rather crude, shrill,
coarser world of the operatic exclamation.

Becky's appreciation exists, but Thackeray loses no opportunity of pointing out its bluntness. He also refuses to make her
too strong an agent of good; Amelia herself brings Dobbin back,
Becky is permitted the gesture but not the responsibility. And
Becky, like the reader, has underestimated Amelia's powers of
action and feeling. But the impression of Becky's resilience and
limited but vivacious sensibility goes on right to the end of the
novel. She really does appreciate Dobbin. She takes a fair
measure of Amelia's strength and weakness. She hankers (almost
pathetically) after the style and wit of Lord Steyne, for an instant
stupidly supposing that she may still have some power over him.
In all these instances, Becky is shown as demonstrating her mind
and feelings. Though she is almost exclusively confined to
histrionic display, she can occasionally behave naturally. She can
also behave fairly well when there is nothing at stake. She can be
kind, understanding, and appreciative of integrity and depth. It
is a point that Jane Austen makes in creating her version of
corrupt wit, art and sexual charm in Mary Crawford. Mary, like
Becky, can act decently and sympathetically to Fanny, for
instance, when the action and the feeling are inexpensive. Jane
Austen and Thackeray both knew and showed that the point
about moral appreciation and sympathy is not that wicked

people are incapable of such acts of love, but that they seldom feel free to perform them. The psychology of moral action and the realistic creation of character are enriched by Thackeray's perception and his dramatic enactment of it.

In such instances, then, Thackeray puts the reader through a process of change and recognition. Not only does he refuse to let us enjoy mind and wit overmuch, but he also refuses to let us indulge too zealously and reverently in moral admiration. Unlike Henry James, he never overrates brains: he endowed Dobbin with 'fairly good brains', and did call him Dobbin. Unlike George Eliot, he never overrates intense feeling either; he knows that the heart can be stupid too (like Amelia's and Dobbin's), and he does not feel that awe, veneration or worship should lie beyond the reach of censure. His criticism of strong feeling is probably one of the chief reasons why he is so uncomfortable a novelist, depriving us of intellectual flattery, moral superiority and emotional indulgence all at once.

There are of course compensations. If our feelings at times appear to expand into unwonted respect or sympathy for Becky or Lord Steyne, only to be firmly constricted and put in their proper place, so there are some characters, like Rawdon, for whom our enlarged respect may be tempered and qualified but survives as a firm gain. This sense of expanded knowledge and respect is fairly rare, but we experience it more in *Vanity Fair* than in any other novel. In Dobbin's case we also see another reversal – the worm turning – but we have absolutely no need to learn anything new about this capacity for devotion, honour or love. What we discover about him is that like Rawdon he is capable of a critical discrimination we had not known about; there is not only the pleasure of having him criticize Amelia, but the additional delight in having him step out of the role of self-effacing hanger-on, spoony and Dobbin. It may be argued – though once more Thackeray leaves us to observe it for ourselves – that Amelia is not unlike Becky in learning to appreciate the quality of a man at the moment of loss. Becky and Amelia are both made to realize that there is nothing like deprivation to make us appreciate what we lose. Moreover, they are both made to feel the attraction of energy and attack. Amelia too sees the man she has underrated turn on her, change roles, attack vigorously and gain a victory:

'Have I not learned in that time to read all your feelings, and look into your thoughts? I know what your heart is capable of: it can cling faithfully to a recollection, and cherish a fancy; but it can't feel such an attachment as mine deserves to mate with, and such as I would have won from a woman more generous than you. No, you are not worthy of the love which I have devoted to you. I knew all along that the prize I had set my life on was not worth the winning; that I was a fool, with fond fancies, too, bartering away my all of truth and ardour against your little feeble remnant of love. I will bargain no more: I withdraw. I find no fault with you. You are very good-natured, and have done your best; but you couldn't – you couldn't reach up to the height of the attachment which I bore you, and which a loftier soul than yours might have been proud to share. Good-bye, Amelia! I have watched your struggle. Let it end. We are both weary of it.'

Amelia stood scared and silent as William thus suddenly broke the chain by which she held him, and declared his independence and superiority. He had placed himself at her feet so long that the poor little woman had been accustomed to trample upon him. She didn't wish to marry him, but she wished to keep him. She wished to give him nothing, but that he should give her all. It is a bargain not unfrequently levied in love.   (ch. 66)

Once more, Thackeray does not show all his hand. In the big scene in chapter 53 there are two important things held back; we do not gather immediately the full implications of the maid picking up the trinkets, and the last paragraph leaves a little serial trail from one chapter to another, adding in delayed effect a small but sharp irony. We also do not know yet the answer (or non-answer) to the question about Becky's innocence. The time-lag here in chapter 67 also involves something small and something large. Becky intends to plot for Dobbin, and the reader is allowed to see her full and disinterested appreciation of his nobility without yet being shown Thackeray's refusal to let her be a good agent. More important, we are shown and told a little about Amelia's surprise, discomfiture and selfishness, but Thackeray leaves the narrative of her feelings incomplete. What the reader is left with is not only a very functional loose end or two, valuable in the plotting, and permitting future tension, surprise and climax, but a surprise in character. Here we see Thackeray's tremendous skill in handling a dynamic plot and in centring attention on the psychic point. Dobbin has changed, is Dobbin no longer, and Amelia and Becky both act as sensitive registers of that change. But the change itself registers impressions of Amelia and Becky: Dobbin turns because Amelia has shown herself intolerably ungrateful and selfish, and his fine disgust, as he throws away Becky's note, is the final touch in this record of his honourable energy.

Once changed, like Rawdon, he remains a finer, larger and sadder character, returning to Amelia, but reserving judgment and heart. The last we see of him is the brilliantly true and hard glimpse at the very end, when we are taking a choric farewell of the characters at a Fancy Fair. At this point we may not be expecting either another development or a reminder of that earlier enlargement. Dobbin, Emmy and their children see and shrink from Becky. Thackeray has on a previous page laconically defined Dobbin's reluctance to leave home in this way: 'The Colonel quitted home with reluctance (for he was deeply immersed in his "History of the Punjab" which still occupies him, and much alarmed about his little daughter, whom he idolises, and who was just recovering from the chicken-pox).' His wife is here conspicuous by her absence, but in case absence is not quite conspicuous enough, the author makes the point more clearly in his final paragraphs:

. . . the Colonel seizing up his little Janey, of whom he is fonder than of anything in the world – fonder even than of his 'History of the Punjaub'.

'Fonder than he is of me,' Emmy thinks, with a sigh. But he never said a word to Amelia that was not kind and gentle; or thought of a want of hers that he did not try to gratify.

This kind of refusal to maintain worship, only sustained, I believe, in *Vanity Fair* and *Esmond*, perhaps explains why some readers consider Thackeray cynical or feel that his is the kind of toughness that is very close to cynicism. He is not cynical: there is a refreshing, exhilarating and even optimistic sense that Rawdon and Dobbin are more sensitive, intelligent and energetic than we supposed, and that virtue need not be self-effacing, docile or wormlike. But there is no doubt that this admission and reversal, especially in Dobbin's case, is proffered as an example of human vanity, neither Dobbin nor Amelia discovering what they expected in attaining what they desired. One might say that the only character who is never saddened by this particular form of vanity is Becky, who lacks the necessary faith and love to encounter loss. As we admire her toughness and resilience, as Thackeray cunningly tempts us to do, we should recognize that the faithless and heartless, the entirely corrupt, lacking any ideal, cannot suffer from lost desire.

This expansion and displacement is, then, the original and complex mode of proceeding in *Vanity Fair*. Scenically and psychologically, Thackeray continued to use the same process in subsequent novels, but it is entirely missing in *Philip* and even in *The Newcomes*,[6] where its absence is one of the flaws in Thackeray's last major novel. The method is particularly appropriate to *Vanity Fair*, showing as it does a process of loss and frustration, chiefly for Becky, but for other characters as well; it also permits Thackeray at once to chronicle loss and a certain sad growth of wisdom, as opposed to wit, in Rawdon and Dobbin. But besides dramatizing vanity and frustration, it expresses a psychological interest which is always developed in the drama of social environment. . . .

Source: extracts from *The Exposure of Luxury* (London,
1972) pp. 23–6, 27–37.

NOTES

1. Among the critics who lack confidence in Thackeray's handling of the big dramatic scene is Percy Lubbock, who set the tone for such apologies when he wrote his celebrated judgement on Thackeray's 'perversity': 'how little Thackeray's fashion of handling a novel allowed for the big dramatic scene, when at length it had to be faced – now he neglected it in advance, if how he refused it till the last possible moment'

(*The Craft of Fiction*, 1921). [See extracts from Lubbock in Part Two above – Ed.] Even Kathleen Tillotson feels constrained to talk about the element of parody in chapter 53 (*Novels of the Eighteen-Forties*, 1954); and Geoffrey Tillotson, brilliantly responsive to details of ironic imagery, is also apparently drawn to find non-dramatic matter to admire in this extraordinary scene (*Thackeray the Novelist*, 1954). G. Armour Craig, in his essay 'On the Style of *Vanity Fair*' (1958; reissued 1968) [included in this selection – Ed.], continues the apologetic or compensatory habit, in his judgement that in this scene 'the collision . . . misses its main issue and prize'.

2. James Hannay, *A Brief Memoir of the Late Mr Thackeray* (1864).

3. Elizabeth Jenkins, for instance, remarks strangely, in the Introduction to the Everyman edition, that Becky never deceives herself.

4. See, for example, G. Armour Craig, 'On the style of *Vanity Fair*'; and Leslie M. Thompson, '*Vanity Fair* and the Johnsonian Tradition of Fiction', *The New Rambler*, c. vii (June 1969) 45–9.

5. G. Armour Craig, 'On the style of *Vanity Fair*'.

6. I am not concerned with *Catherine, Barry Lyndon* and other novels and stories where the action is not psychological.

SELECT BIBLIOGRAPHY

TEXT AND BACKGROUND MATERIALS

Vanity Fair was published in twenty monthly parts from January 1847 to July 1848 (the last a double number), and appeared in book-form, published by Bradbury and Evans in June 1848. The standard modern text is to be found in the edition by Geoffrey and Kathleen Tillotson (London: Methuen, 1963).

The standard biography is
Gordon N. Ray, *Thackeray: The Uses of Adversity, 1811 – 1846* (London: Oxford University Press, 1955).
Gordon N. Ray, *Thackeray: The Age of Wisdom, 1847 – 1863* (London: Oxford University Press, 1958).

Other biographical studies include:
L. Stevenson, *The Showman of Vanity Fair* (London: Chapman, 1947).
L. Ennis, *Thackeray, the Sentimental Cynic* (Evanston, Ill.: North-Western University Press, 1950).

Other relevant works are:
Gordon N. Ray (ed.), *The Letters and Private Papers of William Makepeace Thackeray*, 4 vols (London: Oxford University Press, 1945 – 6).
Gordon N. Ray, *The Buried Life* (London: Oxford University Press for the Royal Society of Literature, 1952). This work is subtitled 'A Study of the Relations between Thackeray's Fiction and His Personal History'.

CRITICAL BOOKS

Of full-length studies primary mention must be given to
G. Tillotson, *Thackeray the Novelist* (London: Methuen, 1954). An examination of Thackeray's characteristic techniques and achievement – continuity, commentary, verisimilitude.

Others include:
J. Y. T. Greig, *Thackeray, A Reconsideration* (London, Oxford University

Press, 1950). Links criticism to biography, and is not always very sympathetic.

J. Loofbourow, *Thackeray and the Form of Fiction* (Princeton, N. J.: Princeton University Press, 1964). Is concerned with parallels, some close, some more remote, in both form and time.

I. M. Williams, *Thackeray* (London: Evans Bros, 1968). A condensed survey of the novelist's work.

J. H. Wheatley, *Patterns in Thackeray's Fiction* (Cambridge, Mass.: M.I.T. Press, 1969). Considers the 'ethical' argument, causality and psychology among other topics in *Vanity Fair*.

Juliet McMaster, *Thackeray: The Major Novels* (Manchester University Press and Toronto University Press, 1971). Examines authorial presence, narrative technique, serialisation.

Barbara Hardy, *The Exposure of Luxury: Radical Themes in Thackeray* (London: Peter Owen, 1972). Has chapters on rank and reversal, the power of money, nature and art, and love.

J. P. Rawlins, *Thackeray's Novels: A Fiction that is True* (Berkeley, Los Angeles and London: University of California Press, 1974). Sees *Vanity Fair* as romantic drama, apologue and satire.

CRITICAL ARTICLES AND ESSAYS

(No reference is made to articles included in the text above.)

G. Tillotson and D. Hawes (eds), *Thackeray: the Critical Heritage* (London: Routledge and Kegan Paul, 1967; New York: Barnes and Noble, 1967). Gathers reviews and articles from Thackeray's own time to about 1880.

Lord David Cecil, 'Thackeray', in *Early Victorian Novelists* (London: Constable, 1934). Sees the ambitious range of Thackeray's purpose in *Vanity Fair*, but feels that he failed to achieve it.

A. C. Kettle, 'Thackeray: *Vanity Fair*', in *An Introduction to the English Novel* (London: Hutchinson, 1951). Sociological approach – 'Thackeray's vision of bourgeois society'.

Russell Fraser, 'Pernicious Casuistry: A Study of Character in *Vanity Fair*', *Nineteenth-Century Fiction*, xii (1958).

Myron Taube, 'Contrast as a Principle of Structure in *Vanity Fair*', *Nineteenth-Century Fiction*, xviii (1964).

Jenni Calder, 'Serpent or Parasite?', in *Women and Marriage in Victorian Fiction* (London: Thames and Hudson, 1976). Considers different types of marriage in *Vanity Fair*, with linking treatment of some of the imagery.

NOTES ON CONTRIBUTORS

G. ARMOUR CRAIG is Professor of English at Amherst College, Massachusetts.

A. E. DYSON is a Senior Lecturer in English Literature in the University of East Anglia, and formerly taught in the University College of North Wales, Bangor. He is co-editor of *The Critical Quarterly* and general editor of the Casebook series. He has written on many aspects of English literature, notably the nineteenth-century novel.

EDGAR F. HARDEN is Associate Professor of English in Simon Fraser University, British Columbia.

BARBARA HARDY is Professor of English Literature at Birbeck College in the University of London, and previously taught at Royal Holloway College. Her writings include studies of Dickens and George Eliot, as well as of other nineteenth-century novelists.

U. C. KNOEPFLMACHER is Professor of English at the University of California, Berkeley, and has written on George Eliot and on religion and humanism in the Victorian period.

JULIET MCMASTER (*née* Sutton) is Professor of English at the University of Alberta and edited the Jane Austen bicentenary volume from that University.

GORDON N. RAY is Professor of English Literature in New York University, and formerly taught in the University of Illinois.

GEOFFREY TILLOTSON (1905–69) was Professor of English Literature at Birkbeck College in the University of London.

KATHLEEN TILLOTSON is an Emeritus Professor of the University of London; she was Professor of English Literature at Bedford College (1958–71). Besides her own critical studies in nineteenth-century literature, she edited *Vanity Fair* with her husband, Geoffrey Tillotson.

DOROTHY VAN GHENT taught English Literature in the University of Buffalo until her death in 1967.

IOAN M. WILLIAMS is a Senior Lecturer in English Literature in the University of Warwick. He has written on Browning and other nineteenth-century writers, as well as on Thackeray.

INDEX

This index does not contain any references to the Appendix of the article by E. F. Harden nor to the Bibliography and Notes on Contributors

Age, The 98
Ainsworth, Harrison 104, 135
Aristophanes 50
Austen, Jane 222

Bagehot, Walter 155, 163
Balzac, Honoré de 47, 118
BAREACRES, LADY 16, 56, 117
Bayly, Thomas Haynes 89
Becher, Anne (*see* Carmichael-Smyth, Mrs)
Becher, John H. 71–2
Becher, Miss Anne 73
Becher, Mrs (*see* Butler, Mrs)
Bell, Robert 13, 14, 28–9, 36–7, 103, 104, 141 n., 169
Beveridge, Henry 77
Blanchard, Laman 89
Boswell, James 15, 185
Bradbury and Evans, Messrs 12, 101
BRIGGS, MISS 34, 50, 135, 137, 198, 215
Brontë, Charlotte 25, 104, 142 n., 178
Brookfield, Mrs 141 n.
Brownell, W. C. 45–7, 129, 141 n., 142 n.
BULLOCK, FREDERICK 27, 196
BULLOCK, MRS FREDERICK 16, 27, 144
Bulwer-Lytton, E. B. 104, 130, 135, 138

Bunyan, John 110, 146, 172, 186 (see also *Pilgrim's Progress, The*)
BURKE, THURTELL AND HAYES 81
Butler, Capt. (later Lt-Col.) Edward W. 72–3
Butler, Mrs (*née* Harriet Cowper 71–6
Butt, J. (and Tillotson, K.) 204 n.

Carlyle, Jane Welsh 96
Carlyle, Thomas 15, 184–7
Carmichael-Smyth, Major-General 12
Carmichael-Smyth, Mrs (Thackeray's mother) 11, 33, 73, 74, 100, 102, 141 n.
Cecil, Lord David 204 n.
Chaucer, Geoffrey 134
Chesterton, G. K. 57–62
Christian, Capt. Charles 72
CLAPP 196
CLAPP, MISS 26
CLAPP, MRS 27
Colburn, Henry 12, 101
Conrad, Joseph 110, 120
Cornhill Magazine, The 12
CRAWLEY, MRS BUTE 27, 89, 119, 148–9, 167, 172–3, 197
CRAWLEY, MISS 27, 48–9, 75–7, 82, 89, 117, 119, 124–5, 148, 156, 172, 178, 196–7, 200
CRAWLEY, SIR PITT 17, 28, 52, 69–70, 102, 117, 119, 123, 125–8,

148, 167, 172, 193-5, 200
CRAWLEY, SIR PITT (the second)
  27, 34, 109, 135, 148, 152, 158,
  197-8, 221
CRAWLEY, RAWDON 14-16, 19-
  20, 26, 28, 31, 35, 42-3, 47-9, 53-
  4, 56, 76, 117, 121, 124-6, 131-2,
  135-7, 148-54, 156-8, 173, 177,
  184, 194-9, 214-21, 223, 225-6
CRAWLEY, RAWDON (junior) 34-
  5, 132, 137, 159, 181, 197, 222
CRISP, REV. MR 149, 192
Crowe, Eugénie 75
CUFF 191-2

DALE, EDWARD 128-9
Day, Thomas 89
Delamere, Rev. L. 75
Delancy, Capt. F. 75
Devonshire, Duke of 34
Dibdin, Charles 89
Dickens, Charles 54, 89, 96, 105,
  107-8, 128, 157, 201
  books: Dombey and Son 157; Little
  Dorrit 107; Nicholas Nickleby 41;
  Sketches by Boz 89. characters:
  Carker 157; Dombey, Flor-
  ence 157; Dombey, Mr 157;
  Dombey, Paul 159; Havisham,
  Miss 120; Jaggers 120; Merdle
  107-8
Disraeli, Benjamin 104-9
DOBBIN, WILLIAM 14, 19-20, 26,
  28, 31-5, 41-5, 50, 60-1, 84, 103,
  118, 132-4, 169-70, 172, 180-1,
  186, 189, 191-3, 197-200, 215,
  218, 221-6
DOBBINSES, MISS 27
Dodds, J. W. 141 n., 202 n.
Dreiser, Theodore 61
Dyson, A. E. 11, 163-82

Eastlake, Lady 15, 30-1, 104
EAVES, TOM 87, 109, 142 n.
Edgeworth, Maria 89

Edinburgh Review, The 96
Eliot, George 130, 216, 223
Emerson, R. W. 110
Examiner, The 26-8

Fielding, Henry 21, 27, 96, 114-15
  138, 147, 153, 165-6, 171, 201
  Tom Jones 114-15, 165, 190.
  characters: Blifil 27, 37, 165;
  Jones, Tom 27, 37, 165-6, 171;
  Square 120
FitzGerald, Edward 12
Flaubert, Gustave 120
Foreign Quarterly Review, The 91
Forster, E. M. 164
Forster, John 26-8, 37, 104
FRANCIS 128
Fraser, Russell 18
Fraser's Magazine 12, 28-9, 36, 91,
  96, 104, 130, 201

Galsworthy, John 110
Gaskell, Mrs Elizabeth 143
GAUNT, LADY 16
Gide, André 95, 110
Gladstone, W. E. 109
Gleig, G. R. 83-5
Gore, Mrs 127
Graham, Mary 74
Greene, Graham 95
Greig, J. Y. T. 141 n., 142 n., 188-
  9, 201, 203 n.

Hallam, A. H. 12
Hannay, James 110, 215, 227 n.
Harden, E. F. 13-14, 188-213
Hardy, Barbara 214-27
Hardy, Thomas 60
Hayward, Abraham 96
Hertford, Marquis of 86-8, 106
Hogarth, William 105
Horace 61
HORROCKS, MISS 125-6

Iliad, The 57

James, Henry 21, 95–6, 110, 114, 117, 216, 223
Jameson, Mrs 141 n.
Jeaffreson, J. C. 104
JENKINS 15
Jenkins, Elizabeth 227 n.
Jerrold, Douglas 148
Job, Book of 57, 60
Jonson, Ben 172

Kingsley, Henry 86
Knoepflmacher, U. C. 13, 65–7

Lafayette, Madame de 119
Lawrence, Thomas 90
Leader, The 142 n.
Lemon, Mark 99–100
Lever, Charles 98
Lewes, G. H. 142 n., 155
Liddell, Mrs 14–15
Lockhart, J. G. 106
Low, Augusta 77–9, 81
Low, John 78
Lubbock, Percy 51–7, 131, 151 (*see* 161 n.), 216, 226 n.
Lytton (*see* Bulwer-Lytton)

McMaster, Juliet 13, 69–70
Martin, Theodore 32–3
Martineau, Harriet 104
Marx, Karl 177
Melbourne, Lord 105
Mill, J. S. 99
Moll Flanders 116, 121
Moore, Thomas 89
Morgan, Sydney 141 n.
Morning Chronicle, The 96
MOSS, MR 15

Napoleon Buonaparte 83, 156
National Review, The 16
North British Review, The 96

O' DOWD, GLORVINA 26, 36
O' DOWD, MRS 26, 36, 56, 84–5, 117, 197
Orford, Lord 105
OSBORNE, GEORGE 14, 17, 19, 27–8, 44–5, 56, 60, 84, 88, 90, 117, 121, 131–3, 136, 140, 157, 168–70, 173–4, 178–81, 187–9, 191, 193, 195–8, 200, 221–2
OSBORNE, GEORGE (junior) 21, 35, 89, 132, 196
OSBORNE, JANE 143–5, 196
OSBORNE, MR 27, 123, 126, 145, 157–8, 167, 174, 178, 196, 198

Peel, Sir Robert 143
Pilgrim's Progress, The 119–20, 146, 161 n., 186
PINKERTON, MISS JEMIMA 26, 170, 192
PINKERTON, MISSES 15, 131, 191–2
Pirandello, Luigi 219
Prévost, Abbé 120
Pritchett, V. S. 71, 77
Proctor, Mrs 141 n.
Punch 12, 89, 90, 96, 98–100

Quarterly Review, The 31, 104

Raffaelle 42, 44
RAGGLES 156, 171, 176
Ray, G. N. 11, 15–16, 71–82, 95–113, 161 nn., 162 nn., 163, 185, 190, 203 n.
Rembrandt 42
Reviss, Theresa 142 n.
Richardson, Samuel 60, 119–20, 164
Rigby, Elizabeth (*see* Eastlake, Lady)
Ritchie, William 78
Roscoe, W. C. 16, 141 n., 142 n.
Rubens 42

Saintsbury, George 203 n.
Satirist, The 98
Scotsman, The 96
Scott, Sir Walter 42–3

SEDLEY, AMELIA 14–21, 26, 28–9, 32–7, 41, 44, 48, 50, 59, 76–7, 81–2, 84, 86, 89, 103, 115, 117–8, 121, 128, 131, 133–4, 138, 144, 149, 156–7, 159–60, 164, 166, 168–71, 174–5, 179–81, 186–9, 191–2, 195–8, 200, 218, 221–6

SEDLEY, JOS 17, 28, 35, 47, 59–60, 71, 76, 80–2, 85–6, 114, 121–2, 126, 131, 133, 135, 150, 173, 188–9, 192–3, 200

SEDLEY, MR 27, 123, 131, 140, 156–8, 178, 181, 187, 193, 196, 198

SEDLEY, MRS 17, 27, 159, 173

Shakespear, George 77–81, 90

Shakespeare, William 167. Characters: Cleopatra 167; Iachimo 195; Iago 137; Imogen 32; Juliet 32; Macbeth, Lady 27; Moonshine 195; Prospero 58

SHARP, BECKY 14–21, 26–7, 31, 34–6, 42–5, 48–56, 59–61, 69–70, 76, 81, 84, 86–7, 89–90, 102, 114, 116–18, 120, 124–6, 128, 131–7, 141 n., 148–56, 158–60, 164–77, 179–82, 184, 187–9, 191–200, 215–18, 220–7

Shawe, Merrick 77

Siborne, William 83

SLINGSTONE, COUNTESS OF 109

Solomon 61

SOUTHDOWN, LADY 27

SOUTHDOWN, LADY JANE 19, 26, 35, 125, 137, 198, 221–2

Staël, Madame de 31

Sterne, Laurence 95, 138, 140, 163, 165–6

Stevenson, R. L. 57–8, 151 (see 161 n.)

STEYNE, LADY 16

STEYNE, MARQUIS OF 16–18, 26, 34, 51, 53–4, 56, 58, 86, 106, 109, 117, 122–3, 128–9, 150–2, 154–9, 176, 181, 215, 217, 220, 222–3

SWARTZ, MISS 26, 89, 157, 196

Swift, Jonathan 20, 61, 163

SWISHTAIL'S 191

TAPEWORM 27

Taube, Myron 14, 190

Tennyson, Alfred 12

Thackeray, Isabella (née Shawe) 12, 74, 141 n., 153

Thackeray, Richard 11

Thackeray, William Makepeace – birth 11; young man 11–12, 73–4, 90, 97; daughters 100–1; periodical writing 12. For Vanity Fair, see under proper heading

Other Works: Barry Lyndon 12, 42, 98, 101, 202, 227 n.; Book of Snobs, The 91, 98, 145; Catherine 12, 42, 97, 135, 202, 227 n.; Denis Duval 12, 201; Denis Haggarty's Wife 97; Great Hoggarty Diamond, The 202; Henry Esmond 12, 110, 138, 201, 225; Irish Sketch Book, The 98; Lovel the Widower 12, 110, 201; 'Mrs Perkins' Ball' 96; Newcomes, The 20, 46, 110, 138, 201, 219, 226; Pendennis 46, 110, 130, 138, 146, 201, 216; Philip 12, 110, 138, 201, 226; Rebecca and Rowena 139; Rose and the Ring, The 167; Roundabout Papers 12, 90; Shabby Genteel Story, A 202; Virginians, The 110, 201; Yellowplush Papers, The 97

Letters quoted 12, 33–7, 96–8, 100–1, 103, 138–41, 155–6, 169, 184

Thirlwall, Connop 97

Thompson, Leslie M. 227 n.

Tillotson, Geoffrey 11, 83–91, 162 n., 190–1, 203 nn., 227 n.

Tillotson, Kathleen 11, 14, 83–91, 127–42, 161 n., 162 nn., 189, 191,

203 n., 204 n., 227 n. (*see also under* Butt, J.)
Titian 42
Tolstoy, Leo 164
TRAIL, RT REV. DR 109
Trollope, Anthony 21, 41–5, 143, 147, 161 nn., 203 n.
TUFTO, GENERAL 17, 117

Van Ghent, Dorothy 20, 114–26, 183
Vanity Fair – characters 30, 129; cynicism, alleged 20; 'images' 120–6; moral commentary 61; narration, mode of 21, 57, 65, 114–16, 118, 138–9, 165, 183–7; publication, mode of 13; reticence 147–8; revisions to

MS. 101–2, 191; scene, management of 51–7; sentiment, excess of 48–9; social commentary 15–17; structure 14, 29, 47–8, 59, 117–18, 130–4, 168–9, 188–213; style 143–61; tone 61, 164, 166–7, 173, 191

Waugh, Evelyn 95
Way of the World, The 48, 58
Wellington, Duke of 88, 199
Westminster Review, The 32–3
Whibley, Charles 13, 47–50, 203 n.
Williams, Ioan M. 15, 183–7
Williams, W. S. 25
WIRT, MISS 124

Zola, Émile 61

PAGE REFERENCES TO QUOTATIONS FROM *VANITY FAIR*

Chapter 1 – 147
2 – 150
3 – 80–1, 114, 138
4 – 115
5 – 191–2
6 – 89, 147, 160
7 – 88
8 – 102, 160, 175, 185
9 – 65, 67, 102, 125–6
13 – 123–4
14 – 70, 124, 148
15 – 70
16 – 136, 149
17 – 129, 136
18 – 21, 157, 181
20 – 156
25 – 136, 199
26 – 159
28 – 83, 158
29 – 56, 132, 179, 181
31 – 85, 133
32 – 140
35 – 178
36 – 21, 51–2

Chapter 37 – 51–2, 137, 159
38 – 21
39 – 125
41 – 116, 128, 130
42 – 143
44 – 129, 135, 156, 159, 182
45 – 137
47 – 109
49 – 55–6
50 – 37
51 – 21
52 – 137, 218
53 – 53–5, 135–6, 150–4, 214–20
54 – 153, 219
55 – 142 n., 156, 158
57 – 21
61 – 140
64 – 150, 153, 167, 182
65 – 135
66 – 224
67 – 133, 141, 182, 225